Exhibit Labels

Exhibit Labels

An Interpretive Approach

Third Edition

BEVERLY SERRELL
KATHERINE WHITNEY

ROWMAN & LITTLEFIELD
Lanham • Boulder • New York • London

Acquisitions Editor: Charles Harmon
Assistant Acquisitions Editor:
Sales and Marketing Inquiries: textbooks@rowman.com

Credits and acknowledgments for material borrowed from other sources, and reproduced
with permission, appear on the appropriate pages within the text.

Published by Rowman & Littlefield
An imprint of The Rowman & Littlefield Publishing Group, Inc.
4501 Forbes Boulevard, Suite 200, Lanham, Maryland 20706
www.rowman.com

86-90 Paul Street, London EC2A 4NE

British Library Cataloguing in Publication Information Available

Library of Congress Cataloging-in-Publication Data Available
ISBN 978-1-5381-6045-9 (cloth : alk. paper)
ISBN 978-1-5381-6046-6 (paperback)
ISBN 978-1-5381-6047-3 (electronic)

∞™ The paper used in this publication meets the minimum requirements of
American National Standard for Information Sciences—Permanence of Paper
for Printed Library Materials, ANSI/NISO Z39.48-1992.

For all the visitors who read labels in museums

Contents

Preface

Welcome to the third edition of *Exhibit Labels: An Interpretive Approach*. We've come a long way. The first edition (*EL1*, 1996) pulled together ideas about planning, writing, and presenting labels by museum staff and research about the impact of exhibitions on visitors. The second edition (*EL2*, 2015) expanded to include the myriad ways that interactivity, digital technologies, and experience design have complicated the basic tasks of writing exhibit labels. In the intervening years, museums have been grappling with and responding to the huge external pressures wrought by social, global health, economic, political, and cultural events of the 2010s and 2020s. Exhibitions worldwide have become more timely, inclusive, and socially relevant. And exhibit labels have improved!

Can *An Interpretive Approach* claim credit for some of that progress? Yes, judging from the positive feedback from readers who have found *EL1* and *EL2* helpful in making exhibits more accessible. While *EL3* continues to be grounded in the same tenets that will be familiar to old friends, there are several changes we hope you will appreciate.

WHAT'S NEW?

We've updated many of our examples to reflect changes in the museum field and society at large. We've also made the book slightly larger, laid out the text to flow uninterrupted, and allowed more room for more legible photos.

More Voices

We wanted this book to reflect multiple voices, so we asked for stories from our colleagues that would inspire readers to do things differently, to want to know more, and perhaps to even reach out to those contributors directly. "Voices from the Field"—a rethinking of the "Case Studies" from the second edition—are concise first-person accounts of our colleagues' experiences. In keeping with our goal of an uninterrupted narrative, those voices are grouped together in their own section of the book.

The biggest change in voice is that this edition was written by two authors. Katherine Whitney, who helped Beverly extensively on the second edition, brings her expertise, shared concerns, and a wider range of experiences to this one. In addition to writing exhibit labels, Katherine has written and edited design guidelines, museum journals, and an anthology of nonfiction from the Iranian diaspora. Her gentle leveling tone and tact helped to lighten Beverly's occasional snarkiness. We hope our lively debates and collaborative writing process are reflected in the text of this edition. And, as two White women, we recognized our inevitable unconscious bias, so we sought prepublication feedback from sensitivity readers, who helped us expand our perspectives.

Community Feedback

As we began this third edition, the first thing we did was reach out to our vast and diverse community of colleagues, including academics who teach museum studies, their students, museum consultants, exhibit designers, and in-house exhibit developers and writers. They told us what parts of the book were most helpful, as well as what needed to change. Later, in the last throes of the editing process, we consulted with our colleagues again, this time to get their opinions about a couple of less traditional approaches we have taken for the third edition.

Eliminated Footnotes

Ah, footnotes! You like them—they are valuable sources of the authors' ideas and provide the "intellectual genealogy" for academic papers. Or you don't like them—they are distracting, and they break the flow of the narrative. Or footnotes make you feel guilty for not using them.

We decided to not use them. We are practitioners, not academics, and this book is meant for practitioners. We have made sure that quotes and examples in the text include searchable keywords. A curious reader can easily find the source material online. In other words, just google it. Also, the sources we cite are in the bibliography.

The Photo Figures

The most criticized element of earlier editions has been the photos. The quality was poor, and the labels depicted were not always legible. In response, we have tried a new approach: photo figures. They include pairs of photos—a label and its context—plus a caption. Again, so as not to interrupt the narrative text, we've grouped the photo figures at the end of four sections of the book. The captions make points that complement the content of the chapters in that section and show good examples of what works as well as what not to do. The photo figure sections are designed to stand on their own and can be read in conjunction with the narrative or as a separate summary of the chapters in that section.

The Essentials

"The Essentials" are new to this edition. They are four fundamental to-do actions that are essential to good interpretive exhibitions. They grew out of the previous editions and evolved further in 2021 as we were editing and writing *EL3*. They came into sharp focus during the pandemic, when Beverly was invited to do a twenty-minute Zoom presentation about labels for a museum group (Gente de Museos) in Bogota, Colombia. Her talk would be live-translated into Spanish, so she needed to be succinct, clear, and fast. She came up with a "holy trinity": (1) Have a big idea. (2) Prototype. (3) Make them shorter. In 2022 we added one more: (4) Don't forget about orientation, because too often its importance is, well, forgotten. These four essentials are equally important and interdependent. They are not only essential to good labels; they are essential elements of good exhibitions in general.

The essentials exist in a concise list in the first and last chapters. Each essential also gets its own chapter, where the ideas and supporting examples are fleshed out. At the end of the book, there's a handy page that you can tear out and post wherever it will serve as a daily reminder. If this were a digital book, you could use it as a screen saver.

WHAT'S NOT HERE

We've opted to not deal with artificial intelligence, augmented reality, and the use of ChatGPT to write labels. Although these are very hot topics, our focus is on helping people use more traditional tools to write good labels for in-person experiences in physical exhibitions with words on the walls, in cases, on screens, in audio formats, and in video captioning. But hey, if ChatGPT can write a great big idea, go for it.

FINALLY

So, welcome again, old friends and new readers. May all your labels be great. Remember this: You are perfect. And the work can always be improved.

PART I

Introduction

1

Guidelines and Essentials

This book is mainly for people who write labels for interpretive exhibitions. They are a lucky group because they get to craft texts that focus on real things in real spaces for visitors in meaningful places with shared boundaries. Label writers come to this task from many vantage points: as specialists in the exhibit topic, as people trained in informal education, as interpreters in the National Park System, as self-educated, interested museum exhibit enthusiasts, and as museum studies teachers and students.

We focus on labels in physical exhibitions. Conveniently, many of the tips, recommendations, and guidelines apply equally well to labels in the less-bounded, unlimited realms of digital content and virtual exhibitions.

Years of practice, research, visitor studies, and evaluation of labels in exhibitions have taught us how to encourage reading and foster engagement, comprehension, and meaning-making. Many books, articles, and people have passed on valuable ideas that have informed our thinking about guidelines and essentials. Shout-outs to those who came before us, especially Chandler Screven for his support and leadership in championing visitor research in the exhibit planning process and to Harris Shettel for being the antagonistic soul he was at challenging our new ideas and reminding us to build on the old ones. Still good advice. The sixteen guidelines listed below are a condensed list—elaborated upon in the body of the book—of the key elements for writing better interpretive labels.

SIXTEEN GUIDELINES FOR MAKING BETTER INTERPRETIVE LABELS

1. Relate exhibit label content to the **big idea** of the exhibition.

2. Emphasize interpretation that offers **provocation** beyond simply presenting information.

3. **Know your audience:** Address visitors' prior knowledge, interests, and/or misconceptions.

4. Have a **recognizable system** and organize labels by their function.

5. **Use chunks** of text in short paragraphs, not large blocks of text in one paragraph.

6. Begin **captions** with concrete, not abstract, information.

7. **Identify the author** or voice that is talking to you in the labels.

8. Write with a **vocabulary** that is within reach of the majority of visitors.

9. **Be as short** and concise as possible or only as long as absolutely necessary.

10. **Use graphics** with the words to reinforce the messages.

11. If you ask **questions** in labels, ask questions that a visitor would ask.

12. Integrate **instructions for interactive** exhibits in logical, intuitive ways.

13. Use **typography** that is legible and easy on the eyes.

14. **Try out texts:** Prototype them in draft form before finalizing label copy.

15. **Put labels as close** as possible to the objects they refer to.

16. **Provide orientation**—physical, conceptual, psychological—to the exhibition space.

These guidelines will help you write visitor-friendly interpretive labels that decrease visitors' efforts to read them and increase the benefit visitors get from them. They will also help you avoid the common mistakes made when writing and designing labels, such as too many words, letters that are too small, too much information, unintelligible icons, and poor placement. A great interpretive label is one that's been guided by a big idea, has been prototyped and tried out with visitors, doesn't have too many words, and exceeds expectations.

FOUR ESSENTIALS FOR MAKING EFFECTIVE INTERPRETIVE EXHIBITIONS

As we developed the third edition of *Exhibit Labels*, in addition to distilling the elements of effective interpretive labels, we have created a short list of the most essential practices for creating effective exhibitions. These essentials did not present themselves from the get-go; they evolved over the first year of editing, rewriting, and adding chapters. These four steps rose to the top as most important for all players in the exhibit planning and development team:

HAVE A BIG IDEA

See chapter 2, page 9

WRITE LESS

See chapter 9, page 83

PROTOTYPE

See chapter 20, page 225

DON'T FORGET ABOUT ORIENTATION

See chapter 13, page 135

These four essentials are discussed in detail in the chapters noted above, and they appear throughout the book. They are also summarized in chapter 25, where, as a bonus, there's an extra tear-out page you can carry with you wherever you go.

PART II

Overview

2

Behind It All: The Big Idea

A powerful exhibition idea will clarify and focus the nature and scope of an exhibition and provide a well-defined goal against which to rate its success.

Writers can do their jobs better and the exhibition team can put together a more coherent exhibition when a big idea sets the conceptual boundaries. Simplicity is not the goal: It's about clarification and focus.

WHAT IS A BIG IDEA?

A big idea is a sentence—a statement—of what the exhibition is about. It is one complete, noncompound, active sentence that identifies a subject, an action (the verb), and a consequence ("so what?"). It is one big idea, not four. A big idea is big because it has fundamental meaningfulness that is important to human nature. It is not trivial.

The definition of a big idea, written as a big idea statement, could read like this: *The big idea provides an unambiguous focus for the exhibit team throughout the exhibit development process by clearly stating in one noncompound sentence the scope and purpose of an exhibition.* This one contains thirty words, but there's no word limit on a big idea. It should be as long as it needs to be.

WHAT DOES IT LOOK LIKE?

The following five big idea examples contain a clear subject, an active verb, and a "so what?". As you read each one, imagine the picture you get in your mind of what you will see, do, and find out in an exhibition with this big idea.

Most of what we know about the universe comes from messages we read in light.

A healthy swamp—an example of a threatened ecosystem—provides many surprising benefits to humans.

Forensic scientists look for evidence of crimes against wildlife in order to enforce wildlife laws.

The conditions for life on Earth in extreme environments help define the ways we search for life on other planets.

Art depicting the California gold rush promoted a skewed, romanticized vision of one of the nineteenth century's most important events.

As you can see in the five examples above, the subject can be stated in one word (*swamp, scientists*) with adjectives (*healthy, forensic*), or more than one word (*most of what we know about the universe, the conditions for life on Earth, art depicting the California gold rush*).

The next three examples do not conform to the Serrell rigors of a big idea statement (subject-verb-so what?), but they do function as a big idea in that they define or describe the content of the exhibition.

Manufacturing a Miracle: Brooklyn and the Story of Penicillin

Sharks are not what you think.

What is it about dogs that strongly connects them to humans?

Some people confuse topics, outputs, or objectives with big ideas. Topics, outputs, and objectives will not help keep the exhibition focused.

These examples are *not* big ideas:

This exhibit is about the settlement of the western United States (a topic).

This exhibit will present the complex historical and scientific information surrounding the questionable authenticity of sculpture (an intended output).

Visitors will learn about molecular structure, chemical reactions, and the scientific process of analyzing unknown substances (an objective).

Visitors will develop a sense of wonder about nature by exploring the secret world of animals (an objective).

These are not big ideas because they don't say what the subject of the exhibition is or tell you what is going on. If "visitors" or "the exhibit" is the subject, you haven't got a big idea yet. If the visitors are doing something, it's probably an objective. If the exhibit is doing something, it's probably an output.

Big ideas work regardless of the type of the institution, the size of its budget, or the nature of the content. Ask: "What is the topic we are going to deal with in this exhibit?" "What is the topic 'doing'"? "Why should anyone care?" Answer these questions to get you closer to having a big idea.

HOW DO YOU COME UP WITH A BIG IDEA?

It takes time—hours, days, even months. It's not a matter of just wordsmithing. It takes a lot of thinking and rethinking. It is messy. There's lots of editing and reediting. Sleeping on it. Often it means tabling it until later or even starting over. Sometimes you go through the whole development process without one. Sometimes you find it after opening. Sooner is better.

There's no formula for coming up with a big idea, but some practitioners have come up with a flexible process of give-and-take until the big idea emerges. Exhibit developer Darcie Fohrman says, "When collaborating on concept planning with diverse teams, I like to keep it organic and cumulative. We get to know each other's perspectives and why they care about it. We look at what we want visitors to know and feel. We test our assumptions with target audiences. On and on until the objectives, big idea, hook, vision, etc., emerge." This process works best when there is a strong and experienced facilitator.

CONSENSUS IS IMPORTANT

Reaching the big idea by consensus is important because it needs to be "owned" by everyone on the team. If you decide on a big idea by voting democratically, the losers will be resentful, and "I told you so" will haunt the process. Consensus means that everyone shares the successes as well as the missed opportunities at the end.

HOW IS A BIG IDEA USED?

Having a big idea does not mean that the exhibition has to insist on communicating it overtly, but it provides a thread of meaning, coherence, and weight. It is primarily a tool for the team, not an actual label for visitors, so although it must be clear, it can use a complex vocabulary.

Exhibit developers use the big idea to delineate what will and will not be included in the exhibition. The big idea also guides the development of exhibit elements and their labels. This means that each element must have a clearly defined objective that supports, exemplifies, or illustrates aspects of the big idea. For each exhibit component, the question "What's this got to do with the big idea?" should have a clear and positive answer.

Some exhibit developers do not exercise self-control when selecting content for an exhibition. They have no limits and do not resist the temptation to try to tell every story. As one developer admitted proudly, "I'm the one who was responsible for the 450 panels on the wall. I wouldn't give up." But what is most interesting to that expert will not interest, engage, or positively impress most visitors. Faced with this type of exhibition, a visitor reported, "My heart sank when I saw all those panels."

Exhibitions that have a big idea can be big or small (e.g., eight thousand or five hundred square feet). Size is not the determining factor. A small exhibit with a big idea can be very powerful. A big exhibit with a big idea can contain many elements that reinforce one another.

ARE THERE ANY EXHIBITIONS THAT DON'T NEED A BIG IDEA?

Some very large, encyclopedic, nondidactic permanent collections may not lend themselves to having a big idea. But even for these, institutions may want to think about renovations and reinstallations that would break up their large mishmash of galleries into smaller, more intellectually accessible units.

Not every exhibition at a children's museum needs to have a big idea, but the teams should be clear about the ones that do and don't. They should decide by looking carefully at the age of the audience, the topic, and whether the exhibit experiences lend themselves to new learning—beyond active, engaging play.

WHAT HAPPENS WHEN THERE'S NOT A BIG IDEA?

Exhibitions that lack a big idea are very common. And they are overwhelming, confusing, intimidating, and too complex. There are too many labels, and the texts do not relate to the objects. The labels contain too many different ideas that do not clearly relate to each other.

Too often, museum practitioners, especially those working in children's museums and science museums, do not ask themselves, "What is the big idea?" Instead, they develop an exhibition as a bunch of "neat, affordable devices that visitors will love and not destroy." These neat exhibit elements are often developed with cleverness and creativity, but they lack a cohesive or logical relationship to each other. They also lack soul—the fundamental meaningfulness that answers the question "So what?"

Neat exhibit ideas without precision, focus, and soul are not enough. There should be more to exhibit elements than having visitors like them and enjoy themselves. Enjoyment is not the only criterion for success. Visitors should be able to understand what an element is about, grasp its context within the whole exhibition (i.e., within the big idea), and find it personally meaningful and useful, especially in exhibitions that claim to be educational.

Without a big idea, the job of the label writer is much more difficult. Their interpretive text contains fragmented, unrelated facts that provide information for the sake of information, not meaningful, useful experiences for the visitor's sake.

ADVANTAGES TO HAVING A BIG IDEA

Exhibit developers who work in teams will appreciate the power of a big idea. It can unify the efforts of the team members by helping eliminate arguments over ego and turf. When all members of the team focus on the same objectives, each person's ideas can be considered more fairly. If an idea works, the team embraces it; if it does not fit, the team can reject it without bias by one member. A clear big idea also protects the team from criticism by sources whose support is needed, such as the director or the board. In an exhibition driven by the team's desire to communicate a big idea, there will be less need for the single job of "educator" because the whole team will share that role.

A big idea works best when the team writes it down—but does not set it in stone—at the beginning of the exhibition development process and changes it when necessary. The operative words are "written down." If the big idea is not written down, different people on the exhibit team will have their own interpretations for it, and conflicts will develop over what is necessary and appropriate in the exhibition. Even when the big idea is written, it is amazing how differently people will interpret it. Members of the exhibit team should all memorize or post the big idea label over their desks so they can refer to it easily.

"The big idea serves as the place to start, a place to come back to, and a place to end as the planning progresses or when the team gets off track. Repeatedly asking the questions what, how, and why helps to define and refine what we want to say," said a museum studies student.

A BIG IDEA AND EVALUATION GO HAND IN HAND

A big idea can be tried out with visitors early in the planning stages, and visitor response can help developers shape or modify it or tighten up the exhibit plan. After the exhibition is completed, evaluation can tell you whether visitors' experiences successfully reflect or incorporate the big idea.

As they exit an exhibition, if visitors can easily, unhesitatingly, and thoroughly answer the question "What was that exhibition about?" and their answers resonate positively with the big idea, you have strong evidence of comprehension and personal significance. If most of them seem hesitant ("Uh, ummm . . ."), uncertain ("I think, maybe, well . . ."), brief and incomplete ("It was about sharks"), or apologetic ("I really wasn't paying attention"; "I just breezed through"), that's evidence that the big idea was not clear.

Summative evaluation can answer the question "To what degree and in what ways did visitors understand what the exhibition was about?" Visitors certainly can create their own meanings in ways unintended by the exhibit developers. This is not a problem as long as the majority of them create something that is not contradictory to the exhibit's purpose or does not perpetuate misunderstandings the exhibit was supposed to correct.

Having a clear big idea in the first place is important because so many other things depend on it—content research, label writing, image selection, design, layout, graphic look and feel, size, evaluation metrics. With a concise statement as the basis for all interpretation, the use of words in the exhibition will have clear direction and defined limits.

For more examples, illustrations, activities, and ideas about big ideas go online for the e-book, free for you: https://serrellassociates.com/store/big -idea-ebook.

3

What Are Interpretive Labels?

Any label that serves to explain, guide, question, inform, or provoke—in a way that invites participation by the reader— is interpretive.

The purpose of interpretive labels is to contribute to the overall visitor experience in a positive, enlightening, provocative, and meaningful way. Interpretive labels address visitors' unspoken concerns: What's in it for me? Why should I care? How will knowing this improve my life? If labels only identify objects, animals, or artwork, they are not interpretive.

Interpretive labels are part of interpretive exhibitions, which are displays that intend to tell stories, contrast points of view, present challenging issues, or endeavor to change people's attitudes. Interpretive exhibitions are found in all types of museums. They are designed to give visitors an opportunity to become engaged in the exhibit environment, be aware of the communication objectives intended by the exhibit developers, and find personally meaningful connections with the exhibits.

SOME BACKGROUND ON THE HISTORY OF INTERPRETATION

But what is "interpretation"? It is more than just presenting information and encouraging participation. It comes to museums (in the United States) from the National Park Service's oral tradition of educational programming. And it is far more interactive than traditional formal educational models of teachers as deliverers and mediators of information.

In the classic *Interpreting Our Heritage*, Freeman Tilden laid out six principles for interpretation, developed from his extensive experience with national park ranger programs, writing labels and designing exhibitions at park visitor centers. Although his 1950s language is non-inclusive (e.g., visitors and interpreters are referred to as "he" and "him") and the photographs are dated, his principles still ring strong and true, presented as they are in a straightforward, down-to-earth style.

Tilden's six principles:

1. Any interpretation that does not somehow relate what is being displayed or described to something within the personality or experience of the visitor will be sterile.

2. Information, as such, is not interpretation. Interpretation is revelation based upon information. But they are entirely different things. However, all interpretation includes information.

3. Interpretation is an art that combines many arts, whether the materials presented are scientific, historical, or architectural. Any art is in some degree teachable.

4. The chief aim of interpretation is not instruction, but provocation.

5. Interpretation should aim to present a whole rather than a part and must address itself to the whole man rather than any phase.

6. Interpretation addressed to children (say, up to the age of twelve) should not be a dilution of the presentation to adults but should follow a fundamentally different approach. To be at its best it will require a separate program.

Tilden proposed his principles in 1957, long before museum educators and other practitioners began using language like the visitor experience, meaning-making, and empowerment. His fourth principle is the most relevant to this book: Revelation and provocation, not instruction, should be the goal of interpretation.

Several other books discuss the importance and describe the history of interpretive exhibits. Two standard references within the environmental interpretation field are Sam H. Ham's *Interpretation: Making a Difference on Purpose* and John Veverka's *Interpretive Master Planning*. In *Interpretive Planning for Museums: Integrating Visitor Perspectives in Decision Making*, Wells, Butler, and Koke situate the role of interpretive labels into a broader consideration of interpretive planning for exhibitions or for interpretive master plans at the institution level. Their book emphasizes how museum practitioners can integrate visitor perspectives into their plans for developing and evaluating interpretive efforts.

Two professional associations are dedicated to issues of interpretation: the National Association for Interpretation and the Association for Art Museum Interpretation. AAMI's online blog has many valuable examples, and its annual gatherings are a good source of new ideas.

LABELS AS STORYTELLING

Interesting similarities tie together interpretation, narratives, storytelling, and exhibit texts. Printed words exist as visual and verbal elements to the reader's eye and mind, and they are oral components to the reader's ear, either read silently or heard as read aloud. Good interpretation, like good storytelling, employs the sound of the words and the images they create to carry the readers or listeners along, and lets them participate by anticipating where the story is going. Our brains are wired for emotional storytelling strategies, says Lisa Cron, author of *Wired for Story: The Writer's Guide to Using Brain Science to Hook Readers from the Very First Sentence*. Says Cron, "All story is emotion based—if we're not feeling, we're not reading." Interpretive exhibit labels tell very short stories. Below are three examples of individual interpretive labels that strike a good balance between what the reader might anticipate is coming next and what does. This balance is a hallmark of good storytelling.

From an aquarium, at a seabird exhibit:
When the tide ebbs, sandpipers fan out across mudflats and beaches to feed. As the tide rises, they retreat, to preen themselves and wait for the next low tide.

From a decorative arts exhibit, as a caption for a pair of textile screens:
These screens were made at the Savonnerie manufactory, which was owned by the French Crown and provided carpets and screens for the royal chateaux. Such screens were known as paravents ("against the wind") and were usually kept folded in the corners of rooms. When the rooms were being used, the screens would be arranged by servants for protection against drafts.

From a history museum, as a photo caption in an exhibition about logging:
The logger needed clothes that were functional and provided freedom of movement. Pants were cut off just below the boot tops to keep the rain out and to prevent snagging. Men working in the woods often had to take off at top speed, and if a pant leg caught it could mean the difference between life and death.

These kinds of labels encourage readers to look back and forth between the label and the object or photo while following the details of the narrative. Readers can imagine action in their minds and memories, aided by the label's concrete references. They may not see the tide rising, feel the cold breezes in the chateaux, or witness the logger running for his life, but these quick stories give visitors a "minds-on" moment.

The Subject and the Action of the Story

People refer to labels in various ways: as blurbs, captions, wall texts, descriptions, titles, legends, cards, and explanations. What changes would it take to get them to call labels *stories* or *conversations*? One way might be to follow the advice of Joseph M. Williams in his very handy book *Style: Ten Lessons in Clarity and Grace*. He gives us excellent guidelines for how to make prose more clear, less passive, and more engaging. His "First Principle of Clear Writing" states, "When we link the simple point that sentences are stories about characters who act to the way we use the grammar of a sentence to describe those characters and their actions, we get a principle of style more powerful than any other."

Williams's principle has two parts:

1. In the subjects of your sentences, name your cast of characters.

2. In the verbs of your sentences, name the crucial actions in which you involve those characters.

Similarly, labels that lack subjects and have unclear action will not tell clear stories that flow easily.

Because many of the stories in museums are about people, labels can be edited to include them as the subjects. In the two examples below, notice how changing the subject of the label from objects to people creates a more engaging story. In the first version, the subject is the object; in the second version, the subject is the people.

Pictograph
Carvings and paintings on rock are scattered throughout California. They seem to have had magical or religious significance related to the hunting of large game. Other rock paintings were made during girls' coming-of-age ceremonies and boys' initiation rites.

Rock Carvings and Paintings—Pictographs

Early people carved and painted on rocks throughout California. The pictographs they created, such as the one on your left, may signify magical or religious aspects of the large game they hunted. Other rock paintings showed girls' coming-of-age ceremonies and boys' initiation rites.

In the first, the subject "they" refers to the pictographs, not the early people, and pictographs are never defined. Pictographs do not have beliefs, people do; the second example actively acknowledges that.

By focusing on people, interpretive labels—as part of interpretive exhibitions—can tell stories that contrast points of view, present challenging issues, or endeavor to change people's attitudes.

What is said in a label will depend on the big idea, the object displayed, the context of the label, and other factors. Below are three drafts with different vantage points. The topic is a lifesaving station that had a key clock post where surfmen who patrolled the beach clocked in during their rounds. What should the subject of the label be: the surfman, the post, or the key? That depends on what you want readers to pay the most attention to and what the label is captioning: an object or a photo. Notice how the emphasis changes with the subject.

Before radio communication, **surfmen** walked regular patrols along the beach looking for mariners in distress. To prove he'd done his job, a surfman punched in at a key clock post, located two miles in either direction from the Life-Saving Service or Coast Guard station.

Posts like these were driven into the sand two miles in each direction from the Life-Saving Service or Coast Guard stations. They were the destination for surfmen, who patrolled the beach on foot looking for mariners in distress. A key attached to the post made an impression on the surfman's time clock, proving he made his rounds.

This concrete post originally housed **a key** used to prove a surfman had walked his two-mile patrol. Stashed inside the metal box, the key was fished out by a surfman and pressed into his time clock, registering that he'd made the journey.

Telling Difficult Stories

Because museums can provide multiple types of experiences for visitors, they are in a unique position to create exhibits that tell stories about difficult or controversial topics, such as race, immigration, environmental disasters, rape, and murder. Exhibitions can be designed to provide safe spaces and to give visitors starting points for critical conversations, collaborative learning, and problem-solving discussions.

The traveling exhibition *Race: Are We So Different?* asked "What is race?" and opened a public discourse on this complicated topic. One of the primary messages was that the concept of race is a human invention and that we are all more alike than different. Individual exhibits encouraged interaction and conversation. Talking circles, mediated by trained docents, gave visitors the opportunity to discuss issues of race raised by the exhibition and from their own personal experiences.

An exhibition about the Japanese internment camp at Heart Mountain in Wyoming walked a line between revealing what happened there and being sensitive to the people who were involved. The exhibition took a clear position: The internment was both illegal and wrong. The labels were written in the first person, and sometimes in the voice of a person who had lived there. Oral histories and interviews prompted visitors to put themselves in the shoes of the interned people and provoked thoughts about modern civil rights issues.

Darkened Waters: Profile of an Oil Spill was about the grounding of the *Exxon Valdez* off the Alaska coast and the aftermath. Like the Heart Mountain exhibition, *Darkened Waters* had a point of view: The oil spill was a huge disaster. But it included other, differing points of view—of commercial fishermen, oil industry workers, government officials, conservationists, Alaska Native people, and others caught up in the spill—letting people speak for themselves wherever possible. It did not, however, try to present those points of view as equally important. Exhibit elements about the transport and use of petroleum, the vulnerability of marine life, and long-term energy needs encouraged visitors to think about the future and to take action to protect the environment.

The Children's Museum of Indianapolis created a traveling exhibit honoring Emmett Till, who was murdered in 1955 in Mississippi. Among the objects traveling with the exhibition was one of the many commemorative road signs that mark and memorialize Till's murder throughout Tallahatchie County. The battered sign held a second story: Vandalized over the years and featured in a racist social media post in 2019, the sign connects the racism of the 1950s to the current day. "We are honored to work with this incredible team including Emmett's family to elevate this important story and bring attention to widespread racism that continues today," said Jennifer Pace Robinson, president and CEO of the Children's Museum of Indianapolis.

When the Isabella Stewart Gardner Museum brought together four monumental paintings by the Renaissance artist Titian, they realized they also had to address the inherent sexual violence depicted in the mythological subject matter. Recognizing that there would be visitors to the exhibition who had experienced sexual assault or rape, museum staff worked with the Boston Area Rape Crisis Center to develop interpretive content designed to be sensitive and respectful for those visitors.

While closed to the public during the COVID-19 pandemic, The Nelson-Atkins Museum embarked on a harm-reduction audit of their exhibit labels. Working across departments, they collaboratively defined what was meant by "harm," drew up a list of fourteen types of harm, and embarked on a label-rewriting program. For example, the original label for a sixteenth-century Italian cassone, or chest, that depicts the myth of Apollo and Daphne presents a romantic story. In the revision, "[W]e explicitly called out the violent nature of this myth as a story of attempted rape," wrote Rachel Nicholson in a four-part blog post about the project. She continued, "Everyone interviewed preferred the shift away from a traditional art historical approach to the new label that was more explicitly tied to a twenty-first-century understanding of the myth and gendered power dynamics. This one was particularly interesting (and exciting) for me, as it proves that people appreciate, and may actually want, culturally relevant discussions and transparent language in interpretation."

In 2012, History Colorado's first attempt at an exhibition about the 1864 Sand Creek Massacre—titled *Collision: The Sand Creek Massacre, 1860s–Today*—was shut down after only a few weeks because tribal representatives resented being excluded from the exhibit development process. The museum then engaged in a ten-year collaborative process with the Cheyenne and Arapaho tribes of Oklahoma. "The main thing we told them when we started out is we want you to tell the truth," said tribal representative Fred Mosqueda. The new exhibition, now titled *The Sand Creek Massacre: The Betrayal That Changed Cheyenne and Arapaho People Forever*, opened in 2022.

Keeping It Real

The nature of interpretation in museum exhibitions and the techniques for doing it well are part of a larger context of issues that surround education, communication, and being human. Bringing forward real objects and real people, exhibits can tell origin stories, envision the future, and give a sense of continuity and purpose. The challenge is to do this in ways that resonate with the communities we serve.

4

Types of Labels in an Exhibition

Every label in an exhibition has a specific purpose that needs to make sense within the organization of the whole. Given the fact that visitors often encounter labels out of order, they also need to function independently.

Museums have yet to coin a universal terminology to identify types of labels. Some institutions use function (e.g., orientation, introduction, caption); others use placement (wall text, case label, freestanding); some have in-house colloquial expressions (chat panels, tombstone labels); and others haven't thought about labels enough to commit to an in-house style with a clear vocabulary or standards. Regardless of the names they are given, labels should be developed as an integrated system, from the single title to the broadest categories to the one-of-a-kinds. And they should all work together.

The most important types of interpretive labels in any exhibition are the title, introduction, section labels, group labels, and captions. These labels help organize the information and present the exhibition's rationale for looking as it does. Although these labels are often developed and written in a linear and hierarchical way, they may not be used in the "right" order by visitors. Nevertheless, the labels still should have internal integrity, organization, and a clear logic to their design. Even if an exhibition or collection is not intended to have any interpretive purpose, the title and introduction should at least briefly describe why it's there. Visitor research studies, such as those described in the special issue of *Visitor Behavior* on orientation and circulation, edited by Stephen Bitgood, have shown that visitors who understand the organization of the exhibition and use it in the intended sequence (if there is one) spend more time and get more out of it.

TYPES OF INTERPRETIVE LABELS

Label Name	Purpose
Exhibition titles	To attract attention To inform about the theme To identify the area
Introductory labels	To introduce big idea To orient visitors to the space To delineate the themes of the exhibition
Section labels	To announce a new area of the exhibition
Concept labels	To add information about more general ideas or explain a specific topic or theme
Group labels	To explain commonalities of a grouping to interpret a specific group of objects to introduce a subtheme
Caption labels	To introduce individual objects, models, phenomena

Exhibition Titles

Exhibition titles identify the name of the exhibition. The best titles will arouse interest and curiosity and give enough information so visitors can decide whether they are interested enough in the subject matter to enter.

Large title labels placed high overhead (i.e., more than eight feet from the ground) may be missed by visitors and will need to be repeated somewhere in their line of sight.

There should only be one title, and the same words should be used consistently throughout the museum: on the floor plan, in the guidebook, on the exhibit itself, and in the press release.

Introductory Labels

Introductory labels set up the organization and tone of the exhibition. A large, simple floor plan and a summary statement will help prepare visitors for the size, sections, and themes of the space, even if it is a small exhibition, and especially if it is large.

Quick, clear orientation is a very important feature for visitors. Many people will not stop to read a long introduction because they are being drawn into the exhibit by many competing and enticing sights, objects, and sounds. If the entryway is crowded, visitors will not want to stop and block traffic flow into the exhibition.

Dense introductory text with many thoughts all crammed into one paragraph is not inviting or easy to read. For all these reasons, keep information short and the print large so that visitors can scan it without stopping.

Even though visitors are more likely to read gallery introductions in art museums, especially in special or temporary exhibitions, the Detroit Institute of Arts found that fewer than one in ten visitors read a section or gallery panel. Recommendations from their summative evaluation included this: Decrease the word limit for introductory panels from 150 to 50, and increase the size of the type to allow reading from a distance and at a glance.

The prominence and importance of an introductory label may make it difficult to get the exhibit team to agree on the text. As one label writer put it, "I can write three dozen captions, and nobody will take any interest in them. But as soon as I write the introductory label, everybody from the director to the janitor wants to fiddle with the wording." This is ironic because visitors use these label types in exactly the opposite way.

A good introductory label can also serve as an exit label. After experiencing the exhibition and all it has to offer, the content can serve as a summary or reflection—sort of a coda that helps readers think, "Yes, I got it. That was good!" and feel inspired.

If an exhibition has more than one entrance, an introductory label should be placed at each.

Section Labels

Section labels introduce themes or areas within an exhibition. These important clues to the arrangement of the content are often missed or skipped by visitors if they only contain words, because visitors' attention is being drawn to the objects instead. Adding visuals and even mounting objects to section panels can create more interest in them. Placing them in the line of sight and keeping them short help too.

Concept Labels

Concept labels play a wide variety of roles, such as setting the stage or mood for an area of an exhibition, explaining a process, or posing and answering a question. They often include graphics that can make the communication more effective. Many words-only concept labels are used to supplement captions and group labels, especially in history exhibitions, where they fill in important information not being illustrated with graphics, objects, or photos. They range in length from twenty-five words to more than one hundred, depending on how much they are trying to say. They work best when they are well integrated with the messages in the surrounding texts, are not too long, and don't stray far from the big idea. They are less successful when they add too many ideas that are not related directly to visitors' experiences with the real stuff.

Group Labels

Group labels inform visitors of the rationale behind a subgrouping of objects, paintings, or animals. "Why are these things shown together?" is a common question in the backs of visitors' minds, and it needs to be answered to help visitors feel comfortable, competent, and in control of their own experience. Even if there is little cohesiveness in the groupings, inform visitors of that so they will not wonder if they are missing something. Do not make area or group labels so wordy that people will want to skip them.

Group labels are also called "focus labels" and "chat panels" because they often contain more content than a title or subtitle and are more general than captions.

Captions

Captions are specific labels for specific objects (e.g., artifacts, photos, and phenomena), and they are commonly used in all types of museum exhibitions. Captions are the "frontline" form of interpretive labels because many visitors wander around in exhibits without attending to the linear or hierarchical organization of information (title, introduction, section label) until they see something interesting. If visitors stop only when something catches their attention, the information in caption labels must make sense independently while also working harmoniously with all the other labels.

Captions should refer to visible specifics—beyond the obvious—of the objects they discuss. If they are abstract or can be read alone without any reference to the object, they are not doing their job. Labels that support the caption information, such as subgroup or area labels, should be close by so that visitors can start with the specific caption or ID, then jump to the broader context, and vice versa. Captions are so important, they get their own treatment in the next chapter.

TYPES OF NON-INTERPRETIVE LABELS

Non-interpretive labels include identification labels (ID labels), donor plaques, wayfinding, regulatory signs, warnings, and credit panels. Labels for interactive exhibits, which have special requirements, are addressed in chapter 17.

Identification Labels

Identification labels contain minimal short details, such as name, maker, date, material, scientific name, and accession number. They are also known as tombstone labels. They are not interpretive, although they are often combined with captions.

Several formats for ID labels are commonly used, but there is no standardized design. Many art museums have their own in-house guidelines.

The examples below show art and animal ID information.

The Abduction of the Sabine Women
Painted in Naples, about 1640
Johann Heinrich Schonfeld
Oil on canvas

PIER FRANCESCO
Italian, 1612–1666
Vision of Saint Bruno 1660–1666
Oil on canvas 89.PA.4

PORCELLANIDAE
Neopetrolisthes maculatus
Anemone Porcelain Crab

DROMEDARY CAMEL
Camelus dromedarius
NORTH AFRICA AND ARABIA

In most cases, what is most important to visitors is *what it is*—its title or its common name, identifiers that they can relate to. The first example shows the most sensitivity to the visitors' interests, vocabulary, and priorities. In the second, an unfamiliar artist's name and three sets of numbers present a jumble of details for visitors to sort through. In the third example, few visitors would even know that the first line was the animal's taxonomic family name and the second its scientific Latin binomial. The final example recognizes the basic information zoo-goers want to know. But zoos, aquariums, and botanic gardens still need to use scientific names to further identify the species on display, because common names do not sufficiently distinguish one animal or plant from another (Which deer? Which snapper? What rose?).

As long as they are legible, identification labels are usually easy for visitors to decode once a person has seen one or two. While consistency of ID information formats is important within each exhibition, format can vary between exhibitions. Different types of objects, artifacts, or animals might suggest or require a different ordering of information. Make a style that works for you, and then be consistent. We are aware of a growing movement to give attribution to makers of things that were formerly identified as objects. For example, an ID label for an Ojibwe basket from the nineteenth century might now include "Unknown Ojibwe artist or maker." In the American Alliance of Museums 2023 keynote panel, C. J Brafford, director of the Ute Indian Museum, reminds us that these are not artifacts or objects but "belongings" and should be referred to as such.

Donor Information

Donor information is typically provided last and in the smallest type. These taglines ("donated by . . ."; "gift of . . .") are not interpretive, and they should not be larger than or mixed in with captions, IDs, or other interpretive labels. Labels that acknowledge funders are best dealt with in their own space, near the end of the exhibition, in a discreet, respectful way. Materials, typefaces, and sizes should be sophisticated but not out of character with the rest of the signage.

Expensive bronze donor or funder plaques next to dog-eared paper interpretive labels indicate that visitors' interests are not being considered first. Donor and funder names mixed into titles, such as "The Webber Hall of Mammals," are ostentatious and confusing. Exhibit designer Paul Orselli has collected good examples of creative donor recognition installations in his blog post "Many Ways to Say Thanks."

Credit Panels

Credit panels recognize the contributions and efforts of all the people who worked on the exhibition. A credit panel does not have to be in bronze, nor does it have to be big, but somewhere, credit should be given. Visitors should see the many people and different skills required to make a good show. Credit panels are also good for staff morale, as well as for reference and accountability. It's nice when the label writers get credit!

Wayfinding and Orientation Signs

Wayfinding and orientation signs help visitors find their way around the museum and orient themselves in each new space (such as when they walk in the front door or get off the elevator at an upper floor). These signs are technically not interpretive labels. But orientation and wayfinding signs play an important role in satisfying visitors' basic need to know where they are, which then makes them ready and receptive for learning. Visitors are not ready to receive interpretation if they feel lost. A secure and comfortable knowledge of their present location—and the subsequent relative locations of exits, restrooms, or food—allows visitors to feel ready for higher level social, creative, and intellectual pursuits. See chapter 13 for more information about the importance of orientation.

Regulatory Signs

Regulatory signs tell us not to touch the art or feed the animals. With a little creativity, prohibitive signs can be made friendly, funny, and positive rather than threatening.

Warning or Caution Labels

Warning or caution labels can alert visitors to the placement of exhibits they might want to avoid, such as nudity, violence, or strong sexual content. The function of these labels is to help visitors make the right choices for where and how to spend their time.

HOW MANY DIFFERENT TYPES OF LABELS IN ONE EXHIBITION?

The number of different types of labels used in any one exhibition will be driven by communication goals, size, budget, and other factors. It is good to limit the types of interpretive labels to fewer than ten. More than that and the exhibition design will look cluttered and feel disorganized, and visitors will have a hard time figuring out what the "system" is and how to follow it. Labels on every available surface—rails, kiosks, walls, stanchions, glass; mounted so that they flip, turn, or flow around and over graphics—plus projected and scrolling electronic labels are too much in one exhibition! For a more thorough discussion of flip labels, see chapter 16, "Labels that Ask Questions."

TRY A "RANDOM ACCESS" TEST OF THE TYPES OF LABELS

Since visitors often read labels "out of order," it's helpful to test individual labels to see if they are able to stand alone or can be read out of order. Take all labels of a certain type (e.g., all the captions, all the section labels) and scramble them up. Pull one out. If this is the first label that a person reads in the exhibition, will it serve as a good entry point? Select a set of three or four at random out of the pile and read them. Do they make sense in that mixed-up order? Will one-fifth of the labels support and convey the big idea? If labels pass this test, they will serve visitors well in the random, out-of-sequence, incomplete way that people typically move through an exhibition.

Good exhibitions will skillfully combine several types of labels and use them in a consistent manner. They need not conform to the exact types described here. But whatever form they take, each type of label should have a recognizable function that is clear to visitors. Size, typeface, color, graphic design, length, placement, and content will all be cues to the label's purpose. Multiple cues ensure that visitors easily follow the logic of the exhibit designers' intent and messages.

5

The Importance of Captions

Captions are used by visitors more than any other type of label in interpretive exhibitions.

Captions are the smaller labels for specific objects (e.g., artifacts, photos, art, and phenomena), and they are commonly used in all types of museum exhibitions. Captions are the "frontline" form of interpretive labels because many visitors wander through exhibitions without attending to the organization of information (title, introduction, section label) until they see something interesting.

Captions should refer to the visible specifics—beyond the obvious—of the objects they discuss. If they are abstract or can be read alone without any reference to the object, they are not doing their job. Group or section labels should be close by so that visitors can start with the specific caption, then jump to the broader context, and vice versa.

One of the most consistent findings from evaluations of museum exhibitions is that visitors read far more captions compared to other types of labels because captions are usually short and placed right next to an object. If visitors stop only when something catches their attention, the information in the caption label must make sense on its own as well as work harmoniously with the other labels.

Label writers might have a bit more editorial freedom with captions compared to other types of labels in an exhibition because stakeholders are more likely to focus on introductory or section label texts—and certainly on the title—than on captions. But visitors have the opposite focus, which is why label writers need to apply their skills carefully to captions.

GUIDELINES FOR CAPTIONS

To help make content for exhibit caption labels work effectively:

- Start with visual, concrete information—what visitors can see.

- Work from the specific to the general, not the other way around.

- Use paragraphs. Do not cram all the ideas into one long paragraph.

- Use bullets to make lists easier to read.

- Make the vocabulary appropriate for a broad range of ages.

The following is an example of a caption from an art exhibition about symbolism that contains several of the above-mentioned characteristics.

Rain Mask with Reptiles, Figures, and Bats

This powerful object was actually a mask used in a rain-petitioning dance at the Santa Anita settlement in the state of Guerrero, Mexico. It includes several symbols for water and rain:

- blue eyes, the color of water
- twisting, flowing serpents
- a vampire bat's head at the top of the mask, included because bats live in caves, believed to be the home of the rain gods

Another meaning of the mask relates to the notion of transformation and power. Lizards were said to be able to whisper secrets to the wearer. By wearing the mask, an individual was transformed into a godlike being with both animal attributes and the power to commune with and control nature.

This "Rain Mask" caption contains numerous references to concrete, visual aspects of the object, and encourages visitors to look for details and think about how it might feel to wear the mask. The final paragraph of "Rain Mask" has fifty words. Does it look too long to you? It reads more like a story than a list of unrelated facts.

What follows are more-detailed suggestions for writing better captions that will be more likely to be read by visitors.

Make Them Short

Help visitors read the caption all the way through by limiting the number of words. Five words per second is an average museum reading speed. Write most of the labels so that they can be read quickly—in ten seconds or less—which works out to about fifty words or less.

Vary Their Length

Don't make all captions the same length. Objects likely to be of more interest (e.g., biggest, most famous) to the majority of visitors can be longer. Objects that give support to the big idea deserve longer captions. But don't feel the need to fill up every caption's space with words. Leave some white space. It's visually relaxing for a change.

Can I SEE them?

Make caption type large enough for readers' range of visual acuity. Your audience includes senior citizens and children, regardless of the type of institution. A minimum 20-point type is strongly recommended. If visitors can't see the words, they can't read them. To increase legibility, use colors that create good contrast between the background and the type. Black type against a white background may be a boring choice for designers, but it's the best for most visitors' needs.

Placement Matters

The placement or position of captions is also important.

- Position captions so they are visible and legible to people in wheelchairs.

- Position captions so they are well lighted and shadows don't fall on them.

- Put the caption as close as possible to the object of the text.

If an object has been removed and the caption is still there, it is a thoughtful gesture to put up a photograph of the piece that is missing. Also, it's nice to say why it's gone—for example, on loan or for conservation purposes.

Design Matters

Captions deserve the same good typography and design as other types of labels. Choose type size, font, and type and background colors to provide enough contrast so the caption labels are legible. The best advice for achieving this? Mock them up and try them out in the context in which they will be displayed to make sure they work.

Captions for Interactive Exhibits

Captions for interactive exhibits follow the same guidelines as above, but the placement and ordering of information are even more important. Text that deals with *interpretation* should have a different design—that is, be in a different font, size, or color—than words that give *instructions*. Instructions need to be placed where people's hands and eyes naturally go.

Outdoor Waysides Caption Nature

Outdoor wayside panels are captions about a landscape. Waysides usually don't have a lot of competition with other texts, being few and far between along a trail or road or over a vista. Without the support of other nearby labels, they must provide context as well as content.

The same rules for captions apply. Waysides should address what visitors can see and should direct attention to a physical characteristic or place. Since the need to provide context might make them longer than typical caption labels, the text should be chunked out into easily readable bits and be accompanied by supporting visuals.

Don't Ask Captions to Do Too Much

Captions are strategic for their immediate context, relating directly to the object and conveying how the object is related to the big idea. They provide points of reference and relevance. Captions answer the question "What's this got to do with it?" and they do so as briefly and engagingly as possible. The goal is to whet the reader's appetite, not to include a ton of unrelated, extraneous information. Captions don't need to include less-relevant information or answer all possible questions when visitors can just google it.

6

Label Systems

The best system for organizing labels is by the type and purpose of each label, not various assumptions about who the visitors are.

Notions of levels, layers, and hierarchies for labels have great appeal to exhibit developers because they offer the promise of something for everyone in exhibitions. But they are often poorly defined and don't provide easy answers. This chapter argues against using layers or levels of information (often referred to as hierarchies) that are based on misguided assumptions about visitors.

We can't expect visitors to read exhibit texts in a particular order or assume that some visitors will seek one style of text over another. The best label system presents a variety of label types, defined by function and purpose. Think of this as a buffet of opportunities for readers rather than what's often called a layering of information. The buffet metaphor suggests a variety of choices *that all fall within one theme (the big idea) for a nonspecialist audience, all of which are important.* Visitors are free to pick and choose the elements that appeal to them, and any of their choices will add up to an experience that aligns with the exhibit developers' goals.

WHAT'S WRONG WITH "LAYERS" AND "LEVELS"?

The next four examples of label systems are common, but they have some serious faults—mainly because they encourage information overload in exhibitions. They are based on false assumptions about differences in visitors' interest, ability, or intelligence, implying a pejorative hierarchy in which those possessing more of these qualities receive priority or favor over visitors with less.

The False Something-for-Every-Special-Audience Layering System

The worst example of layering or levels comes into play when exhibition planners (often large teams of staff members and exhibit consultants) try to accommodate every different learning style, gender difference, developmental category, intelligence type, interest, and experience level. This allows team members to put too many ideas into the exhibition; every addition can then be defended by the rationale: "This part is for young children, or scholars, or women, or intuitive learners, or families," or whomever. What they really mean is "Someone, somewhere, sometime is bound to find this interesting because I do, and I don't want to leave it out." Their evaluation criterion is "If one person in one thousand gets turned on by this, it's worth it to me, so put it in." The result of this something-different-for-each-audience mistaken approach is an exhibition that is overwhelming and underused.

The Misguided "More-Interested-Visitor" Layering System

The notion of adding information "for the visitors who want more" is a well-intentioned idea that is rarely realized through exhibit labels. Dense or specialized texts will not be used by enough people to justify the time it takes to research, write, edit, design, fabricate, install, and light them. More important, there seems to be no good way to signal to those few "serious" visitors which levels are meant for them without demeaning, overwhelming, or confusing the rest of the visitors. For example, after attempting a multilayered label approach to match a variety of visitor knowledge and interest levels in the *Human Biology* exhibition at the Natural History Museum in London, exhibit director Roger Miles concluded, "It is better to concentrate on communicating some basic ideas than to fail to get anything over at all, and we feel that it is better to concentrate on succeeding at one level than to risk failure at two or more."

In the *Prehistoric Journey* exhibition at the Denver Museum of Natural History, planners originally organized the information according to three audience levels of interest: "Discovery," for children and low-interest, low-knowledge visitors; "Exploration," for most visitors, either individuals or in groups, and browsers; and "Study," for "motivated learners who prodigiously read," amateur paleontologists, and more-interested repeat visitors. "Discovery," "Exploration," and "Study" levels were signaled with graphic design cues. For example, the signal for study-level information was a panel shaped like a large open book. A magnifying glass signaled the discovery level. Although the three levels of interest were originally defined by types of visitors, the levels represented different interpretive strategies in their final form, defined by their purpose, with different topics. Summative evaluations by Margie Marino revealed that discovery exhibits ended up being used most frequently, regardless of visitors' prior knowledge or age level.

Sometimes layers of information are hidden by a system of multiple flip labels. This design structure has the advantage of keeping words out of sight and off the walls. In the exhibition *Beyond Numbers* at the Maryland Science Center, little tabs that say "solution" or "more about math" signal users to the nature of information contained on the layers below. Some exhibit developers felt, however, that some of the information was added to appeal more to the advisory group of mathematicians than to visitors.

The disadvantages of the more-interested-visitor layered approach is that it still presents an overload of information that leads to underuse by visitors. Something for almost everyone *can* be achieved by striving for inclusive broad appeal, not by segmenting experiences into mutually exclusive audience categories.

The best way to provide more information is in a form other than labels, such as a brochure, catalog, or website. Better yet, let them google it for themselves.

The Supposed-IQ Layering System

Probably the most common use of levels or layers relates to a hierarchy assigned to the presumed amount of information that visitors bring with them to the exhibition. This hierarchy falls into categories ranging from novice (no prior knowledge) to expert (lots of training, high vocabulary). Inherent in this layering approach is the tendency to appeal to the mythical more-interested visitor and to avoid the dreaded lowest-common-denominator label text. We are all novices at some point. And for visitors to care about an unfamiliar topic, they must first pay attention, which can easily be discouraged by a label with too many words and a high-level vocabulary that leaves them out.

This unfortunate example of layering and levels is based on visitors' supposed intelligence—targeting visitors who lack awareness of a topic or those who are knowledgeable about it—which can result in an insulting, underutilized exhibit where levels of labels either pander or baffle. Too much complexity can make visitors feel stupid. Certainly visitor intelligence varies, but for the developers to make decisions based on assumptions about IQ is unnecessary and degrading to their audience.

Many curators voice their fear and repulsion of dumbing down their content. However, a huge difference exists between simplification and clarity. Simplified content can make visitors feel dumb. Clarity, on the other hand, results from a process that focuses on one big idea and helps more visitors feel competent.

The False Hierarchy of Complexity Layering System

Organizing label information from simple to complex, or from general to specific, works *against* making exhibitions more appealing and thoroughly used.

The hierarchy of complexity model gives rise to trilevel labels, with the most general information appearing first in the largest type, more details next in smaller type, and minutiae in the third paragraph in the smallest type. This hierarchy is based on conceptual, abstract knowledge, where "simple" or "general" may have nothing to do with visitors' primary questions about the exhibition context. Similarly, "complex" content often takes visitors far beyond what's suggested by the exhibition itself. The notion of simple-to-complex lacks sensitivity to the immediate contextual needs of visitors and their curiosity and information priorities.

The assumption that visitors who are in a hurry or are not very interested will read only the first, general text of a three-tiered label is misguided. Most visitors in a fast-browsing mode are scanning paragraphs for concrete, specific tidbits of information.

THE BEST LABEL SYSTEMS ARE BASED ON PURPOSE

We strongly recommend that exhibit developers create systems organized around the purpose of each label.

To increase their effectiveness, labels can be clearly organized by type (e.g., introductory, groupings and themes, object labels, points of view) as the exhibition is developed and designed. Examples of some of these types were discussed in chapter 4. This organization can apply to individual components within the whole exhibition, as well as to the organization of information on individual panels.

Create a system based on the role of the label, and clearly define each type, such as:

Introductory labels will introduce the big idea and the organization of the exhibition.

Group labels will interpret the logic for the group of exhibit elements (e.g., how they are related or what characteristics they have in common).

Caption labels will interpret the most relevant information about the object, artwork, photograph (e.g., what's special about it and how it relates to the big idea).

If the role of the label is to tell a story, add supporting information, or explain a concept that is tied to the big idea, that's good. But if the exhibit developers add more information in the form of concept labels or story labels only because they think the content is "interesting," this can lead to an overload of text that distracts visitors and doesn't advance the narrative of the exhibition.

The question to repeatedly ask during interpretive label development is "What has this got to do with the big idea?"

In any exhibition, the content of some elements and labels will naturally be more complex than others. And if a complicated idea is integral to the big idea, it belongs in the exhibition. For example, when trying out mock-ups for an exhibition about forensics, exhibit developers had trouble with an interactive device about a chemical test for antibodies. The activity was frustrating and unclear to visitors. Repeated testing with prototypes and modifications led to improvements, but the exhibit was not easy for visitors without prior knowledge of protein chemistry. Exhibit developers decided to keep the exhibit element in, even though it was hard for most visitors to understand, because it was one of the most important and commonly used tests by forensic scientists. The point they wanted to make to visitors was that some forensic tests were more complicated than others. Because the exhibit developers had tested the exhibits as prototypes, they knew most visitors would be successful with the other units, and they hoped that would build visitors' confidence with this more difficult one.

Difficult ideas should be selected for inclusion based on their appropriateness to the big idea, not just for "smarter" visitors. During a workshop on labels at the Exploratorium, the group joked about putting a banner across some of the more complex interactives that said, "For rocket scientists only." A label like that would inform visitors that the exhibit was indeed not meant for them, unless (of course) they were rocket scientists.

Design Consistency Supports the Roles and Types of Labels

The organization of the label system must be made logically—and visually—apparent to visitors through label design and placement. Visitors need to figure out quickly which labels go with specific objects (e.g., captions) or which group label interprets a case or area. Placement is crucial. Caption labels located too far from the thing they're describing can be disorienting and confusing.

Typography—typeface, size, and color—should be used consistently to differentiate types of texts and to signal to visitors the role of each label. For instance, information about the donor should be in a different typeface and size than the interpretive text. Labels that lack these systematic differentiations can be hard for visitors to decipher. People will give up reading if they can't figure it out.

Another pitfall is the partially developed or incomplete system, where some label types are clearly defined (e.g., title, introduction, subtheme/area labels) and the remainder are a mishmash of one-of-a-kind designs, sizes, colors, and purposes.

From the planning process to the final realization of the exhibition, exhibit design and communication goals—guided and focused by the big idea—need to be clearly defined and tightly structured together. Types of labels that are defined by purpose will help exhibit planners agree more readily on the content. And because purpose can be matched to outcomes, it will be easier to agree on evaluation criteria. Meanwhile, the label writer will have better direction and clear limitations within which to work.

MODALITIES OTHER THAN LABELS

Exhibit interpretation can and should be presented in formats other than labels on the walls or in cases. This can include single-page handouts, newsprint, or brochures that visitors can use in the museum or take home; books or a catalog to browse through (tables and chairs provided); laminated portable labels to carry around the gallery and then put back; and catalogs for purchase. Dioramas and media, including videos, audio tours, tablets, computer databases, and soundscapes, add interest. In-person demonstrations by staff, docent-led tours, or hands-on activities at certain times of the day will appeal to nonreaders or younger visitors. All these supplemental forms of interpretation will allow interpretive labels to remain brief, as they should be.

Multimodal interpretation also offers a point of accessibility, says museum teaching and learning expert Sonnet Takahisa. At a minimum they can appeal to different visitor preferences. At their best, diverse modalities offer visitors of any ability a good experience.

The best way to develop different modalities is to select the exhibit technology for each element based on the content and communication objectives. Instead of saying, "The exhibit should include videos and computers," exhibit developers should be asking, "What is the best way to tell this part of the story—a photograph, a video, an interactive device, an object, a group of artifacts, a re-creation of an environment?" That way, the variety of modalities evolves authentically and appropriately.

While individual visitors may have preferences for certain modalities over others, a well-designed, well-placed exhibit element can override a prior attitude: "I don't usually watch videos, but this one was really interesting"; or "I don't like to take docent tours, but I overheard this really good one"; or "I don't usually use computer interactives, but I wanted to sit down for a while, and it turned out to be fun."

Different Modalities as Part of the Buffet of Opportunities

When a variety of modalities carry similar reinforcing, overlapping messages, the exhibition will build toward and support a big idea coherently and completely for the greatest number of visitors. Organizing modalities as parts of a greater whole leads to inclusiveness and interconnection for the entire exhibition and the total visitor population. Even a small exhibition can use a variety of experiences. A two-hundred-square-foot multimodal exhibition at Chicago's Shedd Aquarium, *Otters and Oil Don't Mix*, interpreting the *Exxon Valdez* oil spill, included photos, labels, artifacts, a small diorama, a video, and an interactive computer, plus four otter pups rescued from the 1989 spill—all intended for the same audience: people eight years old and up.

It is less helpful to think of a visitor as preferring only a single, exclusive modality or having only one developmental level or learning style. This narrow thinking encourages the design of less coherent exhibit elements that will appeal to a smaller fraction of the audience.

For example, adults often perceive interactive elements as being only for children. They feel silly using them, or expect them to be childish and unappealing to grown-ups. Unfortunately, it is often true that interactives are simplistic or ungratifying for adults. But they don't have to be. Even in children's museums, exhibitions targeted for anyone over the age of six can benefit from the same kinds of conceptual integrity, intellectual clarity, and personal meaningfulness appropriate to all other exhibitions. For an excellent example of this, see Sue Allen's summative evaluation of Secrets of Circles at the San Jose Children's Museum in California.

Virtual, non-real modalities can function well, depending on the situation, availability, and purpose. A replica, a combination of real and fake, a model based on reality, a model based on conjecture, a 3D animation constructed from historical photos—all of these have the power to fire the imagination. It is the museum's job to present them in ways that will help that happen.

A Few Words of Caution About Videos

Are they even watching? Consider the limitations and drawbacks to videos, which often have low attracting power and low holding times. Thus, a video is not a good modality for a message that needs to reach the majority of visitors. And forcing visitors to sit through an introductory video before releasing them to the rest of the exhibits is controlling and unnatural in a free-choice environment, where they should be allowed to stop or move on as they please.

With all videos, there is a question in the back of the viewer's mind: *How long is this going to last?* Visitors can comfortably listen to spoken words at a rate of about 150 words per minute. When a visitor confronts a panel of 250 words with graphics, it is instantly obvious how much time it will take to scan it (seconds) or look at it in detail (one minute, if it's not more than 250 words, at an average reading speed). With a video, unless the time is posted, the viewer is left to wonder. The videos we watch on our phones and computers have a time indicator bar at the bottom that tells us how long a piece will last and how long we have until it's over. We are all used to knowing how long we'll be watching something, and museums should provide that information to visitors. Data on visitors' time spent looking at them can be found in Serrell (2002), "Are they Watching: Visitors and Exhibition Videos."

Keeping It Real

A final thought about the most powerful modality: the real thing. Many museums collect, store, conserve, and display real stuff—and that's what visitors come to see. Forget the label, forget the video, never mind the digital device that gives you access to a multitude of facts about it—you get to see the real thing, be in its presence, find out how big/small/shiny/awesome it really is. For many people, their experience with the real thing will always be of primary importance.

Photo Figures for Part II

Plants are up to something.

Simple, but not simplistic. The big idea is
announced on the door leading into the
conservatory. The subject is plants: They are
up to something. What could that mean?
You'll find out inside.

Altered State

In just forty-six words, this introductory label explains the thesis of the exhibition and the rationale behind laying out the content in ten sections.

Putting a paragraph break after the second sentence would help to separate the two ideas (thesis, layout) for quicker comprehension.

Welcome to the Swamp

Visitors can read the big idea at the top of this floor plan that indicates a one-way flow through the exhibits and the expected amount of time. "You Are Here" should be added to reinforce the arrow and improve orientation.

Beautiful Science

A beautiful title panel announces the exhibition name, subtitle and the four topics that will be explored in a nice combination of type styles, sizes, and fonts.

Inside the doorway, the title is repeated on a curved wall. The adjacent introductory label looks dauntingly long.

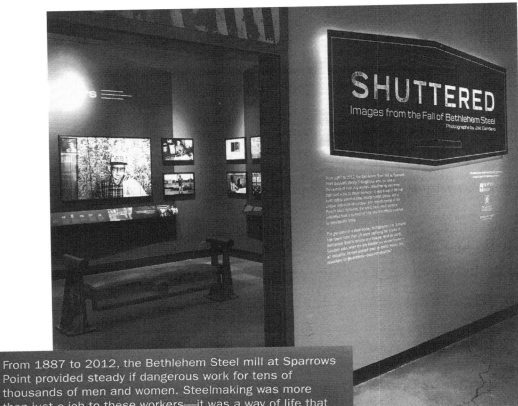

From 1887 to 2012, the Bethlehem Steel mill at Sparrows Point provided steady if dangerous work for tens of thousands of men and women. Steelmaking was more than just a job to these workers—it was a way of life that built stable communities, strong human bonds, and a unique industrial landscape. With the shuttering of the Point's blast furnaces, the world local steel workers inhabited took a number of hits, and the effects continue to reverberate today.

The grandson of a steel worker, photographer J.M. Giordano has spent more than 15 years capturing the impact of Bethlehem Steel's decline and closure. What do you do, Giordano asks, when the only lifestyle you've ever known—an industrial lifestyle passed down by family, friends, and coworkers for generations—becomes obsolete?

Shuttered

This intro label has very readable type that tells an interesting story in not too many words and asks a very empathetic question at the end.

The use of steel for a bench in the gallery is a nice touch.

LOOKING INTO THE MIRROR, THE BLACK WOMAN ASKED,
"MIRROR, MIRROR ON THE WALL, WHO'S THE FINEST OF THEM ALL?"
THE MIRROR SAYS, "SNOW WHITE YOU BLACK BITCH,
AND DON'T YOU FORGET IT!!!"

Mirror, Mirror

A well-written caption in a conversational tone and with easy-to-read typography.

Would the seventy-word label be even better divided into two paragraphs? Start with "A Black woman looks . . .," which is what the visitor sees. Make the second paragraph begin with "Mirror, Mirror is part of . . .," the crucial background story.

Carrie Mae Weems (American, born 1953)
Mirror, Mirror
1987/2012

Gelatin silver print
Courtesy of the artist and Jack Shainman Gallery, New York

Mirror, Mirror is part of Carrie Mae Weems's 1987-88 *Ain't Jokin'* series. The series turns racist humor on its head to call attention to negative stereotypes of African Americans. Weems combines images of Black people with "jokes" drawn from popular culture to make clear that psychological violence that can be inflicted through language, specifically things deemed "just a joke." *Mirror, Mirror* invokes and subverts the fairy tale *Snow White*. A Black woman looks into a mirror, on the other side of which a White woman, dressed as a fairy godmother, looks back at her. Rather than receiving an affirmation of her beauty, the Black woman is cruelly reminded that she does not meet the European beauty standards implied in the name Snow White.

Wine Jug with a Drunk Man Singing

Greek, made in Athens, about 470 B.C.

Terracotta

Red-figured *chous* attributed to the
Oionokles Painter

With his mouth open in song and his arms
outstretched, the man depicted on this pitcher
shows the effects of a night of drinking. His
young servant is ready to minister to his needs,
holding the man's belongings as well as the jug
into which he urinates.

Wine jug

This short caption—only forty-seven words—
tells an animated story with a punchy ending,
drawing attention to a detail visitors might
otherwise miss. The title and identification
information are clearly separated from, and do
not compete with, the caption text.

Compassionate Saint

There are many details in this painting, and an extended caption label with "callouts"—chunks of text with a reference graphic—do that job well.

Located on a pedestal rather than on the wall, this style gives visitors plenty of room to look back and forth from the label to the art.

Find the Compassion of a Saint

Peter Paul Rubens shows a widow and her children begging for help from Saint Ives, the patron saint of lawyers. Rubens's tender representation of the saint, who defended widows and orphans, was new; earlier depictions show Saint Ives by himself, holding a book.

Discover how Rubens invites viewers to connect with Saint Ives's compassion.

The angel crowning Saint Ives with a wreath symbolizes divine acknowledgment of the saint's good deeds.

Rubens shows Saint Ives bent forward, attentive to the widow and children.

Red-rimmed eyes show the widow's anguish and emphasize her sickly yellow skin.

One hand rests on a law book, the other holds the widow's petition for help, suggesting Saint Ives's effectiveness.

Rubens painted these figures life sized, which makes them—and their urgency—more real.

The mother and children are barefoot to dramatize their extreme poverty.

A discarded bishop's hat represents the high church office Saint Ives declined in order to help people directly.

Saint Ives of Treguier, Patron of Lawyers, Defender of Widows and Orphans, 1635–38, Peter Paul Rubens

LIVING TERMITES TURN DEAD WOOD INTO FOOD FOR NEW TREES

Watch these termites nibbling away at a pine stump and you're seeing forest recycling in action. Workers chew and swallow the wood. Then bacteria in their guts help them digest it, converting tough wood fibers into sugars and other nutrients.

Some of the nutrients pass through the termites, in their "frass" (termite poop). The nutrients enrich the soil, fueling the growth of new trees.

Living Termites

Live animals (even sleeping or dead ones) always win in terms of attracting and holding visitors' attention.

In this display, the termites are so small that the label has to tell people to watch closely because they might otherwise miss the action.

Wayside sign

The image of the Goat Mountain landscape matches what visitors can see.

When a wayside sign successfully interprets the view in front of you, looking and reading are reinforced and enhanced in an engaging mental dance.

Avoiding the Reptiles?

We've noticed that some visitors wait outside while the rest of their group goes inside. Fear of reptiles is common to many people. This fear is learned and not instinctive. People can learn to like reptiles, too. Why not give it a try?

Avoiding the Reptiles?

A warning label can help visitors decide whether to proceed as well as be informative.

Layered story

The use of three type sizes and fonts—in a title, a subtitle, and a paragraph—suggests that the content is presented in three levels. Is it helpful or just a design gimmick? The content would work with just the subtitle and a short paragraph.

a layered story

Vertebrate skin is composed of layers

Mammals, fishes, birds, amphibians, and reptiles have skin made of two main layers. The thin epidermis is skin's outermost layer. It covers the thicker dermis, home to blood vessels, glands, nerves, and more. The dermis makes up 90 percent of skin's total weight in some animals.

Fern Room

This room provides a glimpse of what Chicago might have looked like millions of years ago.

Designer Jens Jensen loved midwestern landscapes; the Fern Room is his imaginative tribute to prehistoric Illinois. So natural looking was the result that when the Conservatory first opened, visitors thought it had been erected over an existing lagoon. One of Jensen's chief contributions to greenhouse design was to display plants in a naturalistic setting rather than in groups of pots. This revolutionary approach became known as "landscape gardening under glass."

The Fern Room is home to some of the oldest species of plants on earth.

Many of the plants in this room date to the time of the dinosaurs. They have changed little from their ancestors over the last 200 million years. Our plants, of course, are not that old. The oldest are about 300 years of age.

Fern Room

A title, two subtitles, and two paragraphs introduce the Fern Room. This style responds to the assumption that most visitors will read the headlines, and if they want more information, they will read the details. Actually, the bold statements tend to draw readers' eyes away from the nonbold type. Once distracted, will they go back?

Double V

Despite a hierarchy in the size of the type for the different labels on this panel, all the content is general information, none of which directly relates to the background photograph. Not a good system.

Silver and Gold

California Daguerreotypes

The first photographs made in California, daguerreotypes recorded the Gold Rush on silver-plated sheets of copper.

When I was twelve or thirteen, my best friend's father was an artist who had a small collection of daguerreotypes. I was completely bewitched by the seemingly impossible combination of antiquity and razor-sharp detail. To me they were like tiny time machines. I was hooked. It was that early glimpse of daguerreotypes that put me on the path to becoming a photography curator.

Drew Johnson
Curator of Photography

Silver and Gold

The same font in different sizes in this label suggests the distinct roles or purposes of the content: a title and subtitle to identify the topic; a sentence stating a fact; and a personal, signed quotation.

PART III

Considering the Audience

7

Who Is the Audience?

Museum audiences come to exhibitions seeking a culturally oriented leisure social outing. Although they have a variety of interests and prior experience, they also have many expectations and needs in common.

Many of the current notions about diverse audiences emphasize the differences among people—who they are, what they want and need, and other factors—and these dissimilarities begin to seem overwhelming. Although there is no such thing as "the average visitor," there are many similarities within the diversity. As museums work to increase attendance and reach audiences who have not traditionally visited (non-White, non-affluent, non-college-educated), museum practitioners need not become overwhelmed by the multitude of visitors' demographics, interests, and motivations. Instead, consider the many universal human concerns that can readily be part of exhibition content.

UNIVERSAL HUMAN CONCERNS

While every visitor experience is unique, it is also governed by many factors that most human beings have in common. People's interests, intellects, and educational or economic backgrounds are all grounded in many fundamental similarities, such as the need for physical comfort and nonthreatening spaces, feelings of hunger and fatigue, yearning for continuity, love of a good story, ability to see and seek patterns, grief over loss, natural spirituality, and the desire for self-actualization through personal challenges.

Museums must constantly be aware of these universal factors and integrate visitors' basic needs ("Where's the toilet?") before attempting to help them achieve higher levels of consciousness ("What the heck is that?"). By considering the commonalities among our multicultural, multigenerational audience, exhibit developers can plan displays that will work for more people, and label writers can write texts that will get read.

DEMOGRAPHIC AND BEHAVIORAL SIMILARITIES

Given a representative sample of museum visitors, there are many similarities in who they are, what they like, and how they visit museums. The attributes underlying adults' choices for leisure-time activities include the desire to do something fun and worthwhile as a social group in comfortable surroundings.

In terms of behaviors, museum visitors are surprisingly predictable.

- People tend to turn right and move counterclockwise around a gallery.

- Visitors of all ages are attracted to exhibit elements that are more concrete and less abstract.

- More people read short labels than long labels.

- If visitors cannot understand or personally connect with part of an exhibit, they will skip it.

- Visitors spend less time and attend to fewer exhibits than museum exhibit developers would like to believe.

A striking difference among visitors is age-related, and this is primarily associated with children's uninhibited exploratory behavior. Children instinctively investigate things with their hands and not in a prescribed order, whereas adults may need to be invited to touch and participate ("OK to touch"). Where adults seek structure or directions, children charge ahead without them.

Some of the trends mentioned above are seen repeatedly in general museum visitor surveys. For more specifics see articles by Judy Diamond, "The Behavior of Family Groups in Science Museums"; Randi Korn, "An Analysis of Differences Between Visitors at Natural History Museums and Science Centers"; and "The Relationship between Exhibit Characteristics and Learning-Associated Behaviors in a Science Museum Discovery Space" by Boisvert and Slex.

THE TRAP OF VISITOR TYPOLOGIES

Casual observations of visitor behavior have led some museum staffs to believe that there are different types of visitors who can be identified by the way they use exhibitions, such as "streakers"—people who go through fast and stop at only a few elements; "samplers," "browsers," or "strollers"—people who spend some time and stop at a few things that seem to interest them; and "studiers"—people who spend more than the average time, looking at one thing for a long time, or looking at lots of things. It is easy to accept this "wisdom" without question because it is simple and provides an easy framework for making assumptions about how visitors behave in exhibitions. The activity and practice of systematically tracking and timing visitors can make you see the vast majority of them as curious, interested people who stroll through the exhibits as they try hard to figure out what's going on.

The tendency to subdivide audiences into "types" and pigeonhole them with stereotypic characteristics or predetermined categories of visitor motivations may not be as useful in exhibit design and evaluation as one might think. Instead, exhibit developers should consider the whole audience as time-limited, motivated nonexperts, of which almost everyone is a nonsequential "sampler." This is much closer to the truth. Our overarching challenge is how to encourage more visitors to sample more exhibits and sample them for longer periods of time.

What about Audiences to "Specialty" Museums?

Three friends, a Jew, a Buddhist, and an agnostic, walk into the Billy Graham Museum. The museum feels welcoming. Rather than purely a shrine to Billy Graham—which might be appealing only to evangelicals—the exhibits are informative, engaging, and meaningful to all three of them. They have a really good time watching an old video of Billy Sunday and his whole-body preaching; they laugh while reading the letters addressed to "Many Apples Many Sodas" that still got delivered to Billy Graham in Minneapolis, Minnesota and are thrilled by the experience of going to heaven (white clouds, blue sky, mirrors, J. S. Bach). They learn some amazing things about the history of the evangelical movement, and they leave feeling confirmed as human beings.

Museums that exist to celebrate a particular religious, cultural, or historic community—or personality, product, or object of art—are clearly targeting a specific audience. But those visitors are often in the company of others who may not share their enthusiasm or level of knowledge about the topic of the museum. There is a financial consideration for broad appeal as well. For the specialty museum to stay alive in the current economy and into the future, it needs to court the nonfans, nonbelievers, and the next generation. The Studebaker

Museum, the World War II Veterans Museum, and the Ukrainian Museum have to respond and adapt to the changes in the world and their topics' places in it to be relevant and to welcome people coming through the doors. More so than, say, the Rattlesnake Museum and the Mustard Museum, whose topical relevance might not change so much or so fast.

THINK INCLUSIVELY

Imagine an exhibition where the majority of visitors use the majority of available exhibit experiences: Children work with other children or adults, adults talk and read out loud to each other and to their children, visitors interact with others in different social groups, and people of all ages are tempted to linger longer instead of rushing on to the next exhibit or exiting at the first opportunity. It is possible! Good orientation, a clear big idea, and good labels will all help make it happen, as timing-and-tracking studies have found for topics as diverse as fossilized tree resin (*Amber: Window to the Past*), polar exploration (*Shackleton*), and swimwear (*From Bustles to Bikinis*), all of which are discussed in the American Alliance of Museums (AAM) publication *Paying Attention: Visitors and Museum Exhibitions*.

Several books discuss how to serve diverse audiences. Kathleen McLean makes this point in *Planning for People in Museum Exhibitions*: "If we want exhibitions to be truly engaging, then all exhibit professionals, not only the educators and evaluators, will have to be communicators and audience advocates." McLean argues that this will make exhibitions better for the public as well as make the exhibition development process function better within museums.

Lisa Roberts, in *From Knowledge to Narrative: Educators and the Changing Museum*, reviews the rise of professionalism in the field of museum education and its impact on the ways museums present knowledge. She contrasts the curatorial-positivist stance ("Here is our knowledge and truth for you to learn") with a multiple-meanings context ("Here is what some people believe to be true"). This shift of authority—and the acknowledgment of uncertainties and disagreements about what we know—within museums, whether science, history, or art, is part of a larger academic questioning about our assumptions in every major discipline. Roberts credits museum educators for the trend in making exhibition narratives more inclusive: "It is educators whose sensitivity to visitors has brought them to question the comprehensibility, significance, and voice of exhibit messages." This shift has gained strength among all museum professionals thanks to the COVID-19 pandemic, the environmental climate crisis, the expansion of the Black Lives Matter movement, the increase in awareness of the harm done by colonialism and white supremacy, and new respect for individuals of alternate gender identity.

WHAT ABOUT NON-VISITORS?

Museum staffs have long been thinking about the people who *aren't* coming through the doors, asking, "What do they think about the museum?" and "What is it that we're not doing for them?"

In her seminal 1983 *Museum News* article "Staying Away: Why People Choose Not to Visit Museums," Marilyn Hood examined a large phone survey conducted by the Toledo Art Museum and Ohio State University. The survey identified people's psychographic characteristics (values, attitudes, perceptions, interests, expectations, satisfactions) and how those tracked with their preferences for leisure activities. Hood concluded:

> Individuals do not just naturally gravitate to museums or to any other leisure place . . . no matter how worthwhile or unique it may be. Instead, before making selections, they consider which of several competing alternatives appears to offer them the most rewards, the greatest satisfactions, and they make their choice based on what will satisfy their criteria of a desirable leisure experience. The study found that people who did not visit museums valued being with people (social interaction), participating actively, and feeling comfortable and at ease in their surroundings, characteristics that they perceived were missing from museums.

Hood's research in the 1990s showed that demographic characteristics of museum visitors had remained stable, both over time and across studies undertaken in museums and galleries in many countries. Museum visitors were typically highly educated, with post-secondary education in humanities or the arts; ranged between thirty and fifty years old or were primary-school-aged children; visited as family groups; were in a higher socioeconomic class; and had visited museums as children. Building on her earlier work, Hood identified six factors that affect the decisions people make about their leisure choices:

1. Being with people/social interaction

2. Doing something worthwhile for themselves or others

3. Feeling comfortable and at ease in the surroundings

4. Having challenging new experiences

5. Having the opportunity to learn

6. Actively participating

The data that Hood did not mention was that the visitors were overwhelmingly White. But Hood's findings still resonate with the efforts of twenty-first-century museums to be more inclusive and appealing to non-White audiences. Many of the six factors could apply across a broad, diverse audience. The factor of "feeling comfortable and at ease," however, needs to be addressed in many ways so that all visitors see themselves represented and are able to partake in meaningful, participatory learning experiences.

In another early-1990s study, a consortium of eleven art museums conducted a research project to better understand themselves from the perspectives of their visitors. The resulting publication, *Insights: Museums, Visitors, Attitudes, and Expectations*, reported that no single reason accounted for non-visitation; instead, responses fell into several categories. Visitors reported feeling intimidated by and/or not knowledgeable about art; being unaware that the museum existed or assuming there was nothing there that would interest them; not having the free time to visit a museum; not being interested in art; and being deterred by the location of the museum, either because it was too far away, there was no parking, or the neighborhood was perceived to be dangerous.

In a more recent study, artists Maia Chao and Josephine Davanbu explored what non-visitors had to say about the Rhode Island School of Design (RISD) Museum. They launched "Look at Art. Get Paid," a "socially engaged art project," in 2016. They recruited self-described art museum non-visitors to be "guest critics," paying them seventy-five dollars to come to the RISD Museum and give their input. The guest critics commented on the vast collection of objects presented as art; the silence and stillness of the galleries; the minimal interaction between strangers viewing artworks; the desire to touch the artwork; the presence of guards (some noted approachability, while others expressed intimidation); the "proper" dress and restrained manner of other visitors; the lack of "inner-city" visitors and artists of color; the evident cost and high quality of the building and collection; surveillance cameras; lack of advertisements by the museum in their neighborhood; lack of Spanish labels or guides; lack of proper signage to invite the public into the space; and difficulty engaging with contemporary art.

These three studies at art museums—"Staying Away," *Insights*, and "Look at Art. Get Paid"—across three decades found commonalities among non-visitors that clearly apply to all types of museums. "If we museum professionals are concerned about reaching new audiences," Hood concluded, "we must appeal to them on the basis of what satisfies *their* criteria of a desirable leisure experience." And that requires an ongoing institutional commitment. Chao and Davanbu state on their website, "As pressure builds for museums to change, it remains a challenge to make conversations about the future of museums accessible to individuals who aren't already visiting them—particularly communities of color and working-class communities."

SO WHAT DO THEY WANT?

One way to find out what visitors want is to ask them directly. The Denver Art Museum's Interpretive Project looked closely at its audience and what they wanted. Researchers found that most of the DAM's visitors were "art novices" with high interest in art but limited art backgrounds. The novices' criteria for liking an art object were that it have a pleasing kind of beauty, that it be very intricate and detailed, and that its message be understandable to them.

Finding Out What Visitors Want: Listen to Them

Visitor surveys are a common means of finding out more about who the visitors are. But many of the questions asked do not help exhibition developers and label writers do a better job of giving visitors what they want. Information about a visitor's zip code, income level, educational history, or gender offers little to the label writer. More useful would be visitors' answers to questions that relate directly to their understanding of and relatability to the exhibit's topic, such as, "Do you have any special interest, knowledge, or training in (the subject of the exhibition)?" This question is likely to reveal information about hobbies and other leisure activities and family history, as well as school- or job-related interests. This will give label writers the "hooks" to interest readers. For example, data gathered in Chicago-area museums revealed that the planetarium attracts visitors with interests in telescopes (not an unexpected finding) and surveying (a surprise). Visitors to the natural history museum often have pets, are birders, and have taken courses in biology. Aquarium visitors like to go fishing, eat fish, and keep fish at home (fresh- and saltwater hobbyists). The maritime museum attracts people interested in shipwrecks, boatbuilding, and boat operation. There are also interests that some visitors to a maritime museum, a planetarium, a natural history museum, and an aquarium have in common, such as antique collecting, scuba diving, navigation, and employment as a teacher. Writing labels referencing your visitors' common interests can make those labels more appealing to more people.

A radical transformation in label content and form is needed if we expect to enlarge our appeal to both current and broader audiences. This transformation can be guided in part by listening to what visitors and non-visitors say they want and how they identify the characteristics of ideal exhibitions.

In a study by Alt and Shaw titled "Characteristics of Ideal Museum Exhibits," visitors to the Natural History Museum in London compared old and new exhibitions and, in their own words, described what they thought contributed to the "ideal" one:

> *It makes the subject come to life.*
>
> *It gets the message across quickly.*
>
> *You can understand the point(s) it is making quickly.*
>
> *There's something in it for all ages.*
>
> *You can't help noticing it.*
>
> *It allows you to test yourself to see if you are right.*
>
> *It involves you.*
>
> *It deals with the subjects better than textbooks do.*
>
> *The information is clearly presented.*
>
> *It makes a difficult subject easier.*
>
> *It gives just enough information.*
>
> *It's clear what you're supposed to do and how to begin.*
>
> *Your attention isn't distracted from it by other displays.*

Of the characteristics of ideal exhibitions listed above, more than half are directly related to labels that captivate and communicate quickly, easily, and clearly.

In the "Be a Bird Focus Group" studies done at Brookfield Zoo before renovations to the bird exhibits, visitors discussed the factors they thought would contribute positively to their learning experience at the zoo, using these expressions:

It is memorable.

It's an experience that involves your senses.

You are gently guided to make discoveries.

It is a personal experience.

You get lots of opportunities to investigate and make observations.

For a moment, look at that list and think how it might apply to novices at all types of museums. Change zoology to art, history, anthropology, or science; think about the pleasing beauty and intricacy of an animal, a piece of rock, or an electric engine; and then think about the kinds of labels that would work in each case.

The findings from all the studies above have broad applicability across museums and situations. Most visitors are eager to learn, but they do not want to spend much time or effort trying to figure out things. Short, clear labels, guided by meaningful big ideas, can attract, communicate, inspire, and help visitors get what they are seeking in your designed spaces.

PROVIDING CHOICES FOR VISITORS' PREFERENCES: SIX DICHOTOMIES

The previous discussions revolve around issues of orientation, content, and the cognitive aspects of exhibit viewing. Below we address what kind of environments visitors want. The following lists present opposing choices on six spectrums for informal designed settings. Each set of choices contrasts people's preferences and suggests how to deal with them. They encompass the physical and conceptual layout of the exhibition, the environment and experiences, and the social aspects of visiting an exhibition, as well as verbal information and approaches to interpretation. Exhibit developers need to consider which choices to offer, depending on the kind of experiences they are designing and their assumptions about visitors' needs.

1. Sequenced or Un-sequenced

Visitors' preferences for navigating the physical space of the exhibition range from an orderly, sequenced linear approach to a more free-form, un-sequenced, random, self-selected approach.

Sequenced: Some people like to have the recommended order or pathway laid out for them; they do not want to miss anything, and they want to see things in the "right" order or at least to be aware of what the suggested order is. People who like sequencing will appreciate having floor plans, introductory labels, numbered exhibits, linear or one-way flow, self-guiding materials, arrows, alternate pathways made clear, and choices apparent but not forced. In chaotic or confusing exhibition layouts, these people feel uncomfortable.

Un-sequenced: Other people do not care what order things come in and want to be surprised or free to do it any way they want. People who like free flow will appreciate being able to skip ahead or backtrack, without a one-way path. There can be a sequence, but they feel free to ignore it.

Both? Exhibitions that have a clear sequence or linear structure can also offer the option to skip around, which will satisfy the people who want a plan without annoying those who don't. Smaller exhibitions (less than 2,500 square feet) have the advantage of allowing visitors to get a sense of the whole space at a glance as they walk into it and to decide quickly about their own sequence and pace.

The design of the exhibition environment plays a large role in encouraging a sequence or pathway if there's meant to be one. Boundaries between sections will be much clearer to visitors when the architecture, lighting, and colors of the exhibition support the logic of different thematic areas. Labels alone do not provide adequate cues; multiple methods of orienting visitors need to be used.

2. Pace Controlled or Not Controlled

People have different preferences about having control over their time and the timing of experiences in an exhibition (some of which might also be highly sequenced).

Pace controlled: Some people like exhibit elements that have a built-in structure or pace and a set time limit or duration, such as a video, audio tour, or docent-led tour. If an exhibit element has a set time span, it should be clear to the visitor, e.g., "Push button for a three-minute video," or "Fifteen-minute tour begins here." (Disneyland rides are examples of extremely pace- and sequence-controlled experiences.) Timed ticketing may play a role in limiting time spent overall.

Not controlled: Other people like to choose their own pace, taking a brief glance at one element and spending more time at another one. These people will also appreciate knowing beforehand the time limit of an element, if there is one. They might feel trapped if they find out—after the fact—that they *have* to sit through an introductory video or a media introduction before proceeding to the next exhibit area.

Both? Most pace-controlled exhibit experiences will not be a problem for visitors who prefer to control their own pace if they have the option to ignore them.

3. Peer Group or Expert-Led

People have preferences for how they acquire information in different kinds of social situations.

Peer group: Some people like to talk to their friends and family about what they see, read, or experience. People who like to talk in their groups will appreciate an exhibition atmosphere where they do not have to whisper or worry about disturbing other visitors when they talk out loud. Labels that are easy to read and sound good when read out loud will help promote social interactions between adults and between children and adults. Interactive devices or phenomena that encourage conversation, dialogue, cooperation, or even arguing are appealing to visitors who like to learn in peer groups or casual family groups in which no one is playing "leader" or where leadership is fluid and shared.

Expert-led: Other people prefer to have someone knowledgeable speak to them. Labels written in the voice of an expert will appeal to them. Open-ended questions such as "What do you think about this?" will not be inviting. People who like guided tours will appreciate having them offered at frequent and convenient times.

Both? Tour groups in exhibitions should not hog space close to exhibits, spoiling the experience for self-guiding visitors. Exhibit elements need to be large enough to allow a family group to interact together. Two chairs instead of one at a computer station says, "Work together on this." In addition, both types of experiences should be timed so that visitors who come in social groups can split up, do their own thing, and regroup in a timely manner.

4. Active Participation or Vicarious Watching

Both of these preferences relate to the concrete experiences offered in exhibitions but may involve variability in people's inclinations for participation.

Active participation: Some people like to do and participate, and hands-on interactive elements can appeal to a broad range of ages and abilities.

Vicarious watching: Others like to watch someone else try an activity or perform a demonstration. Although they might not actively have their own hands on, they can vicariously experience an interactive element by observing over the shoulder of a user. Coming to a museum to watch other people—whether you know them or not—can be an important part of the experience.

Both? Exhibitions can easily provide both active and passive opportunities or situations, but interactive devices should not be the only opportunities to access interpretation of the exhibition's main themes. Although the people who use interactives are not a separate population from the people who read, some people do not want to have to use an interactive device to understand what the point is. Good labels on interactives allow observers and readers to experience without touching. Good design allows observers to clearly see (and understand) what the doers are doing.

5. Quiet or Not Quiet

People have different preferences and tolerance levels for the ambience of exhibition spaces. These tolerances can change depending on the time of day, who they're with, or when their last meal was.

Quiet: Sometimes people need areas of rest or contemplation to alternate with, or be available in addition to, areas of high-density sensory and mental overload. Sometimes people have trouble concentrating in the midst of competing sources of noise and distractions. For example, they find it difficult to read a label while a video is playing nearby.

Not quiet: Sometimes people have no problem focusing on one thing amid a roomful of activity. They enjoy the buzz of a noisy environment.

Both? Exhibitions that space elements far enough apart to allow for some separation of activities while still maintaining an overall lively atmosphere will not drive the first type crazy or bother the second type. Half-walls and soft surfaces can be used to create more intimate spaces out of the mainstream.

6. No Labels or Interpretive Labels—Art Museums, a Special Case

In art museums especially, where nonverbal stimuli offer the dominant experience, a dichotomy seems to exist between people who do not like to read interpretive labels about the art and those who do. Whether they are art novices or experts, they have their own opinions for or against reading what someone else thinks.

No labels: For a small but vocal portion of art museum visitors, labels are an imposition. If interpretation is unexpectedly encountered or encountered in a way that feels forced, these visitors are likely to be annoyed. Some people think labels are visually intrusive and that the visual clutter makes an aesthetic experience impossible. But those who do not want *any* information are in the minority.

Interpretive labels: Nonexperts like finding out why a certain piece is in the museum, what makes it famous, what to notice, or why the artist created it. They are, however, sensitive to being talked down to or being told what to feel.

The use of interpretive labels in an art exhibition that is meant to be interpretive, thematic, historical, or narrative will depend on the exhibition's big idea. If a gallery has a declared didactic purpose and uses obvious, legible labels, visitors can choose to bypass the gallery altogether. If they choose to visit, they are still free to use the labels, audio tour, or brochure or not. But every exhibition should have at the very least one main introductory label to reveal the museum's intentions. If there isn't a point, say that.

Both? Nonverbal communication through graphics (e.g., illustrations, icons, photographs) can reach people who do not want to rely on words. On the other hand, for readers, graphics can reinforce and add new dimensions to verbal and concrete experiences. Choices of lighting, color, texture, and sound can change the mood and vary the nature of sensory experiences in nonverbal ways. In most museums other than art museums, these verbal and nonverbal preferences are likely to coexist compatibly in most learners.

Make Choices Clear and Apparent

The type of approach and degree to which the presentations embody one form of instructional design or another should depend on what ideas are being communicated and what experiences are intended by the museum. Some ideas are best communicated in a linear sequence, others by multiple examples, still others through open-ended experimentation or through role-playing or mimicking; and some ideas are best expressed through media. The design of exhibitions and their labels should reflect the exhibit developer's intent, and the intent should be explicit: If it is meant to be open-ended, let visitors know; if it is appropriate to be pace controlled or sequential, make that apparent.

Good exhibit design gives visitors control over their experience. Attractive, effective orientation throughout the museum gives visitors the information they need to make their choices. The interested visitors can find a topic they want; the uninterested are given sufficient information to avoid it. When visitors get to make deliberate, informed choices, they might get more than they expected, become more engaged, even stay longer.

THE AUDIENCE BRINGS THE EXHIBITS TO LIFE

Another way to think about audiences is to realize how they, as an entity, are a vital part of the fundamental purpose of museums as places that exhibit and interpret collections and phenomena. We have been talking about making exhibitions come to life for the visitors; what about the way *visitors* bring the *museum* to life? American artist Michael Asher expressed the visitor's role in activating the museum's purpose through his artwork in the Art Institute of Chicago's 74th American Exhibition. Asher hired groups of viewers to stand in front of two paintings in one of the museum's permanent collection galleries. Asher's Chicago work *was* the viewing process—the intersection of the museum's presentation and the viewer's perception, neither one possible nor complete without the other. When museums recognize and fully appreciate the audience's vital function, they become more willing to integrate new ways to meet the needs of visitors.

WHAT THEY DON'T WANT

The answers to what the audience does not want can be found in the exhibits that visitors never noticed in the first place or forgot about soon afterward. Visitors do not want exhibits that don't attract or involve them actively or personally; are unpleasant, irritating, obnoxious, or crowded; are authoritative, confusing, and condescending; don't allow them to exercise their powers of curiosity and scrutiny; or are foreign, strange, boring, obvious, unclear, overwhelming, or make them feel stupid.

Fortunately, most negative features can be eliminated through more careful planning (refer to discussions of big ideas) and testing (discussed in the chapters on prototyping and evaluation).

To review: Who is the audience? A self-selected group of semi-motivated, time-limited, mostly first-time visitors who are novices but are curious about the subject matter. What do they want? They are seeking gratification through feelings of competence and an enjoyable social experience. If you select elements and write labels for *them*, chances are you will satisfy the vast majority of your visitors.

8

Audience Segmentation

Categorizing audiences into segments can be useful to exhibit planners, who are thinking about visitors' differing needs, and to marketing departments, who are thinking about how to attract visitors to the museum. But the most valuable information about our visitors is gained by watching how they behave once they are at the museum.

Since the 1990s we have seen an expansion in the number of ways to segment and describe learners and audiences in museums. Fortunately, we've come a long way from "grazers" and "streakers" to sobriquets that are less hierarchical and more helpful for exhibition development and marketing. In all the following examples, it should be stressed that the individual intelligences, typologies, motivations, identities, segments, or interests are not necessarily related to any one demographic or psychographic measure. People can be influenced by the situation they find themselves in; that is, context can elicit different kinds of engagement. Depending on the context, a single visitor or visitor group can manifest multiple typologies.

TYPOLOGIES THAT DESCRIBE THINKING AND LEARNING

Multiple intelligences and learning styles, described below, come from studies done with students in formal education classrooms. These educational models and theories have some important, but limited, applications for the unconventional, informal, fast-paced nature of learning (seconds, not semesters) in museum exhibitions.

Gardner's Multiple Intelligences

Howard Gardner's theory of multiple intelligences describes different ways that individuals engage in thinking. According to Gardner, every individual has seven kinds of intelligences: **musical, kinesthetic, logical-mathematical, spatial, interpersonal, intrapersonal**, and **naturalist**. These intelligences link to specific regions of the brain.

Gardner devised his theory of multiple intelligences in the context of the classroom, but his concept of "pluralizing"—described here in the context of general education—has resonance for museum exhibit developers:

> The educator should decide on which topics, concepts, or ideas are of greatest importance, and should then present them in a variety of ways. Pluralization achieves two important goals: When a topic is taught in multiple ways, one reaches more students. Additionally, the multiple modes of delivery convey what it *means* to understand something well. When one has a thorough understanding of a topic, one can typically think of it in several ways, thereby making use of one's multiple intelligences.

McCarthy's Learning Styles

Bernice McCarthy developed a scheme in which she identified four types of learners and learning situations: **imaginative learners, analytical learners, commonsense learners**, and **experiential learners.**

Learning styles refer to the strategies people prefer to use in a learning situation—their preferences for perceiving and processing information. They are based to a large degree on research about how children learn in formal educational settings, especially how students solve problems. Styles are also linked to how our brains process verbal and visual information differently.

People's preferred learning styles are influenced by their genes, their past experiences, and the demands and opportunities of the present environment. It is important to remember, however, that all learners use and need all kinds of learning experiences. One learning style may be more comfortable for a person in one situation, but not in another. While McCarthy's 1978 book about learning styles is no longer valued by educational professionals, the concept is still useful for understanding the needs of people in informal learning environments like exhibitions. Considering a variety of visitor learning styles helps exhibit developers honor the diversity of museum audiences and encourages them to provide a variety of ways for visitors to perceive and process information.

TYPOLOGIES THAT DESCRIBE VISITORS' MOTIVATIONS

Another way of categorizing visitors is to look at what motivates them. The following two models have direct implications for good interpretive label writing.

Jan Packer's Leisure Motivations

Jan Packer and her colleagues measured visitor motivations for educational leisure activities. Using a scale from zero ("not important") to six ("extremely important"), she asked visitors to rate themselves on twenty-five reasons for visiting, which were grouped into five larger categories: **learning and discovery**, **enjoyment**, **restorative**, **social**, and **personal development**.

The Detroit Institute of Arts used a modified version of a longer checklist, based on Packer's studies, for part of its summative evaluation of the visitor experience after the DIA underwent massive restoration and reinterpretation efforts in the 2000s. The adjective checklist questionnaire had eighty-eight items clustered into four main visitor experience dimensions: **emotional**, **intellectual**, **physical**, and **spiritual**. In summary:

> The tool may be especially useful for developing and evaluating special exhibitions, which provide an ongoing opportunity to compare visitors' experiences with exhibitions of different subjects and interpretive approaches. Finally, information about the types of experiences that are most common among DIA visitors could provide a starting point for further research to inform the design of new marketing campaigns.

John Falk's Identities

John Falk, visitor studies and free-choice learning guru, created a model of five visitor identities to help explain the various motivations visitors have for why they visit and how they approach the free-choice learning environment. The five identities are **explorer**, **facilitator**, **experience-seeker**, **professional/hobbyist**, and **recharger**.

Although Falk argues that these identities predict visitors' behaviors and the choices they make during a museum experience, these identities are not immutable dispositions or hardwired in the brain. They can be fluid, depending on the context and content of museum exhibits.

Falk's model seems more geared to visitors in museums, whereas Packer's model was derived from other leisure and cultural sites.

TYPOLOGIES USED TO DESCRIBE SPECIAL INTERESTS

The next four examples of segment studies show how different museums got to know the interests, behaviors, and expectations of potential and actual visitors to their own institutions to help define local marketing strategies and serve their visitors better.

The Tate's Eight

The Tate Museum, testing assumptions about visitor motivations and behaviors, came up with eight segments to describe how its populace engaged with interpretive materials in one gallery: **aficionados, actualizers, sensualists, researchers, self-improvers, social spacers, sightseers,** and **families.** These typologies were defined by cued visitors' pre- and post-visit answers to diagnostic questionnaires, integrated with interviews and observations in a temporary exhibition about the artist Mark Rothko.

Notably, the Tate study was able to relate what visitors said they valued with their observed behaviors involving the introductory label. Different segments found the same label useful for different reasons. The findings also raised questions about the need for more visitor orientation to prepare them for the types and content of interpretive opportunities in special exhibitions.

Field's Five

The Field Museum commissioned a study based on psychographic measures of its visitors' attitudes about digital technology used in exhibit interpretation. It revealed these visitor segments: **curious activity seekers, contemplative, traditionalists, social explorers,** and **parent facilitators.**

Field's exhibit developers used this information when planning new exhibits and media for interpreting them. They were pleased to find that the percentage of types who are motivated to learn, read, and interact with exhibits in the museum far outnumber those who are there just for togetherness or are being dragged along by others.

Shedd's Custom Six

Shedd Aquarium built a custom segmentation picture of its audience from one thousand telephone interviews with local residents (not just visitors). It came up with clusters of people who shared similar attitudes and behaviors. After eliminating the "people whose leisure choices didn't even remotely include a visit to the aquarium" cluster, Shedd concentrated on the remaining six: **young urban explorers, fun-loving suburbanites, idle empty nesters, edutainment enthusiasts, enrichment seekers**, and **Shedd critics**.

Shedd used the audience segmentation data to focus its marketing and advertising campaigns in ways that successfully increased attendance to exhibits, improved communication of Shedd's role in conservation advocacy, and modified its membership strategies to target different consumer benefits.

Pekarik's IPOP

Andrew Pekarik, at the Smithsonian Institution's Office of Policy and Analysis, distilled four typologies that represented visitors' primary interests when approaching museum exhibitions: **ideas, people, objects**, and **physical**. The IPOP model suggested that "exhibitions that strongly appeal to all four visitor typologies will be highly successful with visitors."

He also talks about the notion of how people "flip" from one typology to another:

> Recent interviews suggest that visitors are excited and pleased when some unexpected aspect of an exhibition opens up a preference category relatively unfamiliar to them. Sometimes people can "flip," that is, have a strong reaction to a different type of experience than the one that generally drew them.

Exhibit developers and designers can create multiple opportunities for unexpected positive reactions from visitors who might not have an incoming preference for the exhibition's topic or modalities. This is an important way of thinking about audience typologies and segmentation in general.

INCORPORATING VISITORS' NEEDS AND MOTIVATIONS INTO EXHIBITION DESIGN AND INTERPRETATION

While audience segmentation is a helpful reminder of the great diversity of visitors to our institutions, its most effective use is in encouraging a wider variety of people to come in the first place. Once they're here, it's more useful to study how visitors behave in an exhibition rather than what characteristics they came with. And because the labels will be encountered by many types of people, the exhibition needs to be as inclusive as possible. Ultimately, we want the majority of visitors in an exhibition to stroll more slowly and stop more often. How to encourage that?

There are three keys to making labels and exhibitions appealing to different types of visitors:

1. Provide visitors with a variety of choices;

2. Make those choices clear and apparent; and, most important,

3. Make the variety of choices available add up to a greater whole when experienced together.

Self-selected casual museum visitors have always been in charge of their own goals, used their own strategies, managed their own tasks and time, arrived at their own conclusions and integrations, and not worried much about being extrinsically rewarded for learning or punished for failing to learn. Different kinds of exhibits encourage or discourage assorted aspects of this free-ranging behavior, and some visitors will feel more comfortable with one type of exhibit than another. It is the museum's responsibility to present all information and opportunities for experiences in ways that casual visitors can make sense of for themselves, choose those things they find attractive, and spend as much time they want.

Most options for appealing to visitors' differing preferences are compatible with each other. Careful planning of options most suited to the exhibition's big idea will help exhibit developers pick the right ones. However, while it's worthwhile to consider the preferences, motivations, and abilities of visitors, the options offered should not result in stereotyping visitor characteristics or in an overload of choices.

Museums Control What's Offered, Not Who Comes

Providing for and accommodating people's various motivations, learning styles, personality types, or intelligences is a good idea because it makes exhibitions more appealing to a broader range of visitors. Models, theories, sobriquets, typologies, and segmentation of visitors' motivations and behaviors are useful, but they can give museum practitioners a false sense of security if they equate being informed about these visitor differences with being able to appeal to them successfully in a measurable way. Exhibit effectiveness and impact should be judged by the exhibit's performance, not its presentation of opportunities. The question "How well did the exhibit communicate with visitors and engage them in finding meaning?" should be the driving force in the actual design process and the summative evaluation, not the more preliminary question, "How will we go about appealing to visitors' different learning styles?" Appealing to different identities is not a goal in itself but a means of achieving effective communication. We must thoroughly examine what is presented in the exhibition rather than just who is coming in the door.

A final question about segmentation studies, which require outside consultants and are often expensive: What is a good strategy to get museum directors to put as much money into inhouse interpretive label development, production, and evaluation to make better labels on the wall as they spend on marketing studies that look for identities, segmentations, and audience typologies?

9

The Number of Words

It is a museum exhibition, not an encyclopedia or a library. Visitors should feel they are allowed first and foremost to look and do, not to read. Write shorter labels.

It's safe to assume that the average reading speed for adult visitors who have fluency in the language, who are on their feet, and who have many distractions is about 250 words per minute. In a typical twenty-minute visit, that would be enough time to read five thousand words, but only if they spend the whole time reading. If they spend half the time looking and the other half reading, that allows for about 2,500 words. If they spend three-quarters of the time looking, talking to the other people in their group, and sitting down to rest briefly, that leaves enough time for about 1,250 words. But in real life, the number of words in a typical exhibition is far greater.

The table below suggests lengths for different types of labels, but bear in mind that the question "How many words should there be in a label?" is better asked as "How many words does this label need to have?"

All types of labels should be as brief as possible. Orientation, introductory, and section labels are typically too long, often more than three hundred words. They are more readable when edited down and broken into shorter paragraphs of twenty to thirty words each. A longer introductory label may be necessary if that is the only type of interpretive label in the exhibition, as might be the

Suggested Word Counts for Interpretive Labels

Main Types	Purpose	# of Words
Exhibition titles	attract, inform, identify	1–7
Introductory labels	introduce, orient, delineate	20–200
Section labels	announce, describe	20–100
Group labels	explain commonalities	25–75
Caption labels	interpret individual elements	25–50

case in an art museum. Simple captions (one or two sentences) or extended captions (short paragraphs plus illustrations) should be visually oriented, concrete, and interrelated.

A real life example shows the approximate number of words in labels in a small university art gallery. All labels were in English; no media, no credit panel. The 1,500-square-foot gallery had forty artworks including paintings, sculptures, etchings, and engravings.

Number of Words on the Walls in a 2,500-Square-Foot Art Gallery

Label Type	Number of Labels	Combined Number of Words
Intro panel including donor panel	1	325
Section panels	4	800
Quotes on wall	4	100
Labels for artworks IDs + captions	40	1,200
Caption labels	20	2,500
Total	**69**	**4,925**

To read all the words on all the labels in this relatively small exhibition would take approximately twenty minutes. If a visitor spent half the time looking and half the time reading, their visit would last forty minutes, which is probably longer than most people stayed. A better match between most visitors' short time budgets and museums' desires to communicate interesting, provocative interpretation is to write shorter labels.

When someone says, "I read ALL the labels!" what do they really mean? Probably that they read all the ones they wanted to read, or they are trying to please the evaluator who asked, "How many labels did you read?" during an exit interview. If the labels were shorter and fewer in number, it could be nearer to a realistic claim.

Some curators lament, "Visitors spend more time reading than looking at the art!" But what is their concern? The curator may be worried that the labels are taking time away from visitors' direct experience with the art. These curators fail to appreciate that interpretive captions for art can enhance people's ability to be engaged, to learn, and to find and make meaning. A study by Luise Reitstätter, "Looking to Read: How Visitors Use Exhibit Labels in the Art Museum," confirms several of our claims here.

More text might please directors, donors, funders, founders, or curators who think that more is better, but *those people* are not the primary users of the exhibition. Shorter labels give visitors more time to look at the art.

MAKE THEM SHORTER

Labels with fewer words are read more thoroughly. When a caption, group, or section label has more than two hundred words, in several paragraphs, visitors may appear to be reading when they are really scanning, searching for the most interesting pieces—most likely the interpretations relevant to the objects nearby. If the number of words is cut down to include only those relevant, visually based bits of information, the overall result is that more people will be able to find what they are looking for quickly and easily.

When each label gives them satisfaction, enjoyment, and intrinsic rewards, visitors will linger longer. They will be thinking, "I'm hungry, my feet hurt, and the parking limit is about to expire, but I want to see just a couple more things here."

LESS DRAWS MORE

Shedd Aquarium planned a temporary installation about wildlife forensic science in the 2,300-square-foot special exhibit gallery. Concerned that their visitors might not want to spend much time in a science exhibit that contained no live animals, the developers were conservative about the number of words for each label in the exhibit. The first part of the exhibition contained artifacts and photographs; the second section had ten interactive stations.

At each of the interactive stations, all label copy was written in chunks, and the ordering of the information was kept to a consistent six parts:

1. Title

2. Introductory scenario in fewer than fifty words

3. A challenge, "What forensic scientists know," in twenty words

4. Directions, in twenty words, for what to do and notice

5. A ten-word question on a flip label for visitors to answer by comparing two specimens

6. An answer in fewer than twenty words under the flap that included a sentence about a consequence or result based on the introductory scenario

Each chunk could be read and understood independently of the others, and labels could be read in any order, for a total of about 105 words per station. Each activity was planned to take less than a minute.

All the interactive stations were mocked up and tried out with nonexpert adults and then revised before the final versions were produced. The total number of words for all ten interactive stations, including titles, was about 1,300.

Summative evaluations showed that adults and children spent most of their time using the interactives, reading thoroughly, following directions, congratulating themselves and each other when they knew the answer, reading again or looking harder when they did not, using more than half of the stations, and calling to each other, "Come over here, look at this one!"

The level of visitors' interaction and involvement in this science exhibit surprised and pleased the developers, and they felt that the characteristics of the label copy, especially the brevity and revisions they had achieved through evaluation, contributed greatly to its success.

The exhibition *Whodunit? The Science of Solving Crime* at the Fort Worth Museum of Science and History, was another less-is-more success story. The exhibition presented a "crime scene" where visitors could look for evidence and track down suspects. It was planned by a multidisciplinary exhibit team that included museum educators, designers, curators, evaluation specialists, and marketers, plus a cadre of advisors—scientists, school-based educators, and forensic experts. At an early design stage, they had seven criminal suspects, four computers, and fourteen monitors. They pared those elements down to three suspects, one computer, and four monitors. Prototyping during the design phase and after opening helped the museum continue to revise, compress, and improve the visitor experience.

Summative evaluation conducted in Fort Worth before *Whodunit?* traveled found that visitors spent, on average, about eighteen minutes and stopped at about 25 percent of the exhibits. While the exhibit was well received by visitors and colleagues, the Fort Worth staff thought that more paring down would make for an even better visitor experience. They eliminated exhibit elements that had failed to attract much visitor attention and were deemed not essential to communicating the big idea. Cuts included several wall text panels containing ancillary stories.

The smaller traveling version of *Whodunit?* was 4,500 square feet (down from 6,000), and had twenty-five elements (down from forty). Evaluated again in a new setting, the average time spent by visitors was now twenty-five minutes (up from eighteen), and 60 percent of the visitors stopped at more than half the exhibit elements, making it an "exceptionally thoroughly used" exhibition according to the database of tracking studies. The smaller version successfully attracted more visitor attention to each of the fewer elements.

ACCOMMODATING VISITOR BEHAVIOR

Research has repeatedly shown that visitors often skip the introductory label. But this label often holds important information that sets the stage: It explains the logic of the arrangement of objects in the space and provides context for the viewer's experience. So why do people skip this important label? Because the type is too small? Because they are written for experts? No. Because it's usually hundreds of words too long. (The exception is special exhibitions at art museums, where a high proportion of the nonexpert audience feel a need to read more diligently.)

The Detroit Institute of Arts renovated its building and reinterpreted all the permanent galleries, adding visitor-friendly label copy, interactive devices, and big ideas for all the collections. Summative evaluation conducted after reopening revealed less visitor use of introductory labels than museum staff had hoped for. Based on the evaluation's tracking-and-timing report, the DIA recommended making future introductory labels shorter and the type size larger so visitors could read them easily at a glance and from a distance. On the other hand, tracking studies showed that lots of people stopped and read object labels for highly attractive works. Here the evaluator's recommendation was to experiment with expanded forms of caption labels at works of art that attracted the most attention, sometimes adding *more* text.

HOW DO YOU KNOW WHEN YOU HAVE THE RIGHT NUMBER OF WORDS?

You know you have the right number of words in a label when the content of each type of label has covered the information that is relevant to its role in communicating the big idea or a supporting theme, and when—after prototyping it with visitors—most people didn't tell you it was too long.

Occasionally the need arises for an exceptionally long label. When there is evidence that many people—not just one, not just the "more interested viewer," but a large proportion of visitors—are paying attention to an object, one that is attracting the most eyeballs, raising the most questions in visitors' minds, making them ready, willing, and eager to read, go ahead and write a longer label. But still, keep those paragraphs short.

10

Readability Issues

Readability has to do with how difficult or complex the text is, or the ease with which a reader can comprehend the text. Readability is influenced by writing style, sentence length, vocabulary level and the reader's familiarity with the subject.

Interpretive labels should be appealing and suited to as many visitors as possible: the casual tourist, the layperson interested in the subject as a hobby, the person whose job is related, the family group visiting to entertain the children, the foreign guests with limited English, the new immigrant in the city.

Try this quiz: What is the best way to make sure you are writing at the right reading level for your audience?

   A. Aim for the lowest common denominator.

   B. Use a sixth-grade vocabulary.

   C. Write different labels at different levels.

   D. Write for your peers.

   E. None of the above.

The correct answer is E, but before discussing better alternatives, let's review the answers for A, B, C, and D; why they are misconceptions; and the difficulties they present.

CORRECTING MISCONCEPTIONS ABOUT READABILITY

Don't Aim for the Lowest Common Denominator

There is no point in writing for the so-called lowest common denominator— those who are unable or unwilling to read labels. Nor should you aim for the highest common denominator—the experts or the people who read everything. Give the companions and families of those uncommon visitors a break. ("Brian, come on. The rest of us want to get going!")

Instead, select the content and style that will work for the *commonest* common denominator—the majority who read sometimes (not never, not always). Appeal to the would-be readers who will read if the label is short enough, if it looks easy to read, if it is legible, and if they have time.

Don't Use a Sixth-Grade Vocabulary

Sticking only to words that sixth graders know will help labels have a broad appeal, but it makes them less interesting, less colorful, and less interpretive than if that rule could be broken from time to time. It is all right to aim for a sixth-grade reading level—especially if your museum is only for sixth graders—but do not be a slave to it.

Don't Write Different Labels at Different Levels

Writing for different vocabulary or age levels—content for kids, content for adults—makes labels twice as hard to write and more expensive to produce, and the duality creates visual clutter in the exhibit. Most adult visitors, given a choice, prefer the kids' labels because they look easier, are shorter, and often have larger print. Keep it simple: Write one-level labels.

Don't Write for Your Peers

A label writer who writes for her peers claims, "I'm writing for the more interested readers, and I don't care if people don't read them. Besides, it is our scholarly obligation to present these concepts." This attitude sends a counterproductive message to most visitors: The labels are not meant for you, and the words are not important or essential to your experience in the exhibit. Exhibits displaying this attitude are not visitor centered. Institutions that employ label writers with this attitude are not sincere about seeking to reach a broader audience. This information is better suited for a different modality, such as an exhibit catalog.

CHILDREN'S MUSEUMS ARE A SPECIAL CASE

Labels for children's exhibitions should be crafted for children's developmental levels and not be a watered-down, childish version of an adult label. If children's museums want to fully realize their goals for their primary target audience, they should write for children. They should stick to vocabulary words that are familiar to children, especially avoiding geographical proper nouns and words related to geologic time. Children exist in the here and now and have an age-appropriate sense of extended time (past and future) and of world space (far away is down the block). Children will read labels written for children. Adults often choose to read labels directed at children because they know the labels will be easier to read and understand than most other museum labels. Adults will also read these labels aloud to pre-readers, especially when the language is accessible to a younger age group.

Writing for Families

Making visual comparisons is a natural human activity for all ages. An exhibit case at the Brooklyn Children's Museum contained two masks from Guatemala, three Akuaba dolls from Ghana, and four wicker rattles from Zaire. Labels placed on a panel below the three groups of objects were written to be read aloud by adults and to invite families to make comparisons between objects. The title of the case was "Seeing Individual Differences."

Seeing Individual Differences

These two masks are similar, but there are lots of differences. How are they different?
Masks from Guatemala
Easy to see the differences

These three dolls are similar. If you look closely, you can see differences. What is different about each one?
Akuaba dolls from Ghana
Harder to see the differences

These four rattles are similar. If you look closely, you can see individual differences. What is different about each one?
Wicker rattles from Zaire
Hardest to see the differences

Many good examples of writing for children and families can be found in "Write and Design with the Family in Mind" by Judy Rand. Writing two sets of labels—one for adults, one for children—is not advised. Think of your visitors as one big family, and write for them.

WRITING READABLE LABELS

There is no single "right" reading level, but one good guideline is not to write below a sixth-grade level or above an eighth-grade level. Writing above an eighth-grade level puts text out of reach for a large portion of the audience, especially younger children, non–English speakers, and viewers who don't have prior knowledge of the subject at hand. Writing below a sixth-grade level will sound simplistic or childish to most adults. Beyond that rule of thumb, here are four other tools for crafting readable labels: **readability tests, front-end evaluation, "core" editing,** and **watching out for trickster words**.

Readability Tests

Many computer word-processing programs allow you to check the reading level as you write. Microsoft Word, for instance, does a grammar check that tabulates the average number of words per sentence, the average length of words, and the percentage of passive sentences and uses these metrics to assign the text a Flesch-Kincaid grade level. If your word-processing program isn't equipped with a readability test, calculators are available on the internet.

But don't rely on this method alone. Readability tests are valuable as a check, but they are not sensitive to the unusual context of the designed environment of museum exhibitions, where context can lend clues to readability. Use the following tools to guide you toward colorful, descriptive language that is still comprehensible for children and novice adults.

Front-End and Formative Evaluation

Before writing labels or fully developing all the exhibition components, you can do simple front-end evaluations of concepts, titles, or key ideas with a small representative sample of potential visitors (ten people). Read the concept, title, or key ideas aloud and ask them, "What would you expect to see, do, and find out about in this exhibit?" Or show them (one at a time) the technical words associated with the exhibit concept and ask, "What do you think of when you see this word?"

If you are unsure about an introductory or section label, or any interpretive label, or you are arguing internally about whether visitors will understand it, try this: Take it out on the exhibit floor and ask ten people to read it to you out loud. If they look at it and say, "The whole thing?" it's probably too long. If they hesitate, mispronounce, or stumble over a word, go back to your desk and formulate another draft. If a drawing or photograph needs to be added, try that too.

Relatively quick open-ended user testing like this can give you qualitative feedback from visitors about your vocabulary, their experience, and the expectations they have of your planned exhibition. Front-end studies and tests of prototype drafts often come to the same conclusion: While visitors may be superficially familiar with many of the terms, they do not have thorough understanding of what those terms mean. Thus, if exhibit developers use familiar technical terms in labels, they must not assume that visitors will understand them as well. This underscores the need for labels to be written clearly and simply for readers who do not have sophisticated knowledge of the subject, whether it is microbiology, French impressionism, or the Civil War. Visitors may know the words "*germ*," "*Monet*," and "*Yankee*," but they probably have limited and fragmentary knowledge about them.

Do "Core" Editing

Review the text and cross out words that are above a fifth- or sixth-grade vocabulary. If the label still makes sense, you can leave them in. If it no longer makes sense, consider dropping those words, defining them, or rewriting the label.

A simple example: A sign said, "Free Persian kittens." The middle word, "*Persian*," certainly adds to the meaning of the sign for someone who understands it. But it does not interfere with the basic message or subsequent action. Higher-level vocabulary words that are used as adjectives will add more information to a label without obscuring its core meaning.

The ~~anti-malarial~~ drug comes from the bark of a ~~tropical~~ tree.
These ~~ritual~~ bowls were made from ~~exotic~~ materials like copper and ~~marine~~ shells.
The sea star uses its ~~hydraulic~~ tube feet to open a clam.

The sentences are still clear with the words crossed out: The drug comes from the bark of a tree. The bowls were made from materials like copper and shells. The sea star uses its tube feet to open a clam. The labels are certainly more informative with the additional words, but they still make sense without them to readers who lack sophisticated vocabularies.

OTHER FACTORS THAT AFFECT READABILITY

Vocabulary levels are just one of the factors to consider when writing for an audience with a variety of reading skills. The following advice will help make content easier to grasp.

Watch Out for Trickster Words

The English language abounds with words that are used interchangeably as nouns, verbs, or adjectives. Images that words create in the reader's mind should match what they see, so using the right words is important. Readability and comprehension can be slowed or impeded by words with more than one function and meaning, for example:

cement	concrete	minute	scales
project	fly	envelope	

This goes for spoken words in audio labels as well. Words that sound the same should be avoided.

maze	maize
coarse	course
paws	pause
sales	sails

Good editing eliminates these trickster words.

Consider Reading Speed

Normal reading speed is about 250 to 300 words per minute, and eye movements consist of alternating sweeps and fixations along a line of type, with a return sweep at the end of one line to the beginning of the next. If a person is reading less legible material, the number of fixations increases and reading speed decreases.

Normal reading distance for a seated reader is about twelve to fifteen inches, and normal book or newspaper type is 8- to 12-point type. At that distance, approximately four letters of type are projected by the lens of the eye onto the *fovea, or center,* of the retina, the point of clearest vision. Around the fovea is the area of peripheral vision, which can encompass about fifteen more letters in any direction as our eyes move along a line of type. Peripheral vision helps us anticipate what is coming into focus next—in terms of both legibility and readability.

Avoid large type (bigger than 36 to 48 points) if readers are expected to be only two feet away. Very large, close-up type forces the reader's eyes to see letters instead of reading words, and the reader's eyes must make more fixations to perceive each word. This process is both tiring and distracting because the eyes and the brain are geared to an expected, or normal, perception distance and reading speed. Slowing the eyes down gives the brain time to wander. The reader has trouble concentrating.

Considering Visitors with Limited Vision

Readers with limited vision, such as older readers, will read more slowly. In-gallery aids such as large-print versions of the labels will be appreciated, as will online aids like spoken descriptions of exhibits. An exhibition called *Crip* featured a group of artists addressing disability and intersectional thinking at the University of Illinois Circle Campus Gallery 400. The exhibit's website had an interesting array of alternates to "normal-sized" printed labels, including large type, spoken labels, and spoken descriptions of the exhibits, all of which you could access on your phone while in the gallery.

Readability on Digital Devices

Exhibitions rely on digital devices—computer screens, interactive tablets, smartphones—to deliver content, and the rules for typography outlined in chapter 21 apply to these devices as well. The research is ongoing, but it does seem that technology is changing the way we read. The way our brains interpret information differs when viewing a flat, nondigital surface that reflects light versus viewing a light-emitting device. Maryanne Wolf's book *Proust and the Squid* and Ferris Jahr's article "The Reading Brain in the Digital Age" delve into how our brains react to digital devices. Some research has shown that it is more physically and mentally taxing to read from a screen than from a piece of paper, but these studies usually consider lengths of texts much longer than typical gallery texts.

Earlier screen resolution favored sans serif fonts over those with serifs because sans serif fonts are simpler in design, with fewer details, and are more legible at low resolutions. The resolution of today's screens is such that either font type can be equally legible. The Lucida family of typefaces, designed by Charles Bigelow and Kris Holmes, was the first original typeface designed for both digital printers and screens.

Expert versus Novice Visitors

Readability guidelines should be based on the assumption that the majority of people coming to your exhibition want to read but are not conversant in the vocabulary of the subject, regardless of their age. At the Victoria & Albert Museum, the exhibit development staff knows that typically their visitors are highly educated. But the museum's text-writing guidelines remind writers that "they are unlikely to be educated in the subject you are writing about. [Seventy-four percent] have no specialist knowledge of art and design. If they do have a specialist area, it might be in Renaissance book production, not Buddhist sculpture."

In general, most visitors are not experts, and even if they are experts, chances are they will not be insulted by clear, concise, readable labels that are written with enthusiasm for the subject and respect for novice visitors.

11

Multilingual Labels

Multilingual labels are not easy, quick, or cheap to produce, but they help a museum welcome non-English-speaking visitors.

In many communities in the United States, multilingual labels have become an important, even necessary feature for addressing a multicultural population. Multilingual labels provide critical translation for non-English-speaking visitors. They also make these visitors feel more comfortable and help them create an affinity with the institution.

RESEARCH AND EXAMPLES

The Bilingual Exhibits Research Initiative found that providing labels in Spanish and English helped Spanish-only adults facilitate museum visits for their children, keep up with the group, and feel empowered in an exhibition. In a paper on the BERI, Steven Yalowitz et al. reported that multilingual speakers engaged in "rich forms of language-based interactions" in both languages, going back and forth between Spanish and English to create "a linguistically dynamic social experience."

To welcome local families of Mexican and Vietnamese descent, the Children's Discovery Museum of San Jose, California, translated English labels into Spanish and Vietnamese for the *Secrets of Circles* exhibit. Summative evaluation found that "support for multilingual labels was very strong, not just among speakers of Spanish or Vietnamese (who were extremely supportive), but also across the spectrum and cultures of Children's Discovery Museum visitors."

The exhibition *Giants of Land and Sea* at the California Academy of Sciences included labels in English, Chinese, Spanish, and Filipino, the top four languages spoken by San Francisco residents. This was the museum's first multilingual exhibition. Graphic designers didn't always lead with the English label; sometimes other languages appeared first. A summative evaluation report, published in *MWA Insights*, revealed that the translations increased visitor feelings of comfort and welcome and had a positive impact on family dynamics, relieving English-speaking children of the task of translating and allowing adults to facilitate the experience. Nearly all visitors reported that the multilingual interpretation either positively impacted their experience or had no impact.

Multilingual labels should not be undertaken casually, however. They increase the number of words in an exhibition, and risk giving visitors the visual impression of an insurmountable amount of information. Multilingual labels are also costly to write, design, and produce. They can more than double the lead time needed for developing an exhibition. If you plan to use bilingual interpretation, start early in the planning process. It can save time and money.

PLANNING FOR BILINGUAL OR MULTILINGUAL LABELS

Creating complete sets of labels in multiple languages is most warranted when a large proportion of the local audience speaks a language or languages other than the "official" language, and certainly when it is the law, as in parts of Canada.

Developers need to ask, "Who are we translating for? What are their needs? What should be translated?" It's a good idea to involve the users in answering these questions. In an exhibition about the Inuit people of eastern Canada, consultations with the Inuit community found that they did not want or need to have much of the interpretive texts translated because older Inuit who spoke the language already knew about the objects and customs, and the younger generation spoke English. They were, however, very interested in having the Inuit names identified for places and people shown in photographs.

On the other hand, the original Alaska Native people of the Anchorage area, the Dena'ina, wanted all the texts in *Dena'inaq' Huch'ulyeshi: The Dena'ina Way of Living* translated to encourage the next generation to pay more attention to their language, which was almost lost and is being revived.

An important part of the planning process is taking the time to create an institutional system or set of guidelines for multilingual labels. This is because many people (e.g., museum staff, board of directors, community members) will have a stake in the decisions. "There's no denying that it is complicated, time-consuming, and costly to present text effectively in two languages," said Claire

Champ of the Canadian Museum of History. Canadian law requires all services to be in Canada's two official languages, English and French. In "Champ's Best Practices for Bilingual Exhibition Text," she says, "In our experience, there is no way of getting around this being a lengthy, multistep process that requires different types of expertise."

THE TRANSLATING PROCESS

When translating labels from one language to another, it is best to use a translator who is completely fluent in both languages, as translation is much more than a word-by-word rendering of the text. Interpretation involves subtle forms of communication that must take into account meaning, metaphors, and colloquial expressions. The "standard" version of a language can be incomprehensible to populations that speak a different dialect. Said one professional, "After a while on the job, I realized how we, Mexicans, speak in our day-to-day life in a way that would be nearly impossible to understand to a Spanish speaker from another country."

Before crafting the first draft, reflect on the relevance of the content. Are the situations, words, or examples hyperlocal? Would another audience that lives in a different setting and speaks another language be able to understand it?

Before having the labels translated, keep several other important things in mind:

- Drafted label text to be translated should be edited carefully for readability and clarity of thought.

- The person who is translating must reinterpret the exhibition messages using the style and manner of the given language.

- And before the final translation is approved and put up on the wall, it should be tested with native speakers from the target audience.

The Monterey Bay Aquarium has worked with the same company since the early 1980s to translate its exhibit text from English into Spanish. The company also translates the aquarium's educational materials, marketing and web content, and Human Resources documents. Because of this long-term relationship, the translators now have a good understanding of the aquarium's Spanish-speaking audience. They also fully understand the signature voice of the aquarium's labels. Even so, every project entails a lot of back-and-forth between the aquarium and the translation company to get the rewording right.

At the Phillip and Patricia Frost Museum of Science in Miami, in-house exhibit developer and bilingual communications specialist Carlos Plaza generated a cohesive policy of bilingual interpretation (English/Spanish). These were his initial guidelines:

- Write in the first language, then convey meaning, not literal translation, in the second language.

- Reformulate text in the first language based on insights gained from interpreting the second language.

- Voice, tone, and style should be the same in both languages.

- Use universal terms whenever possible and most-familiar regional variations when necessary.

- Create concise, digestible chunks of information.

- Determine word count based on visitor behavior, graphic design, and readability.

- Develop consistent size, arrangement, and aesthetics for all interpretive text.

- Give equal weight to both languages—font size, headlines, and others.

- Clearly separate the two languages.

- Be consistent with the placement of elements.

- Avoid repeating the same images on one panel.

- Test and modify as necessary.

These guidelines have evolved and been modified as the museum has become more thoroughly committed to bilingual labels, and the museum continues to experiment with effective ways to write and produce them.

The Oakland Museum of California translated primary labels in its renovated art galleries into two languages: Spanish and Chinese. The museum's native-speaking community-based advisors helped choose the translation company most appropriate for the local audience. Once the translations were completed, the museum hired additional external reviewers to look over the translations. This added considerable time and expense to the process, but it was done to ensure that the translations were closest to the original meaning and that they all had a consistent voice. The museum's publication *How Visitors Changed Our Museum* traces the project.

In a primarily English-speaking community, an alternative to multilingual labels is to write label text in a way that visitors who are English language learners (ELLs) are able to understand the basic ideas. Choosing content that's consistent across languages and cultural contexts can help visitors translate for themselves. See the guidelines for readability in chapter 10: Test your text, use front-end evaluation, and do core editing.

THE DESIGN PROCESS FOR BILINGUAL LABELS

The Canadian Museum of History in Gatineau, Québec, has been working on the challenging issues of design and presentation of labels in French and English for years. They have experimented with typefaces, colors, positions, sizes, and other features to ensure that languages are distinguishable and that one language is not given priority over the other. "Visitors scan the labels, looking for their language," said Jennifer Elliott, director, Public Research and Evaluation, "and we need to ensure that the text is always presented in such a way that visitors can find their language easily and consistently."

Distinguishing the Languages

Make the design (colors, typefaces) of the two or more language sets readily discernible from each other to cue visitors quickly into the multilingual system, but be careful not to make one more legible than the other. The type sizes should be the same. The choices of contrasting colors should be balanced equally, although the choices are limited because few colors have exactly the same contrast. And keep in mind that their placement together (right, left, top, bottom) has implications for importance and priority.

For traveling exhibits, separate panels for each language can be rearranged to meet the needs of each venue. For example, in one location the French panels could be placed to the left, English on the right; while the social/political climate in another location might call for the reverse. Another physical option is to install a sliding panel over a bilingual label that visitors can move from side to side, revealing only one language at a time.

Keep It Short

English is one of the more succinctly written languages in the world. One rule of thumb is to assume a 35 percent expansion when writing anything in English that is destined for translation. Remember to provide adequate space on the label panel for all the translated words.

Consider Context and Purpose

When it's not feasible to translate every label, base the selection process on the nature of the audience and the communication objectives for the exhibition. For example, one zoo made labels in Spanish for a temporary interpretation of animals from Mexico and Central and South America. Another zoo put Swahili titles on buildings and services in the exhibition that featured animals native to Africa.

MULTIPLE LANGUAGES IN MEDIA OTHER THAN WALL LABELS

If significant numbers of visitors represent several languages, multilingual signs may not suffice and other forms of translation should be offered. Portable laminated reusable labels can provide two or more languages, as can free handouts, brochures, or audio tours. Museums in large urban centers or those with heavy foreign tourism routinely make use of these devices.

Of course, digital options exist as well. The ubiquity of smartphones has encouraged many institutions to provide translations using QR-coded links to translations of some (but not all) exhibit labels. The Exploratorium provides QR code translations for a selection of its permanent exhibits that it felt couldn't be fully understood without access to the label content.

On-screen digital label texts next to an exhibit element allow visitors to swipe to reveal another language, thus taking up less real estate in the exhibition. Digital labels at the California Academy of Science's Steinhart Aquarium show tabs along the top of the screen that visitors can touch to access label copy in four languages.

The Monterey Bay Aquarium has been experimenting with "blended language" programming, in which the presenter of a training or feeding session speaks in a seamless flow between Spanish and English, alternating sentences, allowing access to the same content simultaneously. Developing this strategy has required hiring bilingual staff, practicing and getting feedback, and supporting the verbal delivery with visual aids. Initial success with blended language presentations has been encouraging. For details, see the *Informal Learning Review* article

"Blended Language Programming: An Emerging Model to Promote Inclusion and Learning" by Amparo Leyman Pino et al.

In addition to words, multilingual environments can include flags, graphic motifs, music, even food (smells) to help create a mood or atmosphere appropriate for a particular ethnic group. It would be disrespectful, however, to use a second language simply as a decorative design motif.

Tips for Multilingual Voice-Over and Subtitling Videos

Guidelines for audio voice-over and subtitle translations are basically the same as for the written word, with a few extra caveats for bilingual videos.

On screen, keep it even shorter.

As with printed labels, translations from English for digital applications, whether as subtitles on the screen or as voice-overs, will run longer than the original wording. Keep subtitles succinct, and place them at the bottom third of the frame so as not to obscure the action. Restrict the number of words in audio scripts.

Be cognizant of what your budget can and can't do.

More text equals more time. Longer monologues or the use of multiple voice actors extends the amount of translation work that needs to be done. Syncing voice-over to on-screen speakers is more costly than an off-screen narrator.

Given that bilingual labels take more time to develop, cost more to produce, and take up more space in an exhibition, what are the implications for museums considering the move to a wide use of translated interpretive labels? To gain the important benefits of creating a better visitor experience and giving recognition to the value of multiple cultures, the same suggestion you've heard in other chapters works here: Make smaller exhibitions with more-focused topics that can be understood, enjoyed by, and engaged in for a broad range of visitor ages, experiences, and ethnicities.

12

The Label's Voice

*Visitors hear a voice—a personality and a point of view—
in interpretive labels, ranging from a single voice to a two-
voice debate on contrasting ideas to multiple voices. Exhibit
developers need to make the voice or voices clear and
consistent.*

"Voice" refers to who is speaking to visitors in the labels. Is it an institutional voice
or a personal voice? Is it a knowledgeable expert? A formerly disenfranchised
person? Should more than one voice be heard? What about the whole community?

Traditionally White-run museums now realize more than ever the importance
of involving other-than-White voices in the exhibit-making process through
consultation, collaboration, and co-development with living representatives.

BEYOND THE DEFAULT INSTITUTIONAL VOICE

The default voice for many labels is an impersonal institutional-authority
museum voice. But this voice can be made more animated and engaging,
depending on the topic and content of an exhibition and its target audience.

Judy Rand describes a process for creating a label voice that has personality,
rhythm, and flow for the messages being communicated. Although this "voice"
still represents the institution, Rand encourages writers to imagine how a real
person might speak about a specific topic or content by using these tips:

- Imagine a real personality.

- Find models and examples.

- Get immersed in the vernacular.

- Use technical guidelines to analyze voice.

- Write style-setter labels for approval.

- Edit labels to match that style.

A key to this approach is reaching agreement on the voice up front with the exhibition team and then sticking to it. Whether the label's voice is institutional, personal, or multiple, it should be discussed and decided before the labels are drafted. It is difficult to insert or change a voice after the fact.

THE NAMED VOICE

If the voice of the labels is unique to a specific real individual who is expressing a personal viewpoint, it should be identified to the readers from the outset. If visitors are not aware that the labels were written by a specific person, they will assume that the institution's view, values, or opinions are being expressed, and that can lead to confusion. For example, labels for an exhibition of historical photographs of Black Americans were written by a descendant of enslaved people of the period who used colloquial expressions such as "mammie" and "boy." Some visitors took offense, thinking that the museum was speaking in a derogatory way. The author of the labels had been identified at the bottom of the introductory panel, which most visitors missed. This misunderstanding could have been avoided by putting the name and a photograph of the author of the labels in a more obvious place or throughout the exhibition, or by putting the author's name on each label. How do you make sure the authorship is obvious? Observe and interview visitors during a soft opening or early after the exhibition opens, and make adjustments if the message is not clear to them.

The exhibition *Jules Tavernier and the Elem Pomo*—co-curated by the Metropolitan Museum of Art and the de Young Museum in San Francisco—explored the intercultural exchange between the artist Jules Tavernier and the Indigenous Pomo community of Elem in Northern California. The exhibition centered on a painting by Tavernier of a ceremonial dance performed by the Elem Pomo in which he placed his White patron, San Francisco banker Tiburcio Parrott, among the Elem Pomo who were watching the performance. The exhibition relates the fact that Parrott was, at the time, operating a toxic mercury mine on the Elem Pomo's ancestral homelands, which had devastating long-term environmental consequences for that community. In addition to museum-authored labels interpreting multiple artworks by Tavernier, curators collaborated with members of the Elem Pomo community, who wrote labels that interpreted nineteenth-century paintings and basketwork from their twenty-first century personal and cultural perspective. At the de Young, every label in the exhibition included the name of its author, including both Elem Pomo community members and de Young curators. The name notation can be enhanced by the author's affiliation—be it museum curator, Indigenous person, or other—so it is clear from what cultural group the voice is speaking.

For an exhibition about Afrofuturism, the Oakland Museum of California invited all contributing and commissioned artists to write exhibit labels for their own works. The artists' names appeared on the labels they wrote. "As a White curator, it was critical that I step away from using my voice," said OMCA exhibit curator Rhonda Pagnozzi in a conversation with the authors. "My role was to be facilitator; this was not my story to tell." The contributed exhibit labels were edited by Pagnozzi and guest curator and arts writer Essence Hardin, then approved by each featured artist. "This experience was about relationship building," said Pagnozzi.

Can there ever be too many voices in one exhibition? Perhaps. In the Native North Americans hall at the Field Museum, renovated in 2022, the strategy was intentionally "polyvocal," wherein visitors encountered short labels in cases and displays authored by more than fifty different named Native people. Some people might find this a bit tiring in printed labels (digital and nondigital) and be more attracted to videos where one can get to know some individuals better in a few minutes of watching and listening instead of a few seconds of reading.

WHOSE POINT OF VIEW IS IT?

In addition to identifying the voice of who's talking, exhibit developers need to clarify whether an exhibition presents a point of view. This is especially important in exhibitions that interpret some form of debate, issue, dialogue, or strongly held opposing views.

In his 1995 *Museum News* article "Exhibiting Controversy," Neil Harris, a professor of history at the University of Chicago, called what happened to museums in the twentieth century "a blurring of cherished artifacts and social contexts, scholarly research and exhibition venues, aesthetic values and cultural meanings." While museums had previously been more about objects and authoritative points of view, they were becoming more about interpretation, and it was important to state whose interpretation was being conveyed. Harris held that if interpretive exhibitions present multiple meanings, and "right" or "factual" are matters of opinion, visitors will have to adjust to a new, unexpected, nonauthoritative stance. It is the museum's responsibility to help visitors see the difference when they make that adjustment. Made in 1995, Harris's statements still ring true today.

Some exhibitions have been picketed, shut down, or not even allowed to open because of criticisms over the points of view portrayed in them. One way to counter these strong reactions is to offer multiple perspectives. Marketing and orientation tools can communicate the exhibition's big idea to visitors before they are confronted with the experience. It also helps when the museum's stance on the issue is both clearly presented and clearly communicated. This allows visitors to think, "I understand what this is about, but I don't agree with it."

Examples of Presenting Multiple Perspectives

In an exhibition about an environmental crisis caused by industry, should visitors be allowed to hear industry's side of the story? The decision should be driven by the exhibition's big idea, and the voices chosen to tell that story should be clearly identified. In *Darkened Waters: Profile of an Oil Spill*, the introductory panel stated that the "we" speaking in the exhibition was the staff of the Pratt Museum in Homer, Alaska, who originally developed it. The Pratt had a point of view: The oil spill was a huge disaster. Throughout the exhibition, other voices were heard as well: industry professionals, spill workers, Native Alaskans, and other residents of the spill zone. The author's name and affiliation or the source of the label's content was written on each label. Their points of view often provided interesting contrasts. It was clear that there was not one simple explanation for the spill, no clear or easy solutions to the problem, and no foolproof way to avoid another spill. The multiple voices gave visitors a variety of perspectives from which to think more deeply about their own prejudices and points of view. But including the other voices did not dilute the force of the Pratt's position that the oil spill was a disaster.

At Brookfield Zoo's *Voices of the Forest* exhibition, four points of view were communicated: the Indigenous people who lived deep in the forest, the Indigenous people who lived at the edge of the forest, the Western zoologists who studied the animals living in the forest, and the local rangers hired to protect the forest. Each interpretive label contained one point of view, and up to three labels were posted together. Contrasting points of view were allowed to coexist; no attempt was made to resolve them. The main message was clear: There were many ways that people use the forest.

The exhibition *Addressing the Statue* presented multiple points of view about what the American Museum of Natural History should do with a statue of Theodore Roosevelt that had been outside the museum's entrance since 1940. The statue depicts Roosevelt high on a horse with two individuals—an African and a Native American—walking behind him. While the statue was commissioned to celebrate Roosevelt as one of the founders of the museum, it also communicated "a racial hierarchy that the Museum and members of the public have long found disturbing," per the exhibition's website. The museum opened a discussion about whether the statue should stay or be removed, engaging a variety of individuals—from academics to artists to people on the street—in an "honest, respectful, open dialogue." In the exhibition, these individuals were named and represented with photos. Their words, both spoken on video and printed on exhibit labels, were included. After the physical exhibition closed, a digital version of it remained on the museum's website. The statue was removed several days before the exhibition closed.

The Native Perspective program of the Metropolitan Museum of Art invites contemporary Native American artists and historians to respond to eighteenth- and nineteenth-century Euro-American representations of Indigenous subjects in the museum's American Wing. In the galleries, the Native Perspective labels sit alongside the traditional interpretive labels, differentiated by background color and clearly identified with the heading "Native Perspectives," along with the author's name and tribal affiliation.

African American community leaders in Wilmington, Delaware, were invited to write personal responses to Danny Lyon's photographs of the Southern Civil Rights Movement at the Delaware Art Museum. These responses were placed on the gallery wall next to the photos. In their statement upon winning a 2019 American Alliance of Museums Excellence in Exhibition Label Writing Competition award, exhibit developers stated that 77 percent of visitors read these "Community Contribution" labels, and 29 percent said the labels changed how they interpreted the photographs.

The interpretive center at the Cahokia Mounds State Historic Site—the remains of a pre-Columbian Native American city directly across the Mississippi River from modern St. Louis, Missouri—created labels that featured two stereotypical voices: one for a female White "Archeologist" in a pith helmet and one for an

Indigenous male "Storyteller" with facial hair, a topknot, jewelry, and body markings. Some visitors were struck by the contrived and inauthentic nature of the attempt to show two viewpoints that were not named and not living. (***Note:*** This insensitive interpretive strategy may have changed. The center was under renovations in 2022.)

Some museums are tapping previously unheard but clearly present voices from within their institutions. Seventeen security officers at the Baltimore Art Museum became guest curators for an exhibition they called *Guarding the Art*. The officers collaborated with museum staff to select artworks, conduct research, determine the scope of the exhibition, weigh in on installation design, develop didactic materials, generate content for a catalog, and plan visitor tours and other public programs. "For the past few years, the Baltimore Museum of Art has tried to bring in new voices that haven't been heard before," said chief curator Asma Naeem in a 2022 *Washington Post* interview. "Our guards are always looking at the art and listening to people as they talk about the art. . . . We wanted to see things from their perspective." In a similar vein, *Beyond the Uniform*, at the Museum of Modern Art, featured first-person audio interpretations of specific artworks in the gallery by members of the museum's department of security.

Drawing from both students and professors, the Middlebury College Museum of Art "Label Talk" series invites three people to share their perspectives on a single artwork from the collection. The authored labels are printed and hung alongside the museum's interpretive text on the gallery walls. Museum visitors can scan a QR code next to the artwork and add their own response on a virtual blog. In a 2021 interview with the *Middlebury Campus*, director Jason Vrooman expressed hope that "showcasing three separate viewpoints will show that there are multiple ways to view art and help make the museum a space where many voices are welcome."

Without introduction and orientation, a visiting voice can sow confusion if it is not supported with interpretation or explanation. In 1992, artist Fred Wilson perused the collections of the Maryland Historical Society and created the *Mining the Museum* exhibition. Wilson's unexpected juxtapositions of objects and cryptic labeling—for example, a case labeled "Metalwork, 1793–1880" contained rusty slave shackles alongside sterling silver vessels—presented a commentary on what museums collect, interpret, and display, and what they omit. Hugely popular, the reinstallation sparked controversy or enthusiasm, depending on the visitor. Wilson was not concerned with orienting visitors or telling them what the exhibition was about. Introductory information was limited to an impressionistic video of the artist walking through the galleries that was meant to tell visitors, "Well, something's going to be odd about this exhibition." As a result, those who knew ahead of time—most often by word of mouth—that this was an artist's reinterpretation of a historic collection were emotionally engaged and moved. The reactions of those who stumbled accidentally upon these galleries—which were drastically different from the other galleries at the museum—ranged from confused to irate.

Fred Dust of design firm IDEO urges institutions of all kinds to "be transparent about what you believe," even when you think your opinions or beliefs are different from those of many members of your audience. Better to have people disagree with you than to misunderstand where you are coming from. Dust also emphasizes the need to understand visitors' hearts and minds. In an email exchange with the author, he suggested that museums must start by making sure they know what *they* stand for and get comfortable "putting it out there."

CAN I JOIN THE CONVERSATION?

While many institutions are experimenting with sharing authority and giving voice to previously unheard histories on their gallery walls, some institutions are taking community collaboration a step further, inviting participation over the entire exhibit development process. The criteria and advice for writing effective museum labels given in this book should be used to guide these new community collaborators, guest curators, and commissioned artists, who can easily make the same mistakes (writing labels that are too long or unfocused) that the more experienced in-house exhibit developers and curators are learning to avoid.

When the Delaware Art Museum reinstalled their eight main-floor galleries, their goal was to make the collections more relevant to the local community. They took what they called a "radically inclusive" approach, involving community members at every step of the interpretive planning process. Their practice of shared authority was designed to center community voices and develop institutional empathy. The museum invited community partners, museum stakeholders, and first-time visitors to give direct feedback through iterative prototyping sessions. Museum staff members listened in during early planning, tested interpretation with visitors, and edited and reedited based on their feedback throughout the process, integrating community voices and perspectives.

Encourage Conversation among Visitors

Let visitors do some talking. Short labels that encourage participation can allow a three-way conversation between the label writer, the reader or readers, and the museum objects on display. In these scenarios, the labels become an easy jumping-off point for visitors to talk to each other in their social groups. In history museums, visitors often share prior knowledge and memories with each other. In a science museum, biology exhibits tend to spark conversations about our bodies. For example, a short label next to X-rays of human bones gave only the person's age and the bone's name, which prompted many memories, like "Remember when Grandma . . ." A 2012 summative evaluation of a Detroit Institute of Arts exhibit of art of the Renaissance found that images of Jesus, Mary, the Nativity, and other biblical stories give Christian visitors a sense of familiarity and connectedness to their prior knowledge. Stimulating conversations can be more than just counting on visitors' natural tendency to reminisce. Paulette M. McManus, in "Watch Your Language! People Do Read Labels," and Lois H. Silverman, in "Of Us and Other 'Things': The Content and Functions of Talk by Adult Visitor Pairs in an Art and a History Museum," point out some socially determined patterns of visitor conversations in museums.

Invite Participation

Ask questions and let visitors post their answers in the form of a "talk-back" panel. Darcie Fohrman, an award-winning independent exhibition developer, has incorporated visitor talk-back spaces in the exhibits she has designed for many years. She says that the secret to getting good feedback and thoughtful answers is to ask a good question. How can you tell if it's a good question? Try it out. Museums must maintain their talk-back panels daily for neatness and to cull rude comments or drawings.

Nina Simon has been the champion of visitor participation in museums at many levels in many ways. Her book *The Participatory Museum* gives advice on how to experiment with audience participation without upending the traditional museum model. She asks: How can cultural institutions use participatory techniques to give visitors a voice and to develop "experiences that are more valuable and compelling for everyone"? Her answer: Participatory experiences have to be successfully designed "so the content that amateurs create and share is communicated and displayed attractively."

If you invite participation, provide a place to do it. There was a missed opportunity for visitor participation in an innovative art exhibition that combined the collections of two museums—the San Francisco Museum of Modern Art (which was closed to the public at the time for renovations) and the Asian Art Museum—under the title *Gorgeous*. Modern and Asian objects in the exhibition were displayed together in the galleries. On first-person authored labels, a curator from each museum spoke about what they found "gorgeous" about selected works of art. Also in the gallery, videos featured people on the street talking about what was gorgeous to them. The premise of *Gorgeous* was that the curators spoke directly to visitors through first-person labels about why *they* thought a particular object was gorgeous. In turn, the curators asked visitors their opinions about what they found gorgeous. The only problem was, there was nowhere for visitors to speak or record their opinions. No iPads in the gallery where they could make comments. No talk-back panel *anywhere*. No place on the website of the Asian Art Museum for visitors to contribute when they got home. Or did the curators mean that visitors should just talk among themselves? The intent was not clear.

Comment Books

Probably the oldest form of inviting visitors' input in a museum exhibition is the comment book at the end, where various scribbles, serious and otherwise, are recorded. Comment books are a unique form of label, totally un-curated. Anonymous writers are usually motivated by extremes of good or bad feelings; younger writers, by mischief. And who reads the comments? Other visitors, maybe the curator. Reading the random remarks, which range in issue and tone from thoughtful praise to naughty pictures, can be a mixed experience. Occasionally comment book data gets gleaned for information about how visitors are relating to and interpreting the exhibitions. Reviewers sometimes look for patterns in critical comments or things that visitors call out as needing improvement. Maybe they get culled from time to time by a staff person. Maybe they are skimmed, counted, or just filed away. On the positive side, they can reveal evidence of personal connections, reminiscence, emotion, empathy, identity, learning new things, and pride. Recent advances in digital tools allow for media displays of visitors' comments. And in more detailed studies of comment book feedback—including "What the books say" on the Informal Science website and Sharon McDonald's 2005 *Accessing Audiences: Visiting Visitor Books*—some researchers see a form of dialogue and discourse between the museum and its audience.

THERE IS NO SUCH THING AS A NEUTRAL VOICE

In 2017 LaTanya Autry and Mike Murawski created the #MuseumsAreNotNeutral campaign "to refuse the myth of neutrality that many museum professionals and others put forward." Launched in a blog post (currently searchable at Artstuffmatters) the campaign has found a more permanent home on Autry's eponymous website.

Only one-third of respondents to the American Alliance of Museum's 2021 Museums and Trust survey attributed their trust in museums to the fact that museums are "nonpartisan/neutral," and White respondents were more trusting of museums than non-White respondents. There is growing awareness in the museum profession that museums are not only not neutral, but that they present a very specific point of view. And if visitors aren't recognizing that fact, it's the museum's responsibility to "show our work." In his 2021 AAM blog post, historian James Gardner states that "every action that we take, beginning with what we collect and what we choose to exhibit, reflects a point of view." He argues that museums should be transparent about how, in creating exhibitions, they "bring together different perspectives, make choices, and present ideas and arguments."

In the twenty-first century, society-wide movements in support of decolonization, Black lives, social justice, economic equity, and greater inclusion of all marginalized peoples have permeated the museum world. Institutions of all sorts are being asked to reconcile with their colonialist and exclusionary histories, to be transparent about them, and to communicate the changes they're making to the public. This change is heralded in the new types of job descriptions, such as head of community engagement, content strategist, and director of diversity, equity, and inclusion. The Hunterian Museum at the University of Glasgow created a new position: a "curator of discomfort." In a February 2021 museum blog post, they describe the job as looking at "ways outside of traditional museum authority to explore the interpretation of contested collections," stating: "What we need to do is collaborate with anti-racist activists, communities, academics, heritage institutions and heritage professionals, to find a way to build a bridge of trust that is strong enough to bear the weight of the truth we are trying it deliver."

Cecile Shellman has spent three decades in the museum field, often as the only Black woman in the room. In her book *Effective Diversity, Equity, Accessibility, Inclusion, and Anti-racism Practices for Museums*, she admonishes:

If museums are expected to share in the social responsibility to champion justice and anti-oppression, it's imperative that we embrace the bravery of taking a stand. Or else there'll be no museums in the future. . . . Museums don't like to be called out on their sins. They like to present the most elegant, tidy treasures on pedestals under gleaming vitrines, as if to say nothing else matters now that there's a three-by-five-inch label exactly at right angles next to the sculpture.

In some cases a museum must make the case for a country's very existence, as did the National Museum of the History of Ukraine in the face of Russian propaganda denying the existence of that country's independent culture. In a May 2023 article in the *Guardian* about why museums are important for telling our stories, Charlotte Higgins maintains:

[T]here is a growing awareness that museums can no longer offer a singular, lofty, purportedly neutral view. Unless, that is, they are content to be mistrusted, or understood as irrelevant to, some of the communities around them. Equally, since there is no such thing as a "neutral" curatorial position, there is a growing realization that museums should be more honest about their own intellectual processes, and more generous about sharing their power (that of amassing, keeping, selecting and displaying objects) with those outside their walls. . . . That makes museums less comfortable places than they were in the days when they could be more or less relied on to be the slumberous resting place of a few Neolithic tools and medieval coins, and no one openly questioned the presence of, say, the African artifacts gathering dust in a corner. But it does make them more vital—because society needs places where debates about history, identity and culture can be enacted, without violence.

Do No Harm

In response to these movements and pressures, museums are looking at different ways to become more inviting and accessible. They are trying to be attentive to the great variety of visitors who walk through their doors. Many are taking steps to reduce harm and increase transparency.

Closed to the public in 2020, the Nelson Atkins Museum of Art looked inward and conducted a harm-reduction audit of its exhibit labels. Borrowing from the discipline of public health, the Interpretation Team examined their labels "through the lens of reducing harm to people who have been historically underserved by our museum." (For more details see "Part VI: Voices from the Field, Examining Labels.")

Rose Kinsley, Margaret Middleton, and Porchia Moore come from three diverse and complementary perspectives to make the case that "words matter" in their article in the Spring 2021 issue of *Exhibition* magazine. Using Middleton's

"Family-Inclusive Language Guide," they lay out how "word choices can hide unconscious personal and institutional biases and assumptions."

The Amsterdam Museum no longer uses the term "golden age" to describe Dutch history of the seventeenth century because that term "tells only half the story." The Harvard Art Museums changed the label on a John Singleton Copley portrait of Nicholas Boylston to reflect the fact that his wealth was derived from the trade of enslaved persons.

Museums (and other cultural institutions) are making efforts to use gender-neutral language wherever possible. But this involves more introspection than one might assume. Alex Kapitan, a genderqueer activist, educator, and founder of the project Radical Copyeditor, advocates choosing conscious language rooted in care rather than correctness. Noting that the etymological root of "curate" comes from the Latin *cura*, which means "to take care," Alex writes, "We must care for not only what's within the museum or cultural institution, but also the people who interact with that content." In a 2022 presentation for the Bay Area museum consortium Cultural Connections, Kapitan identified five important practices:

1. Be appropriately specific; don't use broad language when more specific language would be more accurate.

2. Avoid euphemisms for race, class, disability, and oppression (e.g., don't use "diverse" as a euphemism for "people of color").

3. Avoid dehumanizing language, which includes using adjectives as nouns (e.g., "the disabled"); equating people with a condition or label (e.g., "schizophrenics," "felons"); and negative, stigmatizing, and pathologizing language (e.g., "AIDS victim," "crippled by poverty").

4. Take care in describing identity by respecting the language the people you're writing about use to describe themselves; not making assumptions; and not positioning White, straight, cisgender, male nondisabled people as the "default."

5. Follow leaders on the margins by seeking scholars, activists, and leaders with marginalized identities, learning from them, and hiring them as staff/consultants.

The Center for Gender Equity and Leadership at the University of Berkeley's Haas School of Business has created a terminology guide, "Harmful Terms and Alternatives," which outlines "examples of words and phrases that can be harmful" and suggests neutral alternatives. It also addresses frequently asked questions related to race and language. This living document is a Google spreadsheet designed for business leaders and "other stakeholders to reflect on and improve their language."

Another valuable resource is "A Progressive's Style Guide," a multi-sourced and ever-evolving website giving guidance on terms to be used and avoided in the realms of age, disability, gender, race, ethnicity, and other categories. Their four central principles include using people-first language, self-identification, active voice, and proper nouns.

THERE'S NO SUCH THING AS NO VOICE

Even if there are no words on the walls, such as an art exhibit that uses only an introductory label and no other interpretation, an exhibition will still have a voice that is delivered by the design (e.g., color, lighting, groupings, juxtapositions). These elements, just like words, should speak clearly and appropriately.

Photo Figures for Part III

Douglas squirrel

The typewritten text of John Muir's vivid quote gives it the voice of a personal diary.

Although the vocabulary is a bit high, it might make a squirrel-hater laugh.

DOUGLAS SQUIRREL
Tamiasciurus douglasii

"A firm, emphatic bolt of life, fiery, pungent, full of brag and show and fight—and the acrobatic harlequin gyrating show he makes of himself turns one giddy to see."

—J.M.

Lonnie Holley (b. 1950)
Busted Without Arms, 2016

Dress form, gun grip display,
model handguns

Courtesy of the artist and the Arnett Collection, Atlanta, GA

I have used mannequins in my art since the early 1980s. A few years ago, I came across some old dress forms and also found a Pachmayr handgun display. I loved the way the guns had no barrels (like the one used in *In the Grip of Power*). I made this after years of news stories about black people being killed, only to learn that they weren't armed. One man ran away and was shot from behind. One man was selling cigarettes on the side of the street. It was more than I could handle. A few years ago, I visited Mother Bethel AME church in Charleston, South Carolina. They were redoing their grounds, and I met a deacon there. He gave me some materials from the construction site, and I made art out of it. Six months after my visit, a young man killed nine people there. Sometimes my art comes in the aftermath of pain.

Busted without arms

The artist tells a first-person story, in plain and personal language, that describes his inspiration and process. Because he speaks specifically about the artwork that's right before us, our eyes go back and forth from the art to the words as he brings his story home.

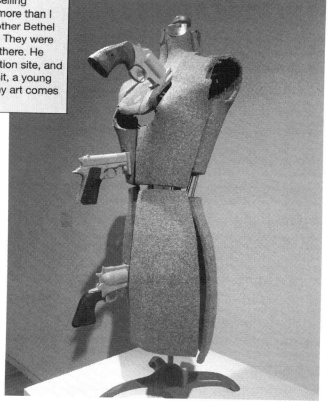

...THEODORE ROOSEVELT
MULTIPLE PERSPECTIVES ON...
...THE STATUE
COMPLICATED LEGACY
IMPORTANT PRESIDENT

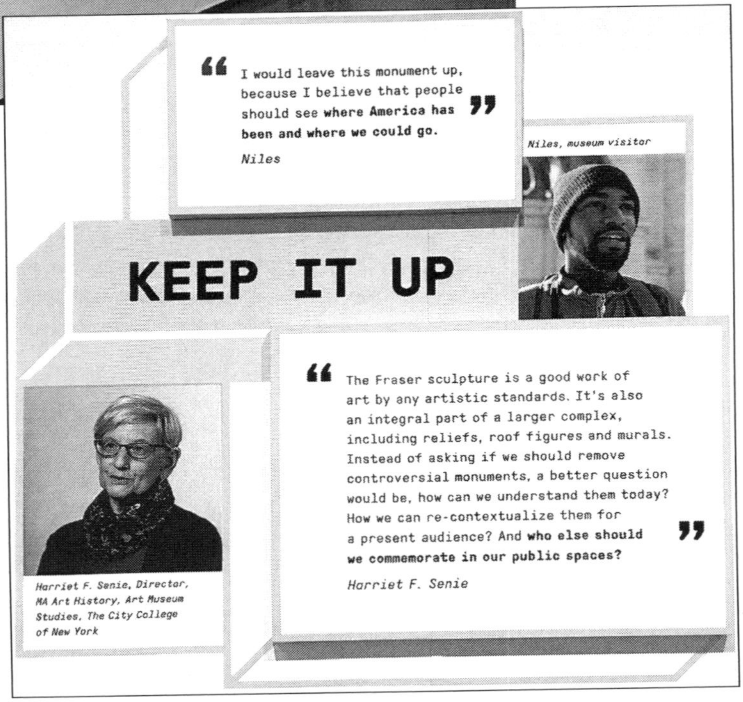
“I would leave this monument up, because I believe that people should see where America has been and where we could go.”
Niles
Niles, museum visitor
KEEP IT UP
“The Fraser sculpture is a good work of art by any artistic standards. It's also an integral part of a larger complex, including reliefs, roof figures and murals. Instead of asking if we should remove controversial monuments, a better question would be, how can we understand them today? How we can re-contextualize them for a present audience? And who else should we commemorate in our public spaces?”
Harriet F. Senie
Harriet F. Senie, Director, MA Art History, Art Museum Studies, The City College of New York

Keep it up?

Multiple first-person perspectives were invited from a diversity of people about whether the Roosevelt statue should remain outside the American Museum of Natural History. While some suggested interpretive recontextualization, the decision was made to remove it.

Reconsidering colonialism

New text affixed to the glass calls out historical inaccuracies and clichés depicted in this 1939 diorama.

Old displays that depict colonialism and white superiority need to be reinterpreted.

What we got from Indians

We don't do this anymore, right?

There's no big idea. There's no logical organization of types of labels. But most of all, the content is condescending.

Are they real— and how did you get them?

All of the specimens in our collection are real. The animals were once alive. In order to study animals for scientific research, scientists must collect real specimens in the wild. When scientists do this, they follow strict state and federal guidelines for treating the animals humanely and protecting species under threat of extinction.

¿Son reales? ¿Y cómo los obtuvieron?

Todos los especímenes de nuestra colección son reales. Los animales alguna vez estuvieron vivos. Para estudiar animales para la investigación científica, los científicos deben recolectar especímenes reales en la naturaleza. Cuando los científicos hacen esto, siguen estrictas normas estatales y federales para tratar a los animales humanamente y proteger a las especies en peligro de extinción.

¿Son reales?

The difference in length of these two labels is typical: Spanish translations of English require more words.

Research has shown that people in Spanish-speaking groups are likely to use both the English and Spanish versions of the labels rather than just one or the other.

Too many words

You don't have to read the words in these labels to know that there are too many.

Why do some art historians and geologists need to say so much? Writers can avoid this when they have a clear and focused big idea, a respect for visitors' limited time and energy, and some self-control.

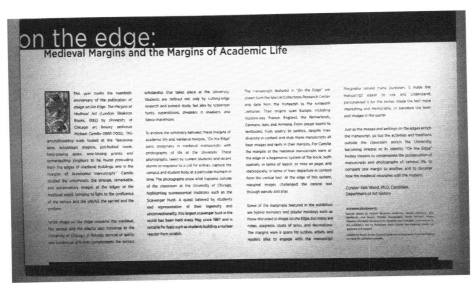

Indians everywhere

The fact that this introductory label begins with short paragraphs makes it easier to start reading; the engaging style then pulls the reader along.

Called "irresistibly readable texts" by art critic Peter Schjeldahl, the exhibit's labels are conversational in style.

Indians everywhere

Indians are less than 1 percent of the population. Yet everywhere you go in the United States, you see images of American Indians. Why?

How is it that Indians can be so present and so absent in American life?

One reason is that Americans are still trying to come to grips with centuries of wildly mixed feelings about Indians. They have been seen as both authentic and threatening, strange yet deeply appealing.

In the 21st century we Americans can surround ourselves with dream catchers and describe a football game as a trail of tears because we know that Indians are in the country's DNA and have shaped it from the beginning. The objects, images, and stories shown here are not what they seem. They are insistent reminders of larger truths, an emphatic refusal to forget.

Officer of the Hussars, 2007
Oil on canvas; frame with gilding

Kehinde Wiley
American, born 1977

This painting is inspired by a long history of European paintings showing military heroes on horseback. It draws attention because of its size, colors, and decorative details, but also because powerful, heroic images of black men are rare in Western art history.

Museum purchase, Friends of African and African American Art
IRA NO. 2008.5A-B

Kehinde Wiley

Alongside Kehinde Wiley's 2007 Officer of the Hussars, interpretive text shows the iconic European painting he "appropriated." It's good to show an image of the referenced work for visitors not familiar with it.

Critics now celebrate Wiley for "reshaping the monumental," not just appropriating it. A step in the right direction for a more current and equitable point of view?

Théodore Gericault, Officer of the Hussars, 1812, oil on canvas. Musée du Louvre, Paris.
Photo: Erich Lessing / Art Resource, NY

In this instance, Wiley appropriated Gericault's painting for his own artwork.

Question flip labels

Flip labels are frequently used as interactive elements in all kinds of exhibitions. A question is posed, and visitors lift the flap to see the answer. Did they guess correctly?

When writing question flip labels, consider the chances of most visitors getting the answer right. If your goal is to trick people into guessing wrong, think again. How do you feel when you get fooled?

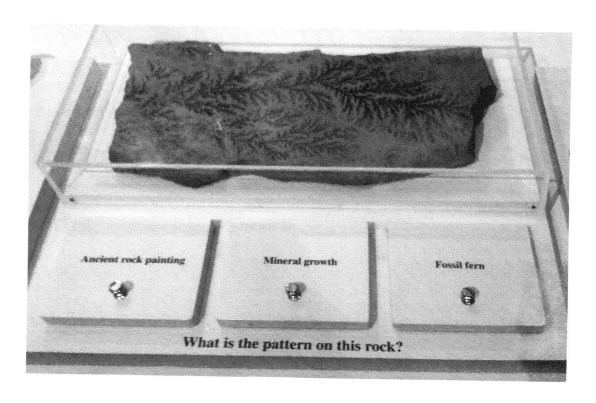

UNICORN

Monoceros mysticus

DISTRIBUTION: Old World with valid subspecies from India, Japan, China, England, and Scotland. No fossil record. First report from India, ca. 1000 B.C.

HABITS: Fierce, strong, solitary, shy, starry-eyed. Attracted to maidens. Feeds on roses.

ECONOMICS: Drinking cups from horn used to counteract poisoning attempts; market declined with advent of gunpowder.

CONSERVATION: General extinction attributed to education. Continues to exist in protected communities such as James Thurber Reserve, Columbus, Ohio.

Unicorn

Labels that attempt to be whimsical can be funny if visitors are in the know. But humor can be harmful if it makes them feel stupid.

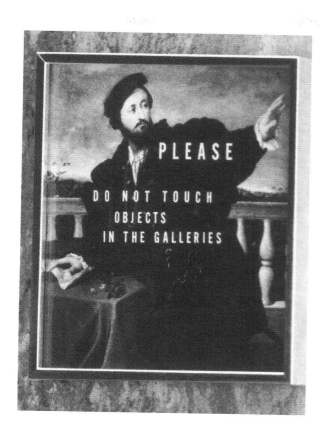

OK to touch?

When the sign starts with "Please," most visitors stop reading because they think the words "Don't Touch" are coming next. Better to say "OK to touch" if they can.

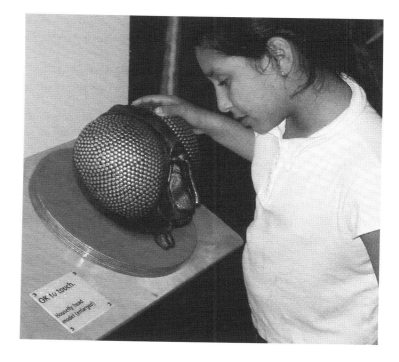

PART IV

Enhancing the Visitor Experience

13

Improving Orientation

Orientation is often the single biggest challenge to get right in exhibitions, and recommendations for improvements often stem from problems that relate to orientation.

Orientation signs are technically not interpretive labels, but orientation and wayfinding devices play an important role in satisfying visitors' basic physical need to know where they are. Visitors are not ready for learning or receptive to interpretation if they feel lost. A secure knowledge of their present location—and the subsequent relative locations of exits, restrooms, or food—allows visitors to feel ready for higher-level social, creative, or intellectual pursuits. If visitors are coming to an exhibition about an uncomfortable topic, it is essential that they are psychologically ready to deal with it or are equipped to make an informed choice to stay away. Other needs that visitors have for orientation, besides physical and psychological, include conceptual, spatial, emotional, locational, and functional.

ORIENTATION ISSUES ARE OFTEN OVERLOOKED

In a Building Informal Science Education (BISE) synthesis study of summative evaluations of exhibitions, the most noted recommendation for making improvements was to improve orientation. Visitors' orientation issues included difficulties in finding the front door of the museum, learning what exhibit topics were offered, finding the caption for a photograph, and figuring out how to operate an interactive device.

Exhibit developers forget about orientation, especially early in the process, when they are obsessed with burning questions about content, design, budgets, and schedules, but also later, when they are struggling with details of design, lack of time, not enough money, and too much content. At either point, they forget to ask themselves these four crucial questions:

1. How will we let visitors know that the exhibition exists?

2. How will we let visitors know who it is for and what it is about?

3. What will we do to make things clear, enjoyable, and relatable?

4. How will we help visitors find their way?

Without adequate orientation, visitors not only miss opportunities to engage with the experiences and messages of the exhibition but also sometimes become stressed, confused, or even irate.

ORIENTATION TOOLS

Abundant devices, tools, and methods are available for communicating orientation information to visitors before, during, and after a trip to the museum. Visitors can be guided by signage, arrows, architecture, staff facilitation, design identity, maps, brochures, floor plans, partitions, boundary markers, videos, and websites, including "Plan Your Visit" pages. A single tool is not enough. It takes a combination of methods at different points along the visitors' path to and around the museum or in an exhibition to reinforce visitors' needs to know where they are, what's coming next, or how to get out. Below, we consider some of the advantages of having these tools and the pitfalls in their absence.

Signage Outside

If a building has been repurposed to be a museum, visitors might need help finding the entrance. It can be a waste of visitors' time to park and walk to the wrong door if the original doorway was changed.

Signage in the Lobby

Visitors want to know who the exhibits are for. If an exhibit's title suggests that it is just for experts, it could drive potential visitors away. The Plant Lab, a room with highly engaging hands-on interactive experiences, needed improvements to let people know that it was meant for all visitors, not just botanists. In children's museums, adult caretakers like to know which places are for the very young or which ones are not for children only.

The information desk in the lobby is handy of course, but if there is a line, if the desk is not occupied, or if a visitor would prefer to figure out the options without talking directly to a person (yet), a brochure needs to be readily available.

The Introductory Panel

At the entrance to an exhibition, introductory panels are imperative. A clear entry message tells visitors what to expect. The absence of an introduction leaves visitors to fend for themselves. This works for those who prefer to wander, but for most people, conceptual orientation is important. The inclusion of clues to the topic, the exhibition's organization, and a reason for why it is worth the visitor's time will be appreciated. Even for a collection of objects that do not have interpretive messages or a unifying big idea, at least have a panel that gives the rationale for the space.

That said, introductory panels are often not read by visitors because they are too long, cause a bottleneck, or are not located in the line of sight. Art museums are different, however. Many people will make the effort to read a long panel in a crowd of other visitors, seemingly hopeful that the information contained there will enable them to enjoy the exhibition. In other types of museums, the effort-to-benefit ratio is not the same, and fewer visitors feel the need to read a long intro panel.

In many situations, a short introductory panel with fewer than fifty words in large type can be read quickly and thoroughly by a visitor who is slowly walking by. They benefit from the panel's orientation function without enduring an undue burden on their attention.

You Are Here

Probably the most underused, underemployed design feature in exhibitions is the floor plan or map of the layout of the gallery. At the beginning, along with the introduction panel, the floor plan lays out the relative size of the space and how it is divided into areas and themes. If the galleries are complicated, or if the exhibition is laid out over two floors, directions along the way are crucial. Physical and conceptual cues help visitors know where they are in space and time and prepare them for what's to come.

While we don't know what percentage of visitors like to read paper maps or feel confident about their ability to do so—especially with people's dependence on GPS or digital wayfinding aids—a basic floor plan of an exhibition will be helpful for those who do like maps, and they can help others in their social group who don't. Visitors who crave orientation will be thrilled by a floor plan; others can ignore it.

"You Are Here" maps should always have a "You Are Here" icon on them, and be positioned so that what the viewer sees to the right and left on the map aligns with what is left and right in real space. Always. (See the bibliography for Bitgood's "Special Issue: Orientation and Circulation" and two other old but good studies: Serrell and Jennings, "We Are Here: Three Years of Wayfinding Studies at Brookfield Zoo," and Marvin Levine's "You-Are-Here Maps: Psychological Considerations.")

To be sure your floor plan is legible, clear, and comprehendible, mock it up and try it out with some visitors before rendering it in final design and materials.

Arrows

Some designers don't like arrows. Some designers like to make arrows that don't look like arrows. But arrows can be familiar, easy to decode, useful, sometimes necessary, and are a great help with navigation. Arrows inform people that they are on the right path and not lost. Visitors feel more confident.

Boundaries

Boundaries are another important feature of orientation within exhibitions. Open floor plans are notorious for confusing visitors. It's hard for visitors to know when they are in one themed area and when they've moved into another. Partitions, low walls, or other boundary markers can help contain interpretive spaces whose exhibit elements go together. When exhibition boundaries are clear, visitors tend to stay longer and engage more because they are not as easily distracted or confused about what is part of the show and what is part of something else.

A FEW OTHER CONSIDERATIONS FOR ORIENTATION

Two considerations about visitors will encourage exhibit planners to focus on orientation. First, base assumptions about visitor behavior on actual audience data before making decisions. Second, adopt a truly visitor-centered attitude, creating an institution that strives to be helpful, welcoming, and accessible to all types of people.

First-Time or Repeat Visitors?

Do first-time visitors to your museum or to a special exhibition outnumber repeat visitors? First-time visitors need more orientation than people who come often. Not surprisingly, repeat visitors who have not been to the museum for a long time will have similar needs to those of first-timers, especially if the museum has been renovated since their last visit and things have changed.

Forced March or Free to Wander?

Often museums will say they don't want to control visitors or overdirect them. They want visitors to decide where to go and discover things by themselves, e.g., "make their own tour." But if visitors are going to plan their own pathways, they need to have adequate and effective orientation tools and a clear sense of their choices so they can make informed decisions about where to spend their precious time.

Marketing

Knowing that the museum exists and what its contents might be are prerequisites for coming to it. Is the Clyfford Still museum named for its donor or the artist? Is the Field Museum located in a field or about the ecology of grasses?

Websites can communicate the types of content and experiences available to visitors through text and graphics, including details for age- and interest-appropriate topics. A "Before You Visit" page can prepare visitors for challenges, such as getting there on public transportation or finding parking, knowing the price of tickets and when the free days are, whether food is available, and the days and hours of business.

What's Orientation Got to Do with Labels?

Good orientation sets up expectations in visitors' minds by telling them the title of the exhibition, introducing them to what it is about, and letting them know who it is for. When those expectations are met in the exhibition, visitors are likely to read the labels, feeling that the interpretation was meant for them and that the experience was worth their time and effort.

14

Being Visitor-Friendly

Visitor-friendly labels appeal to a broad audience, help visitors create positive experiences, and are used by the majority of visitors. They flow from the characteristics of visitor-friendly museums.

Interpretive labels speak to visitors in an appealing voice—not preachy or pedantic, but also not simplistic or condescending. They encourage visitors to begin reading them, to read aloud to others, to read all the way to the end, and to remember what they read. The best kind of interpretive labels are useful and meaningful to visitors.

Marlene Chambers, former editor and label writer extraordinaire at the Denver Art Museum, encourages us not just to write well, but to make our messages useful to visitors. She believes we must offer messages that give visitors something to do—such as agree or disagree with the ideas, use the ideas as building blocks in making conclusions, or make discoveries of their own. Chambers argues that most messages in museum labels are of no personal use and have no relevance to visitors' lives because they are one-way communications of information from curators to visitors. Her advice and philosophy support open-ended interpretation and exhibitions that encourage and present multiple meanings. This emphasis on usefulness and meaningfulness plays a large part in current efforts museums are making to become more visitor centered.

A museum's goal of offering visitors important, interesting messages and visitors' goals of creating personal meaning and enjoying themselves are not incompatible. It just takes more work, because museum practitioners first must find out what visitors know and want, figure out how to design and present what the museum has to offer in ways that will make useful sense to visitors, and evaluate all along the way to make sure that both sets of goals are achieved.

This is not a quick or easy task. It helps if the desire to reach out to visitors is institution-wide.

TIPS FOR MAKING EXHIBIT LABELS VISITOR-FRIENDLY

No book about exhibit labels can tell you what to say, because that depends on the museum, its collection, its mission, its visitors, and the exhibition's big idea. But it can identify guidelines for how to say it, and how to write more user-friendly labels. Whether it's the curator's opinion, the interpretive strategy team's skilled efforts, or a community's issue, the words on the walls will be more effective with the audience when the label writers know and use these guidelines. Many thoughts here are echoed in other chapters as well.

Assume interest. They're here. They're interested. Make labels short enough that most visitors will want to read them. "Tertiary information" with technical and abstract details adds clutter and confusion. Don't write for the few "more interested readers."

Begin with concrete information. Start with information directly related to what visitors can see, feel, do, smell, or experience from where they are standing. You do not know the age, gender, race, or educational background of your reader, but you do know the exhibit's setting and context. You know what your visitors are looking at. Take full advantage of that fact: Use words that are keyed to the most noticeable size, shape, color, position, content, question, or directions to get readers started. What will visitors be likely to notice or do first? Start with that.

Vary the length of the sentences. The longest sentences can be around twenty-five words; the shortest, two or three words; the average, ten to fifteen words long. Sentences that are longer than thirty words make it difficult for readers to follow a train of thought or keep track of the points. A variety of lengths will keep visitors from becoming bored and help them stay alert for the unexpected.

Use short paragraphs and small chunks, not large blocks, of information. A common mistake in label writing is to put too many ideas into a single paragraph. This is especially prevalent in art museums when curators write a lot and designers have to fit it into a small amount of space. Paragraphs serve to separate thoughts and give readers a brief rest between ideas. They also offer visitors a chance to look at the thing being written about—actively using the information or judging the interpretation. Write so that visitors can read a little, look a moment, read a little more, look again—all in less than a minute. Labels that look too long discourage, overwhelm, and frustrate readers. How many visitors walk into a text-heavy exhibit and say, "Oh goody, look at all those words"?

Metaphors are better for other forms of narrative, not labels. Label readers in museum galleries must contend with far more distractions than readers at home in the comfort and familiarity of their own easy chairs. Metaphors—in which one thing is likened to the properties of another—add additional ideas to the already complex environment of an exhibition.

Pick your metaphors carefully. And test them. Exhibit developers planned to use a roulette wheel as a gambling metaphor for taking risks with unsafe sex and HIV. In a prototype test of the element, a visitor talked about how he did not think roulette was an appropriate metaphor for AIDS risk. He said, "My brother died of AIDS, and this isn't doing it for me. It's more than a game—it's a chance, but not a game. You get death, not forty bucks."

Alliteration is an easy device to use. Alliteration—a series of words starting with the same letter or sound—is engaging. When editing, make sure alliteration is necessary, not just a gimmick. It is easy to overuse this technique.

Haiku is like cilantro. Some people like it. Some really don't. Writing exhibit labels in haiku or other forms of poetry can put people off. In most cases, clear writing is likely to be more attractive. If poetry is used, it should be relevant to the content of the exhibition.

Use humor sparingly. Humor is one aspect of label style that should definitely be tried out on a sample of visitors (in context, if possible). If visitors seem misled or confused, or if they don't laugh, drop it. Humor is often an indulgence for the writer's benefit, not the reader's. Puns—if they do not interfere with readers who don't get them—are allowable, but with restraint. Humor is subjective, and it can be hard to find universal standards.

Don't let cleverness or catchy titles rule. A common mistake when using multiple headers is to make titles and subtitles that are clever and catchy but do not advance the narrative. Titles and subtitles should be messages, not isolated, unrelated thought fragments.

Exclamation points in labels shout at readers and force emphasis on them. Let visitors discover and exclaim in their own words (e.g., "Look at that!" "That's neat!" "I never knew that!"). If you are tempted to use an exclamation point, think about what it adds to the label's voice. Some people find them overly forceful!

Use quotations when they advance the narrative and are necessary. They can add color and another "voice" to the exhibition. Or just fill space. Unnecessary, irrelevant, or obscure quotes are worse than no quotes, because they will quickly teach your readers not to pay attention to them.

Don't use newspaper style; it is not visitor-friendly. Newspaper journalism is not a good model for exhibit labels. First, newspaper articles are written with the assumption that most readers will *not* read the whole thing. Second, the body of the newspaper article usually starts with the most general or important content, and then goes into details. This is the opposite of what good captions should do: go from specific to general. Third, the length of newspaper articles is often not dictated by how long it needs to be but by the space available. And finally, newspaper editors assume that their readers are alone and sitting down.

Don't include content for the so-called "more interested reader." If there is more to say in detail for the few more interested readers, put it in a brochure or handout, if the cost can be justified. The assumption that visitors who are not interested in "more" information can just skip it is probably the most significant factor contributing to poor labeling in museums for the past century. Curious and motivated readers often find it difficult to "skip" text. Overall we know that when there are fewer words on the wall, more words get read. As long as museum practitioners use the excuse of "the more interested reader" for adding more words to labels, we will be stuck with too many labels, too much content, and information not used by or useful to the majority of visitors.

Beware of using "you" too much. To appear friendly, many exhibit labels overuse the second person singular "you," which can become annoyingly coy. Avoid this mistake by clarifying the big idea at the beginning and deciding early what voice is speaking and who you are talking to. As with most guidelines about labels, you can break them creatively.

Stay flexible within the label system. Different types of labels usually have recommended word lengths, but some flexibility should be allowed. Caption labels that all have the same number of words make for boring design and a dull writing style. Don't be afraid to leave some white space occasionally. It's easy to design area labels that all contain two paragraphs with four to six lines each, but what if there isn't two paragraphs' worth of something to say about each area? Catchy titles on every label can become annoying and uninformative. Overusing questions gets to be insulting.

Let some labels be longer. Some labels need to be longer because they interpret intrinsically interesting objects, defined by what arouses the most curiosity for visitors. Visitors are likely to read a longer label about an electric eel, Lincoln's bed, or Bruegel's *The Wedding Dance* than about less famous, familiar, common, or seen-one-seen-them-all things.

Break up blocks of text with headlines, subtitles, or phrases. These stylistic devices help break up concept labels and introduce ideas quickly. They also help transitions between thoughts. Each title or subtitle must have meaning on its own, and together add up to a complete idea—the main idea of the panel.

Interrelate labels and their settings. Most of all, do not get locked into a system that does not allow label content and design to be responsive to the setting and context. Information on labels works best when it reflects, enhances, and echoes its environment, placement, or setting as well as the objects on display. Label readers will get more out of the words, and more out of looking at the items in the exhibit, when the words are well integrated with the rest of the exhibit design. When the words, graphics, objects, and media all work together, it's like a 3D graphic novella.

Have a snappy ending. Just as most of your visitors self-select to come to the exhibit in the first place, readers are making a choice when they pay attention to the words. Give them a reward for their effort, especially for reading all the way to the end. Rewards can be some form of closure, reinforcement, or new insight. When finished, visitors should feel glad they took the time to read the whole thing. Here is a nice example from a caption for a large bell at an outdoor history exhibit:

> In 1847 this bell hung in the cupola of the congregational church. It was later used as the village fire alarm. It also sounded the 9 o'clock curfew when every kid was supposed to be off the streets or have a good excuse why he wasn't home. I know, I was one of those kids. *Les Schrader*

A good online reference containing visitor friendly advice is Anna Faherty's "What Makes a Great Museum Label." Rather than a list of guidelines, it's a discussion of the characteristics of great labels accompanied by colorful examples.

USE VISITOR-FRIENDLY DATA

Architects and designers estimate budgets for huge projects based on size—the number of square feet of a building or room. Exhibit planners could make use of similar budget figures based on how much time visitors typically spend in exhibitions.

Consider Time Budgets

Visitors use time budgeting by asking themselves (either consciously or unconsciously), "How long do I want to spend in this exhibition?" The answer is related to the size of the exhibition, its density (e.g., the number of elements, types of activities), the visitor's social group, and the visitor's perceived interest in the subject or activity, as well as the nearness of a restroom or café and when the parking reservation will expire.

Rather than making assumptions about visitors' motivations or internal fortitude, consider two metrics of time: the *average time* visitors might be expected to stay and the sweep rate, which is an index for a rate of time per unit space as visitors walk slowly, looking around, stopping occasionally. The sweep rate is derived from empirical data gathered from more than one hundred exhibitions of varying sizes and topics.

The conclusions drawn from the time database findings in *Paying Attention: Visitors and Museum Exhibitions* stress that visitors by and large do not spend much time in exhibitions, certainly not as much as many museum staffs like to think. The average time spent is around twenty minutes, and the average sweep rate is around three hundred—meaning visitors cover three hundred square feet per minute—which is useful information for planning new exhibitions. What can visitors comfortably do in twenty minutes without feeling bored or overwhelmed?

In exhibitions with an intended educational purpose, communication objectives, and a big idea, every exhibit component or activity can be integrated into a realistic time frame. Each exhibit element in an exhibition can be considered as a unit of potential time; for example, it takes five seconds to look at this; it takes twenty seconds to read that; this video lasts four minutes; or it will take people about ten seconds to figure this out. Then the exhibition can be planned so an appropriate number of elements are used and experienced in the amount of time the majority of visitors are likely to spend. Exhibit developers should clearly understand and define the most logical order in which visitors will use the elements and the amount of time estimated to use each one. Time-budget planning by the team will help create exhibitions that are not overwhelming. Instead of giving visitors fifty choices and activities or labels that take a long time to use, try giving them fewer choices or activities that take less time.

Share your time-budget planning with visitors. People appreciate being given information that will help them make intelligent choices. If an exhibit element has a set time span, it should be clear to visitors; for example, "Push button for a three-minute video," "Fifteen-minute tour begins here," or "This activity takes about four minutes."

Time-use categories are practical, empirical, value-free, clear, and objective for planning and evaluating exhibits. Collect your own user data by systematically observing your visitors: Track where they go in the exhibition and how long they spend. Data collection by staff members can lead to changes in the museum's attitude toward its visitors. By watching visitors closely, staff will become more empathetic toward its visitors—for the number of choices visitors have to make; how much effort it takes for them to read standing up while keeping track of their friends or children; and the amount of time it takes to look at a large number of exhibit elements competing for their attention.

Consider Height

One more example to consider in your visitor-friendly label system bears mention: organization based on physical height from the floor. Introductory and section labels need to be clearly in visitors' line of sight—not too high and not overhead. Visitors tend to look straight ahead or down (at the floor, at their kids), not overhead. Labels with text at eye level for adults and large graphics or small, simple interactives or touchable objects below at a child's eye level can keep everyone's eyeballs engaged.

THE IMPACT OF VISITOR-FRIENDLY LABELS

For visitors, all the tips above can help make interpretive labels easy to read and seamlessly integrated with each visitor's experience, motivations, expectations, and stamina. Visitors should come away from an exhibition saying, "Wow, that was a great exhibition!" not "Wow, those were great labels." The context, content, environment, designed spaces, colors, etc., should all work together. Done right, interpretive labels don't stand out and call attention to themselves or wear out visitors' energy.

In the final installation, if the labels are done right, they will look as if it was an easy and painless process to plan, write, edit, design, and produce them. Done right, it will be hard to imagine that there was any other way to do them.

VISITOR-FRIENDLY LABELS FLOW FROM A VISITOR-ORIENTED INSTITUTION

In the overall analysis, visitor-friendly style means that museum practitioners have learned to put visitors first—respecting and valuing their concerns, wishes, desires, and perceptions. There are many sources for investigating this approach. In her "Visitor's Bill of Rights," museum exhibit developer and writer Judy Rand lists eleven important human needs seen from the visitor's point of view. They include comfort, orientation, welcome/belonging, enjoyment, socializing, respect, communication, learning, choice and control, challenge and confidence, and revitalization. Rand's list and the framework presented by museum researcher and evaluator Deborah Perry in her book *What Makes Learning Fun?* share many ideas. Perry's framework has three complementary perspectives—motivations, engagements, outcomes—each of which is divided into four to six components describing ways to satisfy visitors' needs in exhibitions. Stephen Bitgood has put many of these ideas together in his attention-value model for understanding visitors in museums. Labels created by an institution that is committed to visitors' needs will sound and feel different from an institution where the communication of curatorial knowledge is paramount. Can an institution adopt a visitor-friendly voice in its exhibits without dropping the curatorially driven agenda? Yes, but it's not recommended. It will feel and sound condescending. Do the right thing and become a visitor-centered institution instead.

Becoming a visitor-centered institution that makes visitor-friendly exhibitions does not happen by hiring a consulting firm to categorize your visitors into different types or by spending large sums on a new logo. It happens by caring about visitors' feelings as they leave an exhibition. They should be saying—in the back of their minds—"I feel like that exhibition was meant for me."

Why do museums spend lots of money on marketing and visitor research but so much less on interpretation and evaluation? Probably because truly good interpretation becomes "invisible." It doesn't call attention to itself. It is so well integrated into the engaging experiences that visitors are not likely to think about the labels specifically. They are more likely to recall looking and enjoying. And probably because truly good evaluation often does and should include findings that suggest issues that need improvement, point out missed opportunities, or mistakes—information no director wants to present to the board! Directors like to present marketing data that makes their job look good and secure: "Look at all the great things people say about us; look at the potential for growth and more success!"

Characteristics of a Visitor-Friendly Institution

These features tend to characterize a visitor-centered institution—an institution that puts its visitors first:

- **Top down.** The vision and direction to be visitor friendly comes from the top, from the director to all departments. The director supports and encourages collaboration.

- **Focus on a novice audience.** The institution focuses on novices as their target audience—people without any special interest, knowledge, or training in the museum's subject area; visitors for whom English is a second language; and first-time visitors. Novice visitors need, use, and appreciate extra orientation strategies to prepare for their visit as well as to aid them in making the best decisions about where to spend their time at the museum.

- **Dispersed opportunities.** Visitor-friendly interpretive strategies are dispersed throughout the permanent collection and special exhibits, not reserved for a separate "discovery" room or area.

- **Meaningful experiences.** Evaluation is conducted to understand visitors' experiences in their own words, using open-ended questions and analysis driven by the museum's mission to help visitors find personal meaning. While in-house evaluations will consider how well the exhibit team worked together, or the number of community members that were brought in to partner or advise, visitor-friendly institutions put more emphasis on investigating the impact on users, not producers.

- **Iterative and reflective.** Good approaches that serve decision-making are iterative and reflective, from planning to development to evaluation. Staff members repetitively ask, "Are we doing what we said we'd do? Is it working for our visitors?"

When label writers indulge themselves with catchy phrases and clever style, curators indulge themselves with more and more (and more) words on the wall, or designers indulge themselves in new award-winning graphic styles or personal favorites, they are not being visitor-friendly. The whole exhibit team must agree and care about the primary impact on visitors and carry out that intent in all aspects of the planning and design. Being visitor-friendly means prioritizing visitors' experiences and their participation more than presenting new knowledge. Remember, in the end it's about inspiration, not information.

Examples of Ways Museums Put Visitors First

Museums have evolved many ways in their commitment to being visitor-friendly. Art museums especially have given the profession great examples in the last two decades. Perhaps this is because they can respond more quickly to making changes, given that their exhibition spaces have open floor plans and flat walls and are not bound by dioramas, tanks, live specimens, huge mechanical objects, or permanently installed vitrines.

Detroit Institute of Arts reopened its museum in 2007 with a completely reinstalled collection, guided by the question "How can visitor studies help the DIA become more visitor-centered?" The goal was to become more accessible to more types of people, including those who were not drawn to or felt excluded by the DIA. Its reinstallation guidelines stated: "Interpretation is better understood as a means of communication between the museum and its audience in which (1) the audience is encouraged to engage in satisfying experiences; and (2) the museum deepens its understanding of the audience for the purposes of better serving its visitors." The new exhibits had shorter labels, labels that related to what the visitor could see, and installations that touched on common human experiences. An entire January 2009 issue of *Curator* was devoted to discussing the DIA's reinstallation project.

Minneapolis Institute of Art started a robust evaluation program called "Voice of Audience," which combined quantitative and qualitative data in weekly institutional reports to ensure the museum is listening and responding to visitor needs. Nelson-Atkins Museum of Art and the Delaware Art Museum instigated extensive reviews of their labels for exhibits that needed updating. "Do no harm" was the guiding principle for initiatives that addressed colonialism and increased respect for people's cultural histories.

The Exploratorium is an institution that puts visitors first. The changes to its labels and physical designs over the past twenty-five years have been notable, and the current exhibits reflect a care for design that really does help visitors. Their Department of Visitor Research & Evaluation (VRE) conducts research on learning, largely in the public space of the museum, with studies that address issues that have applicability beyond a specific exhibit or set of exhibits. VRE has conducted more than three hundred evaluations and over thirty research studies. And they share them. All their reports are available for download.

The *USS Constitution* Museum realized that most of its visitors were family groups, yet staff knew little about this population. To better understand and serve families, the museum initiated the Family Learning Forum. Research from this project informed the interactive exhibit *All Hands on Deck*. Extensively prototyped exhibits and label text were so engaging that even teenagers—a typically underwhelmed demographic—participated fully. As for the labels, the developers declared, "Visitors *will* read. We promise. What's more, well-written text will get visitors talking to each other. So keep it short. Try the first-person voice. Use quotes. Ask questions. And don't forget the fun." All exhibitions and programs developed since *All Hands on Deck* was completed have included the process of prototyping and putting families first. The museum offers a comprehensive online resource called Engage Families.

The Children's Discovery Museum of San Jose has been on a three-decade-long journey to make the museum welcoming, relevant, and responsive to its diverse community. Strategies have spanned all aspects of museum operations, including exhibits, outreach, programs, events, trilingual signage, marketing, staffing, and governance. The museum offers cultural festivals each year celebrating Eastern Indian, Chinese, Jewish, Mexican, Vietnamese, Special Needs, and LGBTQ+ families. The "Museums For All" initiative, for people with California benefits identification cards, offers reduced admission tickets purchased in-person without reservations. These efforts go far beyond labels.

The Crystal Bridges Museum in Arkansas is "committed to making the museum accessible for all visitors." In addition to the legally required accommodations for mobility, service animals, and visually and hearing-impaired visitors, Crystal Bridges reaches out specifically to neurodiverse visitors. These visitors are offered a quiet way to enter the museum (through the library), a sensory-friendly museum map for navigation, and sensory-friendly bags containing devices like noise-canceling headphones and communication aids, which they can check out from the lobby desk or library.

Similarly, the Orange County Regional History Museum in Orlando provides Social Narratives in English and Spanish on their website. These documents spell out—in words and images—every step of the museum visit, including what to expect at the front desk and the temperature inside the museum, for neurodiverse visitors.

Not surprisingly, when you make improvements in exhibitions to aid visitors with disabilities, the exhibits work better for all visitors. When you make improvements that will make exhibits more accessible to children, you also make the exhibits better for all visitors. See B. Davidson's "New dimensions for traditional dioramas: Multisensory additions for access, interest and learning" and Clifford Still Art Museum's "Art and the Young Mind Summative Evaluation."

The Pendulum Swings and Questions Remain

Unfortunately, institutional commitment to being visitor centered is not always long lasting. Changes in leadership have halted visitor-centered progress. Interpretation and evaluation departments have been created and disbanded.

Exhibit developers with wide-ranging skills in informal education and design have been hired by one administration and abandoned by the next, resulting in a return to exhibits planned only by curators and subject matter experts. And when external factors of economics, epidemics, and social upheaval lead to institutional layoffs and restructuring, visitor-centered programs are often the first to go.

Almost a quarter of the way into the twenty-first century, the project of being a visitor-friendly museum is becoming more complex. The questions challenging us with greater urgency include:

- How can museums balance the limits of their own authority with the need to share it with others?

- When does the in-house process of incorporating new voices, points of view, and opinions into exhibit planning override concerns about the number of words and the visitors' experience of the final product?

- How much information should be included in an exhibition when visitors are holding personal devices in their hands that can zero in on 19,500,000 possible answers to their questions in 0.36 seconds?

- How can we put more effort into designing accessibility for people with disabilities and co-designing with communities who don't typically visit?

It is still up to the museum to decide what any exhibition will be about, whether it features the museum's collection or highlights the concerns of outside special-interest groups. What is written in the labels depends on the unique set of conditions of that museum, but label writers can consider the guidelines in this chapter for *how* to write more user-friendly labels. Hopefully the writers will be supported by the powers that be.

15

Making Words and Images Work Together

One of the most important and difficult things to achieve with interpretive labels is getting reading and visual nonverbal experiences to work together. This is accomplished through an iterative process of word selection, image selection, word modification, and nonverbal content modification.

Different kinds of nonverbal images, visuals, and experiences accompany labels. They might be illustrations on the label itself, a photo next to the label, objects or artwork referred to by the label, or a combination of all of these. Even though a label may not have images on it, the things around it constitute nonverbal content that visitors will see and experience as they read the label. Those things must be referenced by the label in some way. Labels should also consider content produced by image-triggering sources, such as sounds and smells. Nonverbal content might also be a feeling.

Three-dimensional objects are the most powerful and attractive types of images. Labels next to an object will be read more often than labels next to a photo or a label alone on a wall. But visitors' experience will not be complete or memorable if, once attracted by the object, their interests, questions, or casual curiosity are not addressed by the label.

The label's words and what visitors are seeing and experiencing must work positively together toward the same objectives. If the words on the label do not refer to what a visitor sees, hears, or smells, the label is in a vacuum. And without that connection between the label and its image, the label is less likely to be read and comprehended.

For example, an exhibit of human body slices at the Museum of Science and Industry in Chicago had one label that introduced the exhibit, answered visitors' most common questions, and recognized their feelings. The language is straightforward and frank.

Anatomical Sections: Windows into the Body

These unique displays present a rare look inside the human body. They contain actual horizontal sections from a man's body and vertical sections from a woman's body.

These sections were prepared in the 1940s from a man and a woman who died of natural causes. Their bodies were frozen and cut into half-inch sections with a power saw. The sections are preserved in a solution of chloral hydrate, glycerin, potassium acetate, and water.

Although the exhibit may make you feel somewhat uncomfortable, take advantage of this rare opportunity to view at close range the unseen sections of the human body.

The body slices were displayed in multiple window-like frames positioned at right angles to a short wall. The words *"windows," "sections,"* and *"anatomical"* resonated with the physical layout and content; the words *"frozen," "power saw,"* and *"preserved"* cut to the heart of the matter, so to speak. Showing real but unidentified human bodies in an exhibition today would not go over well.

INTEGRATING VERBAL AND VISUAL CONTENT

Everything in an exhibit or on a label has content, whether intended or not. Images that do not support the words are not neutral. Superfluous content or design is distracting. The same goes for adjunct artifacts or props. Exhibit developers should resist the temptation to add visuals and physical structures just for the sake of ambience, because visitors cannot easily sort out ambience-only elements from message-bearing elements in exhibitions. When all the content is purposeful and integrated, the exhibit communicates more effectively.

A common mistake in selecting an image to accompany text is to choose one because it is available, not because it is the best one to tell the story. To avoid this problem, exhibit developers should over-research and over-collect appropriate images; if a first-choice photo turns out to be unavailable, a suitable alternative will be on hand to fit in its place. If copy has been written first, and the image to be used is not the first choice, make sure the copy is modified to make them work together.

PLANNING AHEAD AND EVALUATING

Choosing the right words and images starts during planning and design. Quick front-end tests are a good way to try out illustrations and/or words with visitors so that writers and designers can make choices that fit with visitors' prior knowledge. If eight out of ten visitors think of malaria when they see an image of a mosquito, exhibit planners can feel confident that those two parts (the mosquito image and the word "*malaria*") will resonate in visitors' minds.

Sometimes exhibit developers use dissonance or a lack of resonance to make a point. It can be a good thing, but evaluation is necessary to make sure the questions you hope to raise with a dissonant combination of words and images are the questions visitors actually ask. If the dissonance simply creates confusion, it will hamper communication, not aid it.

An Iterative Process

Since most exhibitions are planned and built by a team of people, the process of making images and words work together needs to be built into the schedule as a series of iterative, or repeating, steps. This back-and-forth series of refinements results in a better product. The old linear process—in which the writer writes the text, hands it over to the designer to design, who then hands it over to the fabricator to produce, who then hands it to the installer to put it all in place—results in multiple missed opportunities to fine-tune all the parts and make them reinforce each other. If only one person is wearing all the hats, the fine-tuning will happen inside that person's head. By the way, we use the term "iterative" a lot because it is so important during development and design. The repetitive rounds of testing, tweaking, and testing again, looking for flaws, resolving problems throughout the process, are especially useful when new teams are formed with community voices to gain insights into other ways of thinking.

Making images and words work together requires knowing what the images and words will be far enough in advance so there's time for adjustments and fine-tuning. Waiting until the last minute or handing the process off in a linear fashion from writer to designer without back-and-forth consultations will lead to problems.

Knowing what artifacts or visuals are nearby can profoundly influence a label writer's ability to catch visitors' attention and satisfy their most immediate questions. Elevation drawings, detailed dimensional models, and sometimes floor plans can show the relative positions of all exhibit elements, what is next to each label, and how visitors will approach the spaces. Throughout the process, check and check again.

- If the label directs readers to look "on your right," is the object there?

- If the label describes an artifact from the front, will visitors see it that way too?

- If the label makes a comparison with another object, is that object clearly visible from where the visitor is standing?

- Is it appropriate to adjust the type size of a heading (for example, a smaller type size might be more appropriate if a panel is in a narrow hallway) even though all headings were specified at 72-point type?

- Is a larger type size needed, given that the label ended up in the back of a deep case, even though all captions were specified as 20-point type?

- If one artifact had to be substituted for another at the last minute, is the label copy still accurate?

While drawings and models can help with planning, the context will only be complete after the exhibition opens to the public. Then everyone can see what things are influencing each other. Time and money allotted for fine-tuning the relationships between words and images after opening will be well spent.

In the best of all possible situations, the combination of words and images will create a complete experience that neither could do alone. When images and words are working well with each other, visitors will read and look, or look and read, and the result is a gestalt that leaves the visitor feeling that the effort was worthwhile. They will have gotten something more by doing both, even if it only took a total of ten seconds.

Remember, every second counts. If something does not make sense to people in the first few moments, it is likely to be ignored. If people only spend a second or two looking at an exhibit, they're likely to forget it. Every glance is a window of opportunity to create or squelch engagement.

Icons and Words Working Together

In the attempt to reach non-English-speaking audiences in museums, the use of icons or symbols has become more popular, especially with orientation and wayfinding labels. Standard icons, collected in the Department of the Interior's handbook *Signs, Trails and Wayside Exhibits*, are used to identify visitor information, hiking trails, and restrooms for national parks, national forests, and public properties. Only a few icons, however, are truly internationally comprehensible.

Original and unique iconographic labels may win graphic arts awards from other designers, but they don't win any prizes from visitors for clarity. Symbols, graphics, and icons invented for specific use in a single museum will be unfamiliar to most visitors, not just non–English speakers. A three-year study of wayfinding systems at Brookfield Zoo called "We Are Here" found that only seven of forty symbols, which included animals and visitors services, were unambiguous.

Icons should not be used alone. Words are also needed to help reinforce, clarify, and decode the image. Ellen Lupton, in her book *Thinking with Type*, elaborates: "Another common assumption is that icons are a more universal mode of communication than text. . . . Yet text can often provide a more specific and understandable cue than a picture. Icons don't actually simplify the translation of content into multiple languages, because they require explanation in multiple languages." The best way to find out if an icon works is to test it with a sample of visitors and make changes until it does.

The Extensive World of Royalty-Free Art

If there is no budget for imagery or art such as photography and illustrations, there is an abundance of royalty-free and noncopyrighted options available online. This means the images can be used legally by the public. At the time of this edition, sources of royalty-free art include Freerange, Unsplash, and Pexels. If you have a small budget, it's also easy to find royalty-free stock imagery at Shutterstock, iStock, and Getty Images. These sources have varying restrictions for use, however, so it is important to be clear about the copyright before obtaining a "free" image. It is no longer necessary to photocopy or scan images from a book, although this certainly can be done as well. Just be sure to check the copyright information for the art before including it in your design.

GENERALIZATIONS REQUIRE MULTIPLE EXAMPLES

Museums are great places to make generalizations, but too often exhibit labels make generalizations or conclusions without convincingly showing the steps taken to build or reach them. Rather than make generalizations for visitors, we should help them reach generalizations based on their own experience. By giving visitors multiple examples in words, objects, and images, we offer them the opportunity to build conclusions based on what they know already.

A generalization based on only one example is a common mistake in labels. At least three examples are required to build a convincing generalization. Visitors tend to see one example as a case study or a unique item. Two examples are good for making comparisons. Three examples show enough variability to provide viewers with knowledge that can be used in another situation, and that is the purpose of generalizations. If the museum does not have three real examples, it can supplement with models or photos. Without at least three examples for visitors to examine on their own, they must rely on the authority of the label writer. This creates an information-centered, one-way presentation, not a visitor-centered, visitor-friendly experience.

This practicum is based on the three steps of the iterative learning process described as the rhythm of education by Alfred North Whitehead: romance (the wow), precision, and generalization. Museum objects and designs are great at the wow factor. Precision is the process of gathering bits of information and experiences—words and images—to scaffold and build new learning. Generalization is the result. Museums tend to jump from wow to generalization and skip the opportunities for promoting precision.

AVOID MISLEADING IMAGES OR WORDS IN THE ENTIRE EXHIBITION CONTEXT

On a broader scale, images and words need to work together throughout the whole exhibition so that the graphic look and feel of the total environment harmonizes with the exhibition's big idea.

All too often, a discordant situation results when exhibit planners attempt to make a serious subject more "fun." For example, using playful, cartoon-style images to convey complex, scientific information trivializes the content and is misleading to visitors. A "science arcade" or "circus" setting conveys a mood that might not be in harmony with the mindset required for engaging successfully with complex information, experiences, and interpretations of scientific phenomena in a way that truly increases science literacy. The science museum hype that you will have so much fun that you won't know you are learning basic scientific principles is just that: hype. Discordant situations also occur in exhibition design when the materials or colors are selected for visual impact rather than as an integrated part of the overall communication goal. For example, in an exhibit about recycling or conservation, one might expect the paneling, graphics, and labels to be constructed out of recycled materials rather than glitzy steel and neon.

Poor choices of materials, colors, image placement, and image size can affect the mood and atmosphere of an exhibition in ways that contradict and distract from the intended interpretive messages. In the end, it is the visitors who lose. This unfortunate situation will continue to occur as long as the label-writing process is separate from exhibition design. Writers and designers must work together toward the same goals.

The main idea here is that everything counts: Every word, every image, every object has to mean something collectively.

16

Labels That Ask Questions

The best questions in labels are the ones visitors themselves would ask.

You have probably heard that it is a good idea to ask questions in exhibit labels to stimulate visitors to think, look, get involved, and learn. While asking questions may be a good idea, it is important to recognize that there are good questions and bad questions.

The best questions are those that visitors themselves ask. Two ways to learn what those questions are include (1) watching and listening to what visitors say to each other when they look at exhibits in existing situations; and (2) testing mock-ups with visitors during the development of exhibits. The first is the most natural way because visitors are acting spontaneously and the exhibit is in context with all its parts. For example, "Is he dead?" is what aquarium visitors asked at the snapping turtle's tank as they observed the huge, mossy turtle that rarely moves.

Unfortunately, many questions asked in labels are not really questions at all. They are mock queries. The asker (the writer, curator, exhibit developer, designer) is simply disguising the delivery of *more information* in a superficially user-friendly form. This is not good pedagogy, especially on caption labels that accompany static displays of objects, artifacts, animals, or photographs.

A question that does not flow easily from the visitor's interest can feel like an imposition. A question that cannot be easily answered by looking at the objects can be frustrating. And one with an obvious answer can be offensive.

Sometimes questions are used instead of statements or phrases on section labels. This feels like a gimmick when it's obvious that it is not a visitor's question, especially when it's an abstract question; for example, "How can beliefs and practices bind communities and shape daily life?"

A label that asks visitors to guess "Which one?" is also not a good question if they really have to guess. Yet a "Which one?" question can be engaging if the answer can be found by looking more closely at the exhibit. Finding the answers through observation is easy to set up and a worthwhile activity for visitors of all ages.

THE DREADED "WHY?" QUESTION

"Why?" questions are an especially obnoxious form of the mock query. The questions below imply one right answer, known by the expert, that is not visible or apparent to the visitor.

Why do birds form feeding cooperatives when food is in short supply?

Why is Japanese armor lightweight?

Why are insects commonly found in virtually every environment except the oceans?

Why did volcanoes occur in Missouri during the Precambrian?

These are not visitors' questions, and visitors' answers might rightly be "I don't know," "Who cares?" or "Because God made it that way."

The four "Why?" examples could be rewritten into different questions or made into statements that more honestly reveal the asker's intentions or values.

When food is in short supply, a feeding cooperative for birds . . .

Japanese armor is lightweight because . . .

Are insects commonly found in the oceans?

What factors made volcanoes possible in Missouri?

If the point of asking the question is to make visitors see a comparison, think about an issue or explanation, or understand the purpose of a structure or design, just say so; for example, "The factors that made volcanoes possible in Missouri were . . ."

GOOD "WHY?" QUESTIONS

While strong caution is advised against using a "Why?" question, two conditions make "Why?" questions appropriate: when you are sure that visitors would phrase the question that way on their own; and when discordant factors are present, which cause the "Why?" to occur.

The following discordant conditions raised real "Why?" questions from real visitors.

Visitors at an aquarium saw predators swimming with prey.
Why don't the sharks eat the fish living with them in the tank?

Visitors at a zoo saw an indoor free-flight area with birds and an area for visitor viewing with no barrier between the areas.
Why don't the birds fly out?

Visitors in a natural history museum see dinosaur bone jackets (unopened large plaster of paris–coated bundles) with numbers painted on the outside.
Why were these never opened?

Visitors in an art museum see a room full of gaudy chairs, clocks, tables, and tapestries from the Decorative Arts collection.
Why do they call this art?

Anticipating what visitors want to know and in what order they want to know it—that is, which questions need to be answered first—is achieved through a combination of experience, intuition, common sense, trying it out, and then fixing it if it does not work right the first time.

If you decide that you must use a "Why?" question, or any other question, it's usually a good idea to answer it in the first sentence following the question, in one short statement. It frustrates visitors to have their curiosity aroused and then not be able to find or confirm the answer because it is not there, or it is difficult to find because it is buried in the text somewhere twelve lines later.

The information in this chapter so far refers mainly to questions asked on labels in static or nonparticipatory exhibits. Questioning techniques used for labels on interactive exhibits present a different challenge, which is described in chapter 17. What follows here are three other types of questions: flip-label, open-ended, and talk-back.

QUESTIONS ON FLIP LABELS

Labels that flip up, slide, or rotate (with text and/or images on a surface that is revealed) are common, inexpensive, and popular devices in museum exhibitions.

Also called "flappers," they offer visitors something to do—the overt physical action of lifting or sliding the panel—and thus are referred to as interactive or hands-on labels, although the amount of interaction is typically minimal. The most common use of a flip label is to pose a question. Graphics are often integrated with the question and the answer underneath.

Integrated, engaging flip labels give visitors a logical sense of anticipation, a compelling reason to look under the label, and an intrinsic reward for doing so.

For example, visitors might flip a label to

Peek at something hidden, such as a graphic of a desert where flip labels hide pictures that show "What lives underground?"

Confirm an answer to a question and find something else too. A flip label asks, "How heavy is a hippo?" and underneath is not just the number of pounds but also a cartoon of kids piled on one end of a seesaw, with a caption that says, "As heavy as eighty twelve-year-olds."

Compare different points of view, such as having a question with two answers: "Yes, because . . ." and "No, because . . ."; neither one the "right" answer.

The answer to the question under a flip label should be short. For example: A patterned rock in a plexiglass case had a label that asked "What is the pattern on this rock?" Three flip labels suggested possibilities: "Ancient rock painting," "Mineral growth," "Fossilized fern." The answer for mineral growth was short: "Correct: Although it looks like a fossil fern or a rock painting, it is actually a mineral growth of manganese oxide that formed on limestone." The label writers showed restraint and resisted the opportunity to add a lot more information.

The best flip labels don't just reveal text. They include something in addition to or other than text. For example, flip labels can be installed over small wall-mounted cases with clues, rather than questions, for how objects were used. A label tempted, "It was buried with an Egyptian mummy, and it held the mummy's guts"; lifting the flap revealed an ancient Egyptian canopic jar. Another read, "This is used for carrying things, and it helps a woman balance and hold things on her head"; under the flap was a woven African head ring. Finding a real thing is much more exciting than finding more text.

Flip labels are seductive. Visitors can hardly resist peeking under a flap to see what is there. For children, the activity of lifting can be satisfying by itself. For adults, the manipulation is time-consuming and requires effort. Is it worth it, the adult visitor might ask? If a question or statement posed on the outside of a flip label seems difficult to an adult, it can make them feel stupid. For example, on the outside the label says, "When you are done comparing the two artworks, lift the sheet for more information." As one visitor rephrased it, "Lift the sheet and find out how dumb you are." If you're going to take advantage of visitors' natural investigative behavior, make sure the payback is commensurate—useful, interesting, enjoyable, and memorable discoveries underneath, not just more words.

THE DREADED "DID YOU KNOW?" QUESTION

If the flip label cover is asking, "Did you know?" and hiding more information, forget it. Yes, these labels are popular. They are cheap in terms of the effort it takes for label writers to come up with them. But they can be empty calories in terms of what visitors get out of them. Along with "fun facts," they can be distracting from the big idea—and insulting. A visitor's answer to "Did you know?" is likely "No," which puts the reader in the spot of feeling dumb rather than curious, and puts the writer in a superior, know-it-all position. This is not visitor-friendly.

"Did you know?" as a title over a paragraph of text is a missed opportunity to write a more cohesive and inviting introduction/title. Otherwise, it is another label of "fun facts."

DID YOU KNOW?

Cougars are also called mountain lions, although they are not closely related to lions in Africa. They are also called pumas, Florida panthers, catamounts, and painters.

The label above could be rewritten so that the title and text are related: Skip the question and make the title a statement of content that is related to the text. Like this:

A CAT OF SIX NAMES

Cougars are also called mountain lions, pumas, Florida panthers, catamounts, and painters. Different names reflect the many areas where this large cat lives.

In short, think twice before using labels that asks "Why?" or "Did You Know?"

OPEN-ENDED QUESTIONS

Most of the questions discussed so far have had an answer that can be found in the label or the exhibit, and usually just one right answer is implied. Open-ended questions, on the other hand, are answered by the reader.

Well-done open-ended questions prompt visitors to think about their own prior knowledge and experience and construct or retrieve a thought that is their own personal creation. These questions can promote thoughtful, integrated, and competency-reinforcing actions on the visitor's part. For example, wayside signs at the Cincinnati Nature Center incorporated open-ended questions, along with text and graphics, from spots along the nature trail. Using a little icon graphic to set them apart from the rest of the information, the questions included "What can you sense when you close your eyes?" (on a panel titled "Feel the Field") and "What changes has your body gone through in life?" (on a panel titled "It Takes Time to Grow Up," about the life cycle of frogs in a pond).

But these questions can be tricky. An open-ended question can make visitors feel stupid if they can't easily answer it or if they mistake it for a closed-ended question where there is only one right answer.

QUESTIONS THAT ASK FOR FEEDBACK

Questions posed with opportunities for adding responses in exhibitions most commonly come in the form of a talk-back panel associated with a specific exhibit. Visitors post their sticky notes, three-by-five cards, or illustrations to the mix, and other visitors look at them.

The questions asked by the exhibit developers should be ones they care about the answers to. Visitors are more likely to post thoughtful, untrivial answers when the questions themselves are not trivial. Answers in the form of pictures drawn by visitors can be powerful, as art often is.

In an exhibition about the San Francisco Bay, the subject of the Bay Bridge was shown in photos, objects, and text. A talk-back station invited visitors to consider their feelings about the old and newly built bridges by writing a postcard. The label for the talk back said:

Reflections on Crossing the Bay

Did you know the first Bay Bridge was built in 1936?
Now that there's a new Bay Bridge, the old one will soon no longer be used.

Old Bridge / New Bridge . . . What does it mean to you?
Write a postcard and take it with you—or leave it for others to read.

In another section of the same exhibition, a label asked visitors to imagine the transportation technology of the future.

Draw the Future of the Bay

How would you like to get across the Bay in the future? Would you travel suspended above the water? Or submerged below the water? Or in a taxi-boat or hydroplane that travels on top of the water? Draw it!

The creativity and range of ideas posted by visitors was a great source of enjoyment and discussion for others.

Talk-back bulletin boards are an easy way for a museum to encourage participation. The quality of visitor feedback can be raised to a higher level when the questions reflect the context and content of the exhibition in a meaningful way. Good questions will prompt good answers. Sometimes a simplistic question can prompt a simplistic answer: On a timeline of events in history a label asked, "Did we leave anything out?" and invited visitors to add a note to the timeline. Many notes were added, the most common being "My Birthday."

Digital feedback tools allow museum staff to post and share relevant comments with other visitors and edit out inappropriate feedback, but a single screen may not be as eyecatching for other visitors as a wall of notes. Digital applications can also collect and store feedback data. For more ideas about user-contributed content beyond comment books and sticky notes, see *Visitor Voices in Museum Exhibitions* by Kathleen McLean and Wendy Pollock.

17

Labels for
Interactive Exhibits

*Labels for interactive exhibits need to be customized so that
they respond to and serve the specific design of the interactive
and the way visitors use it.*

Many museum professionals have addressed the specifics of what constitutes
an interactive exhibit. In her book *Planning for People in Museum Exhibitions*,
Kathleen McLean distinguishes among "interactive," "participatory," and
"hands-on." She characterizes interactive exhibits as "those in which visitors can
conduct activities, gather evidence, select options, form conclusions, test skills,
provide input, and actually alter a situation based on input." In their *Curator*
article, "Designing with Interactives," the Exploratorium's Sue Allen and Josh
Gutwill say, "At the heart of interactivity is reciprocity of action, where a visitor
acts on the exhibit and the exhibit reacts in some way." Open-ended activities
are those with no predetermined outcomes. Visitors can experiment with
variables provided by the exhibit or their bodies. With predetermined interactive
exhibits, a visitor can initiate and observe one response.

Exhibits that don't react but still require physical input from visitors, such as
lifting a flap, pushing a button, or engaging in a multistep exhibit experience,
will be included here. In art museums, where the artworks are not likely to
react, interactivity can be as simple as asking visitors to use their eyes or move
their bodies.

Regardless of how interactivity is defined, all exhibits that require physical input
from visitors also require carefully considered labels. Most important, labels for
interactive exhibits need to be tried out with visitors during development. Texts
that guide visitors' activities—often in a required sequence—and explain what is
going on are complex and often fall short of the mark on the first draft. Untested
label texts are frequently confusing and can't compete with visitors' impulses to
do rather than *read*.

A SPECTRUM OF SENSES

Interactivity can involve the senses in addition to physical movement. Simple sensory activities include touching, smelling, hearing, seeing, and, less often, tasting. Careful testing during development will help ensure the highest possible inclusion of visitors along a wide range of sensory abilities. Interpretive labels need to take this diversity into account.

Touching and lifting a flip label can be made easier by designing a handle that is easy to grasp. Smell and taste are not universally agreed-on senses, as people's ability and acuity vary widely. Smells can evoke strong memories, but not everybody has the same ability to smell, and some people can't smell at all. Video and computer interactives need to consider vision and hearing accommodations through captions and verbal descriptions.

INFORMAL SCIENCE WRITING VERSUS LABEL WRITING

In a science museum exhibit about imaging, visitors were asked to look into a tube. What they saw was an image of their eye reflected in a magnifying mirror. The label, which contained instructions and explanations, said:

The Peerless, Priceless Imaging Tool

This device is unrivaled for imaging in the visible light spectrum.

Look through this tube to see the most sophisticated imaging tool in existence: the human eye. Much like a camera, the eye adjusts to different light levels and focal distances. When united with the interpretive ability of the brain, the eye far surpasses any imaging machine ever built. However, unaided, it can only see in the narrow visible light portion of the vast electromagnetic spectrum.

This is excellent *science* writing, but it is not good *label* writing because it does not resonate with how visitors are using the interactive device. It is not responsive to the sequenced steps necessary to experience the interactive. It dominates the visitors' experience by providing lots of important, complex scientific information. The vocabulary is too sophisticated for visitors' needs in the complex exhibition environment. It is more appropriate for writing meant to be read for the sake of the ideas themselves, without competition from the noise, distractions, and other concepts surrounding this one interactive device. Interactive exhibits need shorter, more-to-the-point labels, ones that aid and support a visitor's scientific exploration and thinking, however brief that might be.

THE EXPLORATORIUM MODEL

A format for interactive labels was developed years ago at the Exploratorium in San Francisco. The labels contain four sections, telling visitors "What to do" and "What to notice" and asking the questions "What's going on?" and "So what?" The labels also include a title and often a tagline, which help call out the interactive opportunities of the exhibit and are easily distinguished from the "more information" content.

This style and variations of it have been adapted and used by many other museums across the country and around the world. In its longest form, the format provides plenty of room to explain, in detail, the scientific or technological background for the interpretive element, thus fulfilling the exhibit developer's desire to present knowledge.

The next example is a very short version of an Exploratorium-style interactive label for the same eye-imaging exhibit mentioned above.

The Peerless, Priceless Imaging Tool

What to do:
Look close up into the tube.

What to notice:
You can see your eye, greatly enlarged in the mirror.

What's going on?
Your eye is the best, most powerful, priceless imaging tool.

So what?
Even though thousands of dollars are spent on high-technology imaging tools, your eye is still the best.

This "To do . . . So what" organization of information is logical, linear, and systematic. It can be applied to any type of interactive exhibit, and it provides an easy "off-the-shelf" design format.

The main criticism of this formulaic style of labeling is that it is typically not responsive to the physical layouts, components, and conceptual challenges specific to different types of interactive exhibits. It assumes an "empty-headed receiver" role for participation—visitors are told what to do before they are given any reason to perform the action. In addition, the design format (the four sections) dominates the label content and denies the opportunity to emphasize the information graphically. The lead-in words (e.g., "To do") are too prominent and redundant.

The Exploratorium's Department of Visitor Research and Evaluation has conducted extensive research on its interactive labels. In "Label Lessons Learned," evaluators concluded the following:

- Visitors liked labels that pose challenges in the form of questions (Can you get two objects to float in the airstream?) along with suggestions or hints (Try using the whiffle balls.).

- Deemphasizing the explanation or reducing its overall length can increase the amount of time visitors spend in active investigation.

- Titles that clearly frame the experience help visitors understand what the experience will be; for example, "Watch Water Freeze."

- Headers help visitors scan a label for the information they need.

- Shorter labels are read more thoroughly than longer labels.

- Diagrams that illustrate visitor interaction with the exhibit helped visitors figure out what to do.

When the Exploratorium moved to a new location, the staff took the opportunity to review and rewrite many of the exhibit labels. Based on their visitor studies of how people used the exhibits in the old location, writers kept the basic original format the same, retaining information related to "How to do it" and "What's going on," but they also allowed for variation based on the individual exhibits. Some labels were enhanced with "use diagrams" to help visitors get started. Use diagrams are line-drawn illustrations based on photos of visitors using the interactive exhibits. While photos include lots of extraneous details that create visual "noise," line drawings single out and focus on only the most important information.

At least one Exploratorium exhibit received an entirely new label approach. Allen and Gutwill's audience research revealed that *Light Island*, an open-ended exhibit that allows visitors to experiment with different behaviors of light, offered too many interactive options that simultaneously vied for visitors' attention. The traditional "to see, to do, to notice" label didn't fit with the logistics of the exhibit's design. Exhibit developers changed the shape of the exhibit—from a round table with a light source at the center to an amoeba-shaped table—providing users with separate spaces where they could conduct their investigations. The new shape also increased the perimeter of the exhibit, giving visitors more room and providing room for more visitors. The new label has six questions that are arranged around the edge of the table, an excellent fit for the design.

The Exploratorium has a long and studied history with interactive exhibits, and they have published generously on the topic. Chief among these are Sue Allen's *Finding Significance* (2004) and Thomas Humphrey's *Fostering Active Prolonged Engagement* (2005). Joshua Gutwill's 2002 article "Providing Explanations to Visitors Affects Inquiry Behavior: A Study of the *Downhill Race* Exhibit" reinforces the notion that providing too much information decreases visitor engagement. These findings are elaborated upon in Gutwill's "Labels for Open-Ended Exhibits: Using Questions and Suggestions to Motivate Physical Activity."

Interactive exhibit instructions, questions, and explanations need to be responsive to the individual design and content of each specific interactive. In certain exhibitions, a formula might work to present the different parts of the label, but in others a formula might prove to be too rigid. The words, the visitors' actions, the physical mechanisms, and the exhibit developer's intent need to mesh.

BEYOND THE TO-DO-AND-NOTICE MODEL

In a short paper titled "From Hands On to Minds On: Labeling Interactive Exhibits," Minda Borun and Katherine Adams of the Franklin Institute in Philadelphia recommend a promising approach. They describe an exhibit meant to challenge visitors' false assumptions that the spinning of the Earth causes gravity. Through many iterations of both the interactive and the label text, they were unable to change visitors' minds, even when the label explicitly stated, "Spinning does not create gravity." Visitor understanding changed dramatically when wording in the prototype label was changed to avoid saying what something is not, and instead promoted a more active visitor role: "If the earth stopped spinning, gravity would still hold us down. Can you prove it? (Use on/off switches.)" The label asked a question rather than delivering information. And it linked visitors' actions to the device's phenomenon, helping them anticipate and formulate meanings. When the question was integral to visitors' experience, use of the interactive communicated the exhibit's main message. Doing and understanding the experience became interdependent and mutually reinforcing.

Applied to the label draft shown earlier, "The Peerless, Priceless Imaging Tool," it can be edited to read:

What tool is the best, most powerful, priceless imaging tool?

Look close up into the tube.

The new label invites visitors to try the interactive and answer an explicit question at the same time. When this label was installed at the science exhibit about imaging, comprehension improved. In addition, visitors' descriptions of the exhibits during evaluation interviews were much more appropriate and accurate when this new style of label was used: "You can have all the machines in the world, but unless you use your eyes to look, you can't tell what it is"; and "Technology can see beyond, but you need your eye to understand."

What makes this question strategy work well is that visitors can do something to answer the question rather than just reading the answer. The concept brought up in the question encourages the visitor to use the interactive device, and using it answers the question.

Another important advantage to this shorter, more direct style is that it is more accessible, especially for parents and teachers, who can help children use and understand the exhibits by simply reading the question out loud. As Borun et al. reported in "Families Are Learning in Science Museums," intragroup reading aloud is one of the observable behaviors that indicate learning in museum exhibitions.

Below is another example of a rewrite of an interactive label that eliminates a "Why?" question and gets rid of the "to do" in favor of a more dynamic question. Note the difference between what you can imagine just from the question in the second case compared to the first.

Why is a bur so sticky?

What to do:
Look at the piece of bur and wool under the microscope.
Compare them to the hook and loop pieces of Velcro.

After, with concept and action incorporated into the question—

What do the bur and wool have in common with the pieces of Velcro?

Look in the microscope.

Although it looks easy, this style of label is much harder to write because each label must be individually crafted to include the context of the message, the visitor's role, and the action required. The "formula"—a question followed by a short instruction—is deceptively simple. As with labeling in general, the best product, in the end, looks obvious, but it can often take more than five drafts, plus formative evaluation, to get there successfully.

Improving Interactive Label Questions

Here are some drafts of another interactive question written to get visitors to put their hands on a temperature-sensitive wall and see how the warmth in their hands is imaged by the material. Instead of "Why does the panel change color?" consider other questions:

What makes the panel change colors when you touch it?

How can you make something change color by just touching it?

What do the changing colors on these panels show?

What does heat look like?

By touching the wall, what can you see that is usually invisible?

Which one worked best? The last one contains the prompt for action (touch), where (the wall), what to notice (see), and a clue about the concept (seeing the invisible). The other questions lack one or more of these.

MAKE WORDS AND ACTIONS WORK TOGETHER

Another important ingredient for successful interactive exhibit labels has to do with their design and placement. Buttons must have labels right next to them, not inches or feet away, and the labels must say more than just "Push." Let visitors know what to expect when they push: "Push to hear an owl call," or "Push to release gas." (Um, to fill the hot air balloon.)

Visitors read labels very literally. If the label can be misunderstood, it will be. Here are five examples of how things can go wrong, and what could be done to correct the mistake:

- On a gorilla graphics panel at a zoo, visitors were asked a question and told they could find the answer on the back of the bench next to the panel. Visitors read as far as "on the back" and walked around to the back of the gorilla graphic panel. Visitors soon created a little pathway through the bushes, reinforcing the notion that the answer was back there.

Solution: The zoo added the answer to the back of the panel in addition to the back of the bench.

- On a panel at an aquarium about how fish hear, a little silhouette graphic showed visitors how they could hear like a fish by putting their hands over their ears and putting their heads against the panel to sense the sound vibrations through their skull bones. The graphic, however, showed a person standing with his head *almost* touching the panel, with a tiny distance in between. So visitors carefully stood with their heads *almost* touching the panel.

Solution: The graphic was redone, showing contact between the person's head and the panel.

- In an art museum, supplementary information about two paintings was supplied on large, laminated sheets tucked vertically in a pocket next to a bench in the center of the room. The label on the wall next to the paintings said, "Pick up the label near the couch." But few visitors connected the word "label" to the laminated sheets or the word "couch" to the bench in the gallery.

Solution: The label holder was colored red, and the label was edited to say, "Find more information about these two paintings in the red pocket by the bench."

- In a science museum, an exhibit invited two people to sit facing each other, looking through a glass while at the same time adjusting the amount of light shining on them to create a blend of their reflected images. The label told visitors to sit and "line up their noses." Some visitors responded by mushing their noses together against the glass. "Not only did this make doing the activity difficult, it also left lots of noseprints on the glass," reported the exhibit staff.

Solution: The revised label showed a drawing of two people sitting with their faces properly aligned and text that read, "Sit so that you and your partner are about the same height." More visitors used it successfully and left far fewer noseprints.

- In a science and nature museum, an interactive exhibit meant to model good hiking practices in alpine zones consisted of a series of graphic rocks that children could hop on, from one to the next, like a hopscotch game. The goal was to avoid stepping on the dense mat of wildflowers that grow between the rocks. The simple instructional label stated, "Save the plants—cross on the rocks!" During evaluation, exhibit developers consistently heard adults *misreading* the label out loud to children: "Save the planet—cross on the rocks!" The text hewed too closely to a familiar environmental catch phrase, turning a simple message into hyperbole.

Solution: The final label read, "Save the flowers and plants. Stay on the rocks."

KEEP IT SIMPLE

As museums incorporate more technology and create complex, in-depth immersion experiences, it is refreshing to think about how effective some of the simpler interactive techniques can be. Labels that encourage visitors to do something with their own low-tech bodies can work in a variety of settings.

Next to a natural history diorama—
Can you find 15 beetles, 7 mushrooms, and 2 snakes?

In a marine mammals exhibit—
To make a sound like a whale, hold your nose, close your mouth, and say "OH!" three times.

Next to an art sculpture—
Make a pose like hers.

Next to an art sculpture—
Walk around the sculpture to see it from all angles.

A simple label can still be about something complex. For example, a complicated story about amino acids is elegantly displayed on a long, curved wall at a natural history museum. The molecular chains for sixteen mammal species are laid out in long lines, one above the other. The label instructs you to compare the chains. By comparing the rows of molecules in the different chains, you can see similarities between closely related species. The interactivity is strictly up to the visitor: how many species to compare; how many chains to follow around the wall. Touching the wall with your finger helps you keeps your place.

ALWAYS EVALUATE INTERACTIVES DURING DEVELOPMENT

Think ahead and anticipate, then mock it up and test to see where visitors' hands and eyes go when they approach and manipulate the interactive. When visitors reach over to grasp a lever or push a button, will their arm cover up or cast a shadow on the label, making it difficult to see? Will a handle accommodate a child's arm length as well as an adult's? Will visitors' eyes go naturally from what's moving to the label that explains what's going on?

More than any other type of exhibit text, labels for interactivity need to be prototyped and evaluated. This is because interactive exhibits are often designed and built in a process that doesn't include a writer or editor. Trying them out, modifying, trying them again, and modifying again will lead to interactive labels that get read, are used appropriately, and are remembered.

18

Digital Label Strategies

Advice for written content on digital devices is the same for nondigital labels: Be short, be concrete, do prototyping and evaluation, and use good type design.

A digital device is a tool. Like any other interpretive strategy in museum exhibitions, the device is only as good as its content and design make it. It is only useful if it is well integrated into the intended themes and messages of the exhibition and easy for visitors to use as intended.

Nondigital labels will continue to be a favored form of in-person interpretation because screens—which invite the inclusion of more content and media—often take more time and attention than visitors are willing to allocate to them in an exhibition. Nondigital labels are quicker to access, can be viewed socially, and allow the users to start and stop paying attention without losing their place. Digital interpretive strategies complement and expand on the content when they add audio, multimedia, apps, interactive games, video, and links to the internet.

In this chapter we will review examples of how digital labels have been used for in-person exhibitions (in real life, or IRL), as well as examples of online exhibitions (virtual). We will also consider the application of long-standing fundamentals for developing digital programs.

AT THE MUSEUM: DIGITAL LABELS, IN PERSON, NOT ONLINE

Exhibit developers choose to use built-in digital labels for a variety of reasons: aesthetics, space, interactivity, flexibility, and preference over freestanding digital consoles. Mounted on wall brackets, with tethers, in kiosks or consoles, digital labels can offer many in-person choices: changeable text size, audio labels, another language, music, graphics, diagrams, games, and animation, as well as more and more (i.e., too much more) content.

The Anchorage Museum's Arctic Studies exhibition, "The First Peoples of Alaska," employed digital labels in its galleries. The placement of video introductions close to the floor so as not to interrupt sight lines helped maintain an aesthetic focus on the cultural objects in the large cases. The videos featured first-person narration, images of objects, and scenes that played in a loop. Digital consoles, placed off to the sides, allowed visitors to search for more information about individual objects in the cases.

Many aquariums present fish ID labels digitally, meeting the need to update the labels quickly when the live species in the habitats change. Digital labels solve two problems for aquariums: They give visitors information about each fish in a habitat without plastering the wall with labels; and they create legible labels in a low-light environment. The California Academy of Science's Steinhart Aquarium fish ID labels have gone through multiple iterations, reflecting changes in technology and the evolution of visitors' familiarity with touching and swiping the iPad-size screens to find photos and facts. In the first iteration, each habitat had one digital screen that automatically cycled through individual ID labels for each species. These labels presented a couple of problems: Visitors couldn't control when the content switched from one fish to the next; and the cycle was too fast to look at the label, find the fish, then go back to read more. Newer formats allow visitors to swipe through or pause the label cycle, consuming the content at their own speed and decreasing user frustration.

The *Arctic Adventure* at Boston's Museum of Science presented all content on interactive consoles designed by Richard Lewis Media Group. This company, which has a long history of museum interpretation, has adapted to the ever-changing pre- and post-pandemic "touchability" issues. For a while, RLMG was concerned with modifying digital exhibits into touchless versions. But as the pandemic wore on and the Centers for Disease Control (CDC) learned that transmission through touch was not as hazardous as it first seemed, touch screens reemerged as a reasonable option.

The Chicago History Museum used large screens as section labels for *Out in Chicago*. Instead of using written words, videos of people talking to the camera welcomed visitors and explained each section's theme. Narrators for *Out in Chicago* were gay, lesbian, bisexual, and transgender people who were represented in the exhibition. It was a very personable way to draw you in.

After realizing that visitors were not stopping to read gallery introduction labels, the Monterey Bay Aquarium replaced some with wordless videos. The videos depicted colorful scenes of the natural environment featured in each gallery. The hope was that this nonverbal introduction would set a mood more quickly and effectively than words could.

Advantages and Drawbacks to Digital Labels in Exhibitions

The use of digital labels in exhibitions unfortunately enables the irresistible urge to include too much content. Digital labels give the overzealous curator a place to bury a great deal of extra information for the supposedly dedicated visitor who will presumably "drill down" for more facts. When visitors say they *like* the opportunity to get more information via digital labels in an exhibition, they might be saying it because they expect the museum to offer this technology, not because they actually *need* all those layers of information. Visitors may like that it's there, but how much do they actually use it?

Output costs versus impacts and outcomes

Is the impact of digital information—measured by user time spent, number of options started versus completed, and prolonged engagement with exhibits, art, objects, or phenomenon—worth the output, measured by the staff's time and money spent to create, test, update, and maintain it? Rather than create rabbit holes of information that visitors are unlikely to access in the gallery, why not put that information on a website? Then visitors can find it from home, where they can access it comfortably, sitting down, at their leisure.

Nonportable screen-based digital interpretation located on the wall or on a reading rail or kiosk has the advantage of being easy to update. But how often are these labels actually updated? Writing new label copy takes time, and there is rarely money left over for remedial corrections, especially in a temporary exhibition. According to exhibit developer and evaluator Jessica Brainard, "Content developers bump up against the myth of updatability: It may be easy to upload new text and images, but good label writing, image research, and acquisition still take time up front. There are no shortcuts when it comes to the actual content development."

Digital labels are usually somewhat interactive, allowing visitors to swipe for more information or other forms of media. But whether it's one visitor or a group interacting with a digital label, that experience is still limited to one user's choices. The initial screen of general information gets buried, and other readers will have to wait their turn. Some visitors may struggle with the interface, not knowing how to use the device to get to the information stored there for them, or how to decipher the icons we've put on the screen.

Tips for In-Person Digital Label Success

Ben Gammon has excellent advice about making effective digital labels, based on his experience at the Science Museum in London. Gammon says that many studies have come to the following conclusions about placement, ordering and navigating the screen options, and engagement:

- Digital labels can be very successful—popular with visitors, extensively used, and successful in increasing people's engagement with objects—contrary to what is often assumed.

- For this to be achieved, however, the digital label must be positioned close to and directly in front of the object(s) it refers to, and the user must be able to easily view the object as they stand at the screen.

- The top page (not the attractor screen but the first page visitors interact with) must clearly identify its purpose and what it has to offer. It must contain an inviting and relevant "call to action."

- The most popular content—animations, videos, audio clips, image libraries—needs to be as close to the first screen as possible.

- The label needs to be designed for visitors who are browsing rather than searching for something specific. Therefore, the content hierarchy needs to be relatively broad and shallow—several options on the top screen, each of which provides three or four layers at most.

- The label must have a prominent "Home" or "Menu Page" button, because most visitors navigate by returning to the first screen and then navigating to another topic.

The above issues are visitors' interactions with the digital screens themselves. In addition, one of the greatest challenges with digital labels is having power to drive the devices that are placed in the exhibition, especially in older buildings. No one wants to cut holes and run wires through gallery walls, and no one wants to see wires running up the walls or across the floor. Until someone invents safe, wireless power, this will be one of the greatest limitations of stationary digital labels.

AT THE MUSEUM: ON YOUR PHONE VIA QR CODES

A quick response, or QR, code is a type of barcode that, when read by a smartphone, links the phone to a website or application. QR codes are now ubiquitous in our daily lives: restaurant menus, social media sites, billboards, parking lots, and many other places. They are also becoming more common in museums.

Using QR codes became easier when Apple incorporated a QR reader into the camera app on the iPhone. (Android phones had included one earlier.) No longer do visitors have to go through the cumbersome process of downloading an app to access what a QR code has to offer. Now it's just point, scan, click, and the content appears.

Multiple Uses for QR Codes

QR codes might be posted at the visitor services desk, in a brochure handout, at the entrance to an exhibition, or on labels throughout the space. Wherever the QR code is posted, the content the QR code is linked to should be identified specifically by title, purpose, or intended audience. Avoid using QR codes with just the curiosity killer, "For more information." User uptake data for this invitation is often too low to warrant the effort to produce it.

Many museums use QR codes to help visitors access label texts in different languages. Of the several advantages, most beneficial is the reduction of clutter on walls, panels, or labels in cases. Printing two, three, or four languages takes up space and makes exhibits look more text heavy than they are.

QR codes can increase accessibility in many ways. They can give visually impaired visitors access to larger type or audio versions of exhibit labels. In places such as historic houses or outdoor gardens, a handheld device might be the only way to access interpretation in the absence of a docent-guided tour. QR codes can also be useful for orientation and navigation. Visitors can find out what's available, see a floor plan or map, and get help finding their way to their choices. Good orientation helps visitors be ready for engagement.

In many exhibitions, QR codes allow visitors to access audio or video of a person talking (the maker, the artist, the storyteller) that can enhance their experience. The Chicago History Museum's exhibition of photographer Vivian Maier presented this reclusive artist's short stories about her methods and opinions. The personal voice really brought her to life.

Bisa Butler, a textile artist, included songs from her playlist on the nondigital labels at the Art Institute of Chicago as part of her *Portraits* exhibition, which reimagined and celebrated narratives of Black life. Visitors could use their phones to connect to Spotify and listen to the suggested music, adding another dimension to her vibrant quilted portraits.

Challenges to using smartphones and QR codes in exhibitions

Perhaps the current abundance of QR codes comes from the desire to provide more digital media without having to invest in high hardware costs incurred by installing screen-based digital labels. But delivering content via cell phones also creates the following barriers for visitors:

- Exclusion of those who don't have smartphones

- Difficulty using phones to scan the QR codes

- Concern about running out of memory

- Concern about running out of battery

- Confusion about what the app offers (e.g., what is the content?)

- Confusion about who it is aimed at (e.g., who is it meant for?)

- Confusion about how long each segment of media lasts, especially videos (seconds? minutes?)

- Time spent looking at the phone instead of having social interactions

- Privacy concerns, knowing that the website accessed by a QR code might collect their data

- A website that, when opened, is not optimized for handheld devices (a modified design to fit different screens and orientations)

- Insufficient broadband, which limits the number of visitors that can use the free Wi-Fi

Of course, the content that visitors access by reading a museum's digital label or by scanning a code needs to be worth the effort it takes to find and pay attention to it. There are advantages of having a short physical label to read immediately instead of fumbling with a phone and reading on a screen.

OUTSIDE THE MUSEUM: ONLINE EXHIBITIONS

Online museum exhibitions have arisen from a desire to share content more widely, converting an in-person experience to something that can be experienced remotely. This was especially true in 2020, during the early months of the COVID-19 pandemic, when museum buildings were closed to the public. It quickly became apparent that online exhibitions offered accessibility to a much larger audience. People were welcome to visit from all corners of the globe at any time of day or night.

Online versus In-Person, Briefly

Before we consider the types and examples of online exhibitions, let's recall the definition of an in-person, in-real-life (IRL) visit and the experiences it affords. For our purposes in this book, an interpretive exhibition is a space with defined boundaries with multiple types of media, organized in thematic groupings, that uses a variety of labels to identify and interpret objects (specimens, artworks, phenomena) and is self-guided. Three-dimensional objects and the designed environment are primary features.

In-person experiences in an exhibition are social and sensory. Visitors are able to

- Hear ambient sounds

- Feel floor and wall textures

- Instantly perceive the relative size of things

- Make unlimited choices about where to stop

- Read any available label in any order they want

- Touch the touchables

- Interact with other visitors

- See a wide field of view

- Look from a label to object—read-look-read-look—seamlessly

- Move closer to look at the details

- Turn around quickly; retrace steps

- See high-resolution of any chosen view

- Talk with their co-visitors about the real objects they see

Nevertheless, online exhibits do have attractive qualities: They are available any time, at no cost; they offer unlimited repeat visits, making them a great teaching resource; digital navigation links enable users to jump from one area to another with ease. And, for some people, the opportunity to view a digital exhibit experience without any distractions from other visitors (talking, crowding, children crying) can be a plus.

Caution: Not all online exhibits are online exhibitions.

Some "online exhibits" turn out to be video-recorded tours of a physical exhibition, interpreted by a guide. On these tours, the visitor is led on a prescribed path and cannot move around, jump to, or revisit areas. There are no digital labels; sometimes exhibit labels are visible in the background, but they are not legible. These programs should be called guided tours, not exhibitions. But they can be great, as in curator Allison Glenn's nine-minute virtual tour of *Hank Willis Thomas: All Things Being Equal* at the Crystal Bridges Museum of American Art. COVID-19 forced the museum to close just a few weeks after this exhibition opened, so Allison brought it to life on YouTube.

Online programs that tell a linear story in text printed over graphic images scroll like well-illustrated articles or stories. Text for this category of "online exhibit" can work well if it follows some of the guidelines that appear in this book. One such example is *The Station Renovation* story at the Musée d'Orsay. This program about the evolution of the old railway station into the modern museum includes the right number of images and the right amount of text. It pulls the reader along, and if you look at the whole thing, you get a prize at the end.

Web pages that use images of objects supported by text, but with no sense of a designed environment or content that references itself, are more like catalogs than exhibitions. Google Arts and Culture offers lots of these types of catalogs.

To be called an online exhibition, a program should mimic the strongest features of what an interpretive exhibition is or does, suggests Cait McQuade, consultant to museums on exhibit development and interpretive planning. She shared this thought about what characterizes an online exhibition:

> I believe that grouping things because they have a concept in common, for the purpose of communicating the idea they have in common, is itself an interpretive act. And that is something essential to exhibitions, whether they're physical or online. There might be degrees of "exhibit-y-ness." An online story seems more exhibit-like when structured as a set of objects with accompanying text that, taken together, support an interpretation. Whereas a story that uses images almost as background, without specific reference to the images and without characterizing them as objects, is more like an article.

Online programs can enhance in-person exhibitions.

Then there are online programs that are extensions of physical exhibitions. The Isabella Stewart Gardner Museum provided an extensive online gallery guide for *Titian: Women, Myth & Power*, with abundant examples of details, close-ups, media, history, multiple points of views, and additional resources. The only thing that kept the gallery guide from being totally overwhelming was the fact that the exhibition consisted of just six paintings, so the viewer didn't get lost or confused.

The online gallery guide for the Met's *Alice Neel: The People Come First* had extensive offerings: a floor plan of the nine galleries of the physical exhibition; four audio recordings (six to nine minutes each) of Alice Neel being candidly interviewed about her life and art; photographs of the Met galleries showing the layout of paintings; and digital images of all 118 artworks. Some, but not all, included their caption labels (approximately one hundred-plus words each). Navigation of the digital guide was tricky, with dead ends where a back click of the mouse took you to the top of the category, not where you left off; no search function; and cutoff label copy with images overlapping the text. You would probably appreciate sitting at your home computer to thoroughly view *Alice Neel* because it is a time-consuming experience to see, read, and hear. Yet the content is so fascinating that it inspires a strong desire to be there in person with the real things.

ONLINE SELF-GUIDED VISITS BASED ON IN-REAL-LIFE EXHIBITIONS

Google Maps' "Street View" features 360-degree panoramic photographic maps that enable users to choose a starting point, move down a street, and look all around them in a "3D" view. Street View has limited capacity to zoom in for a closer view of houses, storefronts, etc., as you move down the street, but it is still an excellent orientation tool for locating and seeing a destination before you go.

The "museum street view" strategy creates an online visit to an IRL physical museum exhibition, using a 360-degree camera to photograph a walk-through of the exhibition. It is a useful tool for getting a good overview of an exhibition. The camera does not differentiate within its field of vision, as our eyes and brain do. So in these street-view exhibitions, glaring lights have the same prominence as objects and labels, making for a more cluttered view than we experience in person.

If the quality and precision of the original camera are good enough, zoom-in opportunities allow visitors to see objects up close and read the actual labels. The advantage of the high-quality photography is that the original graphic design of the labels is preserved, giving visitors access to the design aesthetic of the whole experience.

These are good large-scale examples of this street-view strategy:

- *Deep Time*, at the Smithsonian's National Museum of Natural History, has fantastic photo resolution that allows zooming in on label text, which means you can read the labels in their context. This 31,000-square-foot space needs to be visited multiple times to see it all, perhaps an unreasonable expectation for most people in person. But online it could be done . . . in theory. A floor plan tool allows users to skip around to different areas.

- *The Road to Independence*, at the Museum of the American Revolution, has a digital self-guided online tour of the 120,000-square-foot immersive space (a more linear layout than *Deep Time*). This program presents photographs of the graphic wall labels in pop-up windows, which preserve the labels' original graphic design. Unlike visiting in person, however, you cannot look back and forth at the object and read the label at the same time.

- The nine thousand square feet of *Cyrus Tang Hall of China* at the Field Museum has most of its labels produced as digital reading rails in its physical galleries, with multilevel texts and graphics that address five thousand years of Chinese civilization. In the online version of the exhibition, a helpful floor plan and a chance to jump to the highlights mitigates the feeling one gets in the galleries of being overwhelmed by unfamiliar objects and layers of text.

While these qualify as good examples of an emerging genre, they are not without their shortfalls, such as problems with wayfinding or orientation, not being able to see things up close, not being able to read labels, or being overwhelmed by a sometimes unknown number of choices. In addition, these examples also required a sizable amount of time just to gain competence with the navigation tools and to understand all the possibilities and limitations. The shortfalls of these three high-quality (and presumably expensive) production examples hint at the drawbacks that are also encountered in less costly productions.

Online Exhibition Walk-Throughs Created with Matterport

As of the publication date of this edition of *Exhibit Labels*, Matterport, Inc., a platform created for the real estate industry, was being used to create online versions of in-person exhibitions. Matterport was popular with museums, especially after the 2020 pandemic began, because of its comparatively low cost, relative ease of use, and because it offered an alternative to engaging high-budget virtual-exhibit professionals. For real estate marketing, this technology "enables viewers to feel like they're really there" as they explore room by room during a virtual open house.

Museums use Matterport to create a self-guided virtual exhibition walk-through that shows the layout of the galleries and the placement of the exhibit elements. The user controls the direction of their movement through the spaces and has the ability to stop at exhibit elements. But the location and number of stops is often predetermined, so viewers can't stop anywhere they want. In addition, the amount of zoom-in power is limited. Depending on how close the camera gets to the individual exhibits, the original in-person labels are sometimes readable, but more often the label text is out of focus and inaccessible due to poor resolution. Labels can be re-created with a Matterport-designed pop-out element in a box with white type and a limited word count. But the original typographic design is lost, and full content may not be included.

Selected Examples of Lower-Cost Online Exhibitions

In preparation for the updated digital label chapter of this edition, the authors looked online for formerly on-view IRL exhibitions that used the Matterport program to create a virtual museum experience. The following examples were selected to show commonalities and differences in size, purpose, and ways of portraying exhibit labels.

The Detroit Institute of Art made its first online re-creation of its popular annual exhibition, *Ofrendas: Celebrating el Diá de los Muertos*, in 2020 to reach visitors isolated during the COVID-19 pandemic. The DIA wanted to present the same content that was available in person: thirteen altars with bilingual labels created by local artists and community members. The designers considered their first use of the Matterport platform an experiment and hoped to use what they learned for future projects, and also share their findings with the museum field. The lessons they learned appear in the "Beyond the Walls" 2021 edition of NAME's journal, *Exhibition*, where they discuss their planning, design, and evaluation processes, as well as user outcomes. "If we try it again, our conceptualization and execution need strengthening," they reported. The article included thoughtful introspections and discussions of short timelines, budgets, limitations of the platform, and the need for more prelaunch user testing.

At Milwaukee Art Museum's online version of *The Quilts of Pauline Parker*, only nine of the twenty-five quilts had interpretation. Those elements each had three clickable pop-outs: (1) a text label with ID information (some also had thirty to fifty words of interpretation and a quote by the artist); (2) a musical intro with a two-minute spoken label containing complementary interpretation by Parker's daughter; and (3) a closer photo of the quilt with a limited zoom-in function. Some viewers will find the limited choice restricting.

The *Salem Witch Trials 1692* exhibition at Peabody Essex Museum had fifty-three stops with pop-out ID information and a photo of the object with a limited zoom-in function. Quotations high on the walls were legible; the largest wall labels were legible, but just barely; the other labels were not. Many of the pop-out labels were only IDs, not interpretive captions.

More recent examples, such as Arizona State Museum's *Wrapped in Color: Legacies of the Mexican Sarape* exhibit, use a higher-resolution 360-degree camera, which allows users to zoom in close enough to exhibit labels to see them, but not to read them clearly when letters-to-background color contrast is low.

More Types of Matterport Tours in Museums

In addition to walk-throughs of exhibitions, the authors found Matterport tours of whole museums, of one special area, or of a single large object. At the Cardinals Hall of Fame and Museum in St. Louis, a virtual tour of the whole museum seemed designed to sell the idea of renting the museum after hours for an event. It even marked the best locations to put the bar and the appetizers. The Will Rogers Memorial Museum self-guided tour included a special room with small dioramas called *A View through the Life of Will Rogers* by Jo Mora, with "classical miniature figures cast in hydrostone and done to scale in fine art form." Each of the twelve dioramas had its own label that was not very long, centered on the window of the diorama. The titles were legible, but the text was disappointingly out of focus. The Museum of Flight in Seattle had Matterport "3D step inside" tours of twelve aircraft, including the Concorde. This one works well because it's based on a familiar space—you might have been inside an airplane—so the text didn't feel as necessary (and general information was located elsewhere). You've probably never flown in a Concorde, and now that they no longer fly, you never will. Don't bother with the VR or 3D that need special headsets or glasses. Just gawk.

The above examples shared the following features: (1) navigation circles that identified "stops" where (2) some additional information was provided; (3) a floor plan overview that gave a sense of the shape and size of the gallery and partitions; and (4) a "dollhouse" view that shows a "3D" zoom of the space. It was possible to jump from the floor plan to a spot in the exhibition and back to reorient yourself, but in larger exhibitions or whole museum tours, this can be difficult when the floor plans are highly complex.

Suggestions for Making Better Street View-Style Virtual Exhibitions

In a virtual exhibition, the users should have control over what they look at and the order they look at things by using a cursor to move through the virtual environment. Keep in mind that in an online exhibition, users are more likely to want to casually browse for minutes, not study for hours.

- Start with features that provide orientation, such as a floor plan or map of the exhibition, to give a visual overview of the spaces.

- Include a short text introduction to the show, including what it's about and who it's meant for.

- Use callouts on the map to name the main sections.

- Make a hybrid combination to allow users to navigate overviews and see close-up details. That is, combine a walk-through "street view" of the exhibits plus have zoom-in controls to read the actual label texts. Or use the highest-quality camera.

- When planning new exhibitions, think about how the spaces will read virtually.

- Resist the urge to make too many clickable layers of information or details. Select a limited number of high-definition "stops," enough to whet visitors' interest.

- Use the online version to sell the idea of coming to see it in person, if possible.

Online Collections

A final category of online exhibits is the posting of images of entire collections. This invites the temptation to add interpretive text, but by whom and to what end? Depiction of objects with no interpretive connection to each other or to a theme is essentially an online catalog. Google Arts and Culture provides some groupings based on artist, era, color, and medium, but a user can become overwhelmed by too many choices. To the point, the Google Arts URL includes the term "asset." Users of these resources can capture images of objects to create their own exhibits to share or not.

TEST AND CRITIQUE

There is much to learn about the effectiveness of these new digital combinations of software and devices for museum interpretation. We need more studies (small and large) that evaluate the use and impacts of digital components in the hands of real visitors. The studies should include and share recommendations for both small tweaks and big improvements, as well as hints of missed opportunities. They should be clear about what did not work or if the devices fell short of the developers' expectations. The "Beyond the Walls" issue of NAME's journal, *Exhibition*, included critical reviews alongside the glowing reports (e.g., news releases, marketing campaigns) of the recently installed latest shiny digital thing.

Lessons from a Digital Media Evangelist

Scott Sayre has gleaned many lessons in his more than thirty years of integrating digital media into museum displays and interpretive strategies. Most relevant to the concerns of this book are these:

- When developing digital interpretive technology, recruit cross-departmental teams that draw on the expertise of all participants. This approach not only produces superior content but will also provide an excellent opportunity for internal team building and professional growth, and generate museum-wide ownership in a project.

- Audience research, formative and summative evaluation, usability testing, and usage statistics should be built into every digital technology project plan. We are never good at assessing our own work without input from the end user.

- Our visitors expect interpretive technology to be up to date and reliable. While in-house support is essential, with knowledgeable staffers who can troubleshoot problems and address visitor questions and issues, online help and external support contracts may be necessary.

Web developers generated best practices for web writing much more quickly than it took for museum label guidelines to come along. Also, web developers relied on audience research and prototyping—user testing—right from the beginning. The not-so-surprising parallels between writing for exhibits and writing for the web (commonly called "content writing") exist because there was always more money available for the internet than for museums.

Digital Strategies Related to More Assistance, Not Just Content

Digital devices have the capacity to create better experiences for visitors in exhibitions. They can help visitors with the primary features of wayfinding, agenda setting, and introductions. They can also flag the hot spots and invite annotation.

Wayfinding and orientation

Both physical and conceptual wayfinding can be accomplished digitally. Instead of a paper map, electronic maps with GPS can continually update and indicate that "you are here" as you move around the space. Orientation with a digital device should be coordinated with standard nondigital signage so that the visitor experience is reinforced in both modalities. Any new system will require vigilant iterative testing to get it to work effectively.

Offer an agenda

Because many visitors arrive without an agenda, a digital strategy can offer them one. By presenting a few options or asking personal questions about topics of interest and time budgets, the institution can make some individually calculated suggestions that are accessible via a digital device.

For example, in Paris, the "Louvre Trails" include a path that follows Jay-Z and Beyoncé's APES**T trail through the famed museum. The web itinerary gives specific directions—"Enter through the Denon wing. After the ticket check, continue on up the stairs . . ."—for visiting each of the artworks featured in the power couple's music video.

Flag the "hot spots" and highlights

When a visitor moves into the vicinity of an exhibit that has a high attraction rate (greater than 50 percent as determined by tracking-and-timing studies of visitor behavior), a digital device could suggest that they take a closer look, tell them why it is so popular, or invite some form of participation, including plugging in a number or scanning a QR code to access other media.

Let visitors annotate the labels

Instead of encouraging or facilitating the use of social media outside the walls of the museum, the museum could invite visitors to talk back to the label writers themselves—with their reactions, corrections, questions, or elaborations. More than a talk-back sticky note, this kind of interaction would welcome visitors into a conversation about the actual scripts of the labels. As technology evolves, more features will promote visitors' comments on the labels and replies from the exhibit developers. Social media experts on staff can assist with ways to do this. Hopefully the discourse would be focused, informal, civil, and helpful for all, with the shared goal of effective and lively communication. "Let visitors annotate the labels" reminded us of the experimental "ASK" mobile app program at the Brooklyn Museum that invited visitors to message with a museum staff person about works on exhibit. Shelley Bernstein and Sara Devine were the brains behind the program, and they have generously shared their lessons learned online.

Provide easy and free access to Wi-Fi

Museum audiences are accustomed to easy access to digital networks in other parts of their lives. Visitors depend on the museum to not just allow the use of phones but also to encourage their use and to provide the broadband Wi-Fi connections that make digital interactivity possible. They grow increasingly impatient when an internet connection is not possible or is prohibitively expensive. Although they can use their phones without Wi-Fi in the museum, free, secure, and dependable access lets visitors know that phone use is encouraged.

While static wall labels and graphics will continue to play a primary role in affording visitors meaningful interpretations in exhibitions, the digital opportunities are also here to stay.

May we continue to improve them both.

Photo Figures for Part IV

Rocks talk

The caption for El Capitan Granite speaks in the first person, and its location encourages close looking, reading, and even touching the object. Truly visitor friendly.

Plant petting zoo

What to do and notice is clearly stated in words and shown in the gender-neutral drawing.

The label could be even shorter by leaving out the second sentence of the first paragraph.

198

Reading rail videos

Small, short, silent, constantly looping videos—like the one at the far right on this reading rail—can bring belongings to life by showing how people use them.

White school Black school

Great example of how images, words, and objects
work together to clearly and strongly communicate
the ideas.

Olives

The thought-bubble design suggests that the
plant is thinking, but the voice is impersonal.
The design and the content don't match.

Butterfly connection

The interactive station shows two butterflies: One was wild, the other was farm raised. Which is which?

When visitors can answer the question posed by looking closely at clues given in the interpretive labels, the experience is more engaging than just guessing.

Sticky notes

Visitors like to give feedback, and good questions encourage thoughtful responses.

Here, lots of emotive feedback resulted from the prompt to share a personal story about a local fire.

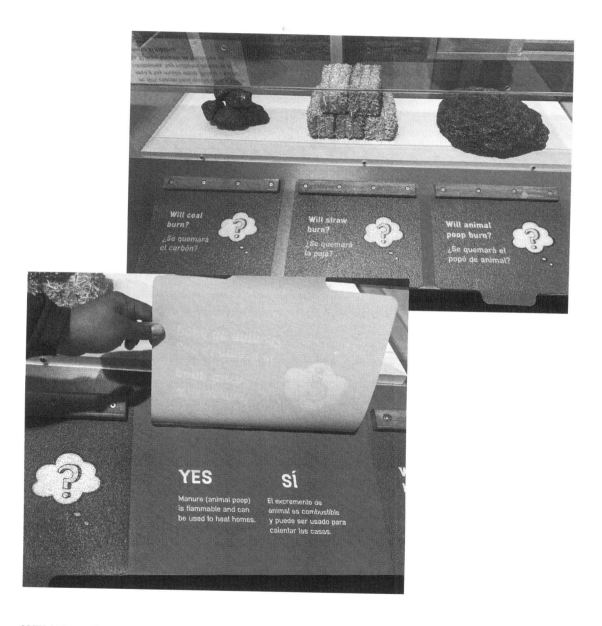

Will it burn?

The answer to all three of these questions is "yes," which builds to a generalization about the combustible materials of typical homes and barns in 1871 Chicago.

It's often a good idea to show multiple examples of the same idea.

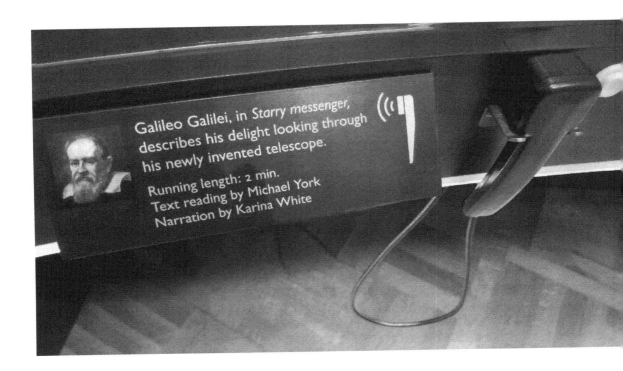

Galileo Galilei, in *Starry messenger,* describes his delight looking through his newly invented telescope.

Running length: 2 min.
Text reading by Michael York
Narration by Karina White

Galileo handset

Two important things to tell visitors about audio experiences: What the topic is and how long it will last. These orientation cues help them decide if they want to pick up the headset, press the button, and start listening.

How much time visitors spend with AV depends on how engaged they become with the content. Two minutes is a long time in museum time. Keep it short.

Ball launcher

Drawings known as "use diagrams"
work better than photographs or wordy
instructions to quickly explain how to
operate an interactive element.

Listen to Vivian Maier experiment with a tape recorder.

Escuche a Vivian Maier experimentar con una grabadora.

Audio recording
1978
Courtesy of Maloof Collection
© The Estate of Vivian Maier

Cell phone QR code

The graphic of the cell phone gives the QR code context. Adjacent text tells visitors what they'll hear. Links to audio and video are much more rewarding than links to more text.

Iguano

If there is room on the sign for a caption, put it there. Don't bury it in a QR code. Words on the sign offer quicker access and easier sharing with others in a social group.

Welcome to Evolving Planet

It's a complicated set of halls in a one-way layout.

Drawings or icons and words would be easier to read than photos on this exhibit floor plan. But nothing can fix the fact that this kind of huge exhibition is a daunting challenge for many visitors.

Vikings entrance?

This doorway looks like an entrance, but it's not.
The "EXIT ONLY" text on clear glass is hard to read.

Entrance letters and arrow need to be much larger to
improve orientation.

Arrow

It takes more than an arrow taped to the floor to overcome visitors' natural tendency to turn right.

A well-designed environment will use multiple clues—including architecture, light, and signage—for clear orientation to the correct entrance of an exhibition.

PART V

Tasks

19

Getting Started and Getting Done

Resist the temptation to write label copy until all the front-end exhibition tasks have been done. The writing is easier when you can see the way to the end from a solid beginning.

Once you have the big idea formulated, the front-end evaluations conducted, the floor plans roughly laid out, and the modalities chosen for the different types of exhibition elements, you are ready to start writing. These are a lot of things to have in place beforehand, but the more you know about what you want to say, to whom, and for what purpose before you write, the faster and easier the writing will be.

Some writers prepare a general narrative or walk-through of the exhibit experience before writing labels. This can help exhibit developers and label writers imagine how visitors might interact with individual exhibit elements. Thinking of conversations you'd like visitors to have in the gallery can help inspire label copy. Narratives and walk-throughs also give funders or the marketing department an idea of what the exhibit might be like. But the narrative walk-through should not be set in stone. It will become outdated as the exhibit progresses. Trying to keep the narrative and actual label copy in agreement is difficult once label drafts are started.

WHO SHOULD DO THE WRITING?

Who should write the labels? The answer is the person who has the time, the enthusiasm, and the willingness to learn this specialized skill. This person can be a content or subject expert, or a nonexpert. The subject specialist might need help writing labels that speak in visitor language, keeping in mind the most basic questions a novice visitor has about the topic. Writers who are not intimately familiar with the topic, on the other hand, will need a little help making labels accurate and comprehensive and not trivializing important points. Enthusiasm is necessary in either case to get the writer through many drafts and repeated rounds of feedback and critique from the team.

More and more museums are contracting with freelance writers because there is no one on staff who has the time, enthusiasm, or expertise to write the labels. Sometimes the writer is a guest curator from outside the museum who is an expert in the subject. Sometimes it is a person skilled in writing. No matter who does the writing, the museum has the ultimate responsibility for the voice and the content of the labels, and the museum must give the writer clear guidelines for what those are. The earlier an outside writer is brought into the process the better; it takes time to get a new person up to speed with the project if they are brought into it in the middle.

Multiple Writers

Sometimes a project requires more than one exhibit writer. When the Detroit Institute of Arts reinstalled its entire collection all at once, it hired a team of freelance label writers to help. The DIA provided writers with detailed guidelines informed by extensive evaluation and a well-developed big idea. These included a style primer for visitor-friendly writing and templates spelling out the location, purpose, and recommended word count for each type of label. Writers were given content for each label—usually reduced to a single page of text—that summarized what DIA curators wanted visitors to know. Even though different sections of the museum collections were written by different label writers, the style guide and review process ensured that all the labels spoke with the "voice" of the DIA.

Including New Voices

When an exhibition presents a new perspective, an alternate opinion, or a previously unrepresented community, it can be important to invite new voices to write exhibit labels. Combining the authenticity of new voices with the constraints of visitor-friendly labels can be tricky, but there are ways to do it. The De Young Museum felt strongly about including the voices of current-day Elem Pomo in their exhibition *Jules Tavernier and the Elem Pomo*. They asked their Elem Pomo collaborators to write a one-thousand-word blog post related to the exhibition, which was posted on the museum website. Label writers took the collaborators' words from the blog, edited them to label length and style, and then ran the labels by the original writers for approval. The final labels included the names of their authors.

The Southern Vermont Arts Center recruited community members to write labels for the exhibition *Our Tangled Choices: Art and the Environment* to emphasize storytelling and peer-to-peer sharing. Curator Alison Crites hoped that visitors "would feel they were gaining insight from a group of friendly and informed neighbors rather than a room full of climate change experts." The community labels were the only interpretive text in the exhibition, except for the introductory label. The SVAC did not establish a word limit for the contributed labels, and they ranged from eighty to nearly six hundred words (although most were two hundred to three hundred words). Crites hoped that the novel first-person writing would be more engaging for visitors, who might be willing to read longer labels as a result. The SVAC did not have the resources to conduct summative evaluation to find out. In their *Exhibition Magazine* article, "Toward Shared Authority," Melanie Parker, Alison Crites, and Amelia Wiggins raise the question: Should we uphold the same word count limits and other standards that we have for institutionally authored interpretation? The authors of *Exhibit Labels* believe the answer is, most likely, yes.

While there is a reluctance to hold community contributors to in-house standards for fear of being disrespectful, we can respect outsider voices while still applying guidelines for making good label texts. An overabundance of first-person voices can be just as mentally numbing as any other technique used without restraint.

MANUALS OF STYLE

Many institutions have developed label-writing guidelines and made them available to the field. The Getty Museum, the Victoria & Albert Museum, and the Australian Museum have posted theirs online. Look around to see if your institution has produced guidelines; something may be stashed in the back of a file cabinet. Or consult the excellent examples from these institutions: Te Papa, Australian Museum, Oakland Museum of California, and Liberty Science Center. One of the newest resources for label writing is the Smithsonian Institution's "Guide for Interpretive Writing for Exhibitions." It contains excellent advice for all steps in the process, is nicely designed, in color, and it's free. The SI's guide uses "big idea" in a different way than we do, and has text hierarchies that are not the same as *Exhibit Label*'s examples. Our advice: Inform your own approaches through the advice of more than one source.

SCHEDULING THE TIME

How long will it take to write the labels? This is a loaded question and a difficult one to answer. "Everyone is in denial about how long it takes and how much it costs," says Judy Rand, an experienced and well-known museum label writer and exhibit planner who has managed many writing projects. Many museums have unrealistic expectations for the number of labels a writer can crank out in a week, uninformed conceptions about how long the editing and review process can take, and naive notions about what is involved in transforming words into a well-integrated typographic presentation in exhibition design.

Depending on the purpose and length of the label (function, number of words), the complexity of the content (subject matter, big idea), and the amount of background research required, it can take from fifteen minutes to two hours per label to research and write a first draft. It can take another fifteen minutes to two hours per label to get through various editorial and review stages. It can take another fifteen minutes to two hours per label to integrate the words with the images in the design process. This gives a range of forty-five minutes to six hours *per label* to get from research to final integrated copy. If there are twenty-five objects needing caption labels, an introduction, three group or section labels, and a credits panel, that's approximately thirty labels. Thirty labels multiplied by four hours each (a rough and low estimate) gives us a total of 120 hours.

However, that figure is deceiving because it is not 120 continuous hours. It is not a three-week job at forty hours a week. It takes much longer. Many critical tasks happen in the hours "in between."

It takes time to

- Get references on line or from a library

- Get calls back from information and image sources

- Submit rough drafts and hear back from reviewers (weeks!)

- Make appointments with busy designers to hash out layouts, images, communication goals, and a host of other design decisions that must be made jointly by the writer and the designer

- Review rough layouts, revisions, and "final" PDFs containing images and type in place

Time is also absolutely necessary for the evaluation and editing necessary to ensure that the labels are effective and accessible. And most labels benefit from a writer putting them aside for a time during the writing process, then coming back to them with fresh eyes.

A rough rule of thumb: Multiply the number of labels by three hours each for how long it will take, then triple that figure. "Yikes!" you say. "That's unreasonable, impossible; we don't have that kind of time!" This hypothetical scenario will hopefully make you think carefully about allowing more time for labels. There is no denying that good ones take longer to make.

GETTING ORGANIZED

When it is time to write, it's helpful to have the following items handy: research notes, the exhibition floor plan and elevations, the big idea, and pictures of the objects or other visuals of what the "stuff" of the exhibit looks like. Imagine you are a visitor, with limited time and no special vocabulary to understand the topic. What would you want to know first? What would probably catch your eye first?

Some writers ask themselves, "What is this label supposed to do?" and "What is the most important thing to say here?" Then they align the answers to those questions with the exhibit content documents and the big idea. There's always more content than the label word count or visitor attention span can support. It helps to prioritize what's most important.

Independent exhibit writer Mike Rigsby told the authors that he starts by collecting and reviewing all the background material provided by the museum that hired him, including big idea, messages, and research resources. He tries to get a feel for the institution by looking at its website and talking to its visitors, if possible. He asks himself, "What is it that they think they want?" and "How wedded are they to this content?" Then he tries to find a unifying thread that he can use to weave all the material into a coherent whole. He writes the label text in a Word document, identifying each label by number, and uses customized styles with a distinct format (font, size, color) for each type of information (label text, note, research citation) on the page. Once he starts writing, he just "keeps going until he gets it done."

Write the first draft freely, without thinking about the word count, then come back and edit later. In this way, a writer loosens up and gets the creative juices flowing. It won't all be good, but often this process provides nuggets that make their way into a final label.

Even in a first draft, label writers should be imagining what visuals will work well with their words. "But I'm a writer, not a designer," a label writer might say. You need to be a bit of both if you are writing for exhibitions, because words in exhibits cannot, do not, and should not stand alone. You should write with both verbal and visual elements in mind.

When making the first draft, try a two-column setup: words that describe possible visuals on one side, words for label text on the other. The visuals list should be thought of as an aid to visual thinking at this point. The designer can use the suggestions or not, or come up with their own ideas, as designers often do. The writer is not dictating anything, only suggesting and thinking visually.

In the first draft, don't worry too much about close agreement between the suggested visuals and the text. Beginning with more visuals than you need will allow for more flexibility and choices later. If one of the suggested images turns out to be unobtainable, it will not leave a hole in the layout.

DOCUMENTATION

As you write and research images, be sure to keep good records. Documentation of authors, titles, sources, and dates will be valuable when you must go back and look up something to verify a fact, defend an argument, relocate the source of a photograph or illustration, or remember when and why you decided to do something a particular way. Some writers keep this information in the label document itself, in a smaller type size and a different color, so it's close at hand and easy to find.

Keeping track of drafts by date and number will help the writer, editor, designer, and other team members stay in sync. Drafts of online documents made available in editing apps, such as Google Docs, can become hopelessly mixed up, and errors that got corrected once can reappear when files are shared and modified. One person needs to be responsible for knowing where the text document is located and what stage it is in. Methods for keeping track of evolving changes should be established before you start writing, not halfway through.

To keep track of research sources, writer Rigsby recommends a bookmark manager (Raindrop.io). During the writing process, he organizes all the documents in digital file folders and keeps all versions of text documents so he can trace changes back to earlier versions.

WRITING AND EDITING

The basic content of the label is laid down in a rough first draft of text. Most of the writing time happens next, in the editing process: refining stylistic subtleties; responding to editorial suggestions from advisors; matching words to visuals; honing text so that it expresses the communication goals with economy, efficiency, and effectiveness; evaluating text with visitors, putting the copy away for a week and coming back to it for a fresh look. All these things take time. Schedule it in.

It is not uncommon to have five to seven drafts between the first and the final, most often with very minor edits, but sometimes with major ones due to changes in emphasis; new information; disagreements about style; or the photograph, object, or artifact finally being in hand. By doing all the right things before you start writing (getting to consensus on the big idea, types of labels to use, voice), the editing can be relatively quick and painless, even though many drafts may be necessary. Editing is much easier when it involves polishing rather than major overhauls or redirections.

At the Minneapolis Institute of Art, the label-writing process begins with a conversation between the content expert (usually a curator), who identifies what they want the labels to say, and the content strategist, who represents the visitor experience. Then, assisted by an agreed-upon list of visitor experience goals and motivations specific to the exhibition at hand, the content expert writes a first draft of label text. The content strategist streamlines and shortens that first draft with an eye toward visitor accessibility in the areas of concept, vocabulary, relevance, and visitor interest. The two parties pass the document back and forth a few times, tracking changes and comments. Generally, the content expert gets the last word.

Cutting Down the Word Count: Focus, Focus, Focus

The editing process should make the labels *shorter*. Following are three examples of copy that has been edited to reduce the word count and make the content more related to what can be seen by the label reader.

In the first example, the original version below contains too much subjective interpretation, which gives the impression that the label writer is trying to dominate the visitor's experience. The second version was shortened to make the text more specific and subtle. The label is for one photo, "*Industrial Detail*," from an exhibition of black-and-white prints by German photographer Albert Renger-Patzsch.

Original version:
Renger-Patzsch always photographed his subjects with an objective eye, yet his photographs often transcend the literal and present a magical transfiguration of the object. Here his subject was a row of freshly milled metal castings that had just been planed smooth, their residual filings still accumulated in the crevices. He angled his lights to cast a silvery sheen over the surface of the castings and the filings, which punctuate the composition with tiny specks of luminosity. The factory assembly line has been transformed into a hypnotic maze of interlocking abstract forms. (91 words)

Edited, shortened version:
A row of freshly milled metal castings had just been planed smooth, with residual filings still accumulated in the crevices. Renger-Patzsch angled his lights to cast a silvery sheen over the surface of the castings and the filings, which punctuate the composition with tiny specks of luminosity. The literal factory assembly line has been transformed into a hypnotic maze of interlocking abstract forms. (63 words)

The original version of the next label accompanied the 1936 painting *Longshoremen Returning from Work* by Alice Neel. The second version was shortened and edited to focus on what the visitor could see.

Original version:
The title of this nocturnal cityscape alludes to contemporary headlines about labor strife among ship workers. Widely publicized battles over union formation for fair hours and wages pervaded the 1930s, both domestically and internationally, but Neel's painting concerns a particular strike involving New York longshoremen in 1936 and 1937, organized partly by Pat Whalen (Neel's portrait of Whalen appears in the section "Counter/Culture"). Among other reports of this extended conflict, Neel read about the strike in the leftist newspapers to which she subscribed. She shows workers walking nonchalantly down the street, presumably on their way home, and commingling with other residents who appear oblivious to their fraught predicament. (108 words)

Edited, shortened version:
Neel's nocturnal cityscape shows longshoremen workers walking nonchalantly down the street. Presumably on their way home and commingling with other residents, they appear oblivious to the widely publicized battles about labor strife among ship workers. Neel read about the strike in the leftist newspapers to which she subscribed. (48 words)

This next label introduced an exhibition about a wildlife hospital associated with a wildlife museum. The first version is an early draft, and the second is the final label copy.

Original version:

If you find an injured animal
More than 98 percent of the animals treated at our hospital are admitted due to adverse contact with human activity. Animals are brought to the museum by the public and the county animal service agency. Twenty percent of the animals treated in our wildlife hospital have been caught by a cat. To save the lives of thousands of birds and other animals every year, please keep your cats indoors. (75 words)

Edited, shortened version:

Meet some of our patients
Most of our animal patients are injured when they come in contact with the human world. Some get hit by cars or are caught by house cats. Others fly into windows or get tangled in netting. Fortunately, people like you find these animals and bring them to the hospital. (54 words)

Keep the Writer Involved

The designated label writer usually sees the draft texts through the entire editing and design process. The writer needs to have control over what happens to the copy to keep the process on track and to keep one clear vision of where it has been and where it is going. This also helps the writer retain enthusiasm and "ownership" of the labels.

When the writer writes and hands label copy over to editors, who make changes and then hand it over to designers, who mark it up and add illustrations, the end product will lack the cohesiveness and consistency that can only come from having one person in charge. A better process is more iterative, where the steps overlap and the different players consult with each other to refine the final label.

REVIEWING

Reviewers should be asked to respond on the draft copy and return it to the writer on time. The team of reviewers should be large enough (five or six) so that if one person is out of town or cannot perform the job in the allotted time, there are enough other reviewers to cover the task adequately. The team should also be small enough (fewer than ten) so that integrating comments does not become a herculean job. Reviewers should include people with different responsibilities, such as content accuracy or fact-checking, and alignment with the museum's mission and institutional style. The person who has the last word (usually the director, curator, or project manager) should be identified early in the process and should be available to help consolidate comments from all the reviewers, resolve any contradictions, and provide one marked-up document to the writer in a timely manner.

Circulate revised drafts as quickly as possible, before the reviewers forget what they last saw. Tell reviewers that you will not respond to or incorporate all their edits and that they should keep a copy of their own comments. If the reviewers understand that their edits are suggestions, not the law, the label writer will be able to function in a more professional manner. Reviewers should review, not rewrite.

Do not sit down at an in-person meeting with reviewers early in the process and try to write the labels as a group. The group setting is better toward the end of the process. A group read-aloud of the final batch of labels will reveal any inconsistencies or typos that get missed when writers become too familiar with their work. This setting also provides an opportunity for all the stakeholders to collectively approve the label copy before sending it to production. In the era of pandemic-induced remote working, this group work was often done over Zoom.

A smooth editing process is most likely to happen when the reviewers know and trust the label writer. But that is not always the case. Sometimes it is necessary for writers to respond individually to a reviewer's comment—to say why they are not accepting the suggestion and to argue for their choices. This is a time-consuming mentoring process, and it can add significantly to the editing turnaround schedule. If the reviewers are not comfortable allowing the writer some amount of freedom, the review process should have a longer timeline. When everyone on the team wants to be intimately involved in the label creation, it takes a very long time to produce a finished product.

Several things can slow the editing process:

- The need to find more up-to-date reference materials

- Editors or reviewers rewriting or retyping the label text instead of editing directly on the draft provided for comment

- Editors or reviewers failing to provide comments within the designated time schedule

ALMOST FINISHED

There is no such thing as "final" copy. Even after it has been printed or mounted on the wall and the exhibit is open, changes can be made if necessary. Still, allow some flexibility and graciousness in letting things go, even though they are not perfect. You do the best you can, in the time you have, within the budget you have. "Don't get it right, get it written" can be watchwords to keep you from getting bogged down. Again, a clear vision of the communication goals, shared by the exhibit team, is invaluable.

20

Prototyping

Prototyping is evaluation with visitors during an exhibition's design development phase. It provides the most useful information and is the best value for the money and time.

Reading this chapter can be a start to—but not a substitute for—learning about evaluation from other resources in which the philosophies, rationales, and methods of collecting, processing, and reporting data are covered more thoroughly. In this discussion, we will focus on prototyping done early in the process, which is useful for all types of labels and is essential for labels for interactive exhibits. But first, some general thoughts on evaluation.

WHY WE ALL SHOULD DO EVALUATION

In the new paradigm of visitor-centered museums with narrative interpretive exhibitions, evaluation is essential to making these educational institutions inclusive, equitable, and socially responsive to their communities. Evaluation can help exhibit developers better understand their visitors and encourage and enable their visitors to feel competent and confident. Visitors will leave the museum feeling that it was a place for them.

Labels play a very large role in creating positive feelings for visitors. When visitors do not have successful learning experiences, the failure to communicate may lie to a large extent with the labels. Harris Shettel, who had a long and influential career in museum evaluation, says, "In every exhibit we evaluate, labels are key to the problems."

One of the biggest mistakes writers make, especially writers who are experts in the subject they are writing about, is to assume that "people will know that—it's obvious." Equally dangerous, however, is to assume that the audience is stupid and the only way to reach them is to simplify text to a childish level. Neither assumption is true. Evaluation can help sort out what visitors know, what is or is not obvious, and whether the assumptions made by exhibit developers about the audience are grounded in some form of shared reality. Evaluation is about making changes that will help visitors use and enjoy the exhibits more.

Museum practitioners who have not spent time systematically and unobtrusively watching visitors may remember only the people who act rudely, break the rules, or don't pay attention. After watching visitors carefully, however, you will have a better understanding of their behavior. As art educator Danielle Rice put it, "Indeed, it is possible to fall in love with one's visitors and to respect and value their wishes, desires and perceptions." You will get to the point where you thoroughly appreciate what *they* can teach *you* about exhibits and labels.

When visitors cannot figure out what labels and exhibits mean—when they fail to understand or make a connection—many will blame themselves, saying, "I didn't have enough time to look carefully," or "I don't have any background in art," or "I'm just here because my friend wanted to come." The fact that visitors are so willing to blame themselves as opposed to blaming the museum indicates the respect they hold for the institution. We, in turn, should be more respectful of them.

WHAT EVALUATION CAN TELL YOU

Exhibit evaluation can be done in many ways, and many benefits can come from using it. The types and benefits are often broken down into four major categories, depending on when they are done. This short review will show you where prototyping fits into the bigger picture.

Front-end evaluation. At the beginning of an exhibit project, you can get feedback about exhibit ideas from the potential audience. Developers can find out what visitors know, what their expectations are, and what vocabulary they use to describe your exhibit topic. Finding out at the beginning of a project what visitors know and what they expect can help shape the exhibit's big idea, communication goals, and educational objectives. It will help you choose the vocabulary and examples that will resonate with the largest percentage of the audience. Front-end evaluations (surveys, focus groups, interviews) of any type that probe for what visitors know are especially relevant to label writers. Finding out what visitors are concerned about, what knowledge they feel confident about, what they are less certain of, or what misconceptions they have is crucial for creating interpretive opportunities that will help them make new connections and to recollect old ones. Front-end surveys that only ask visitors to state likes, dislikes, income levels, zip codes, or other target marketing questions are less useful to exhibit designers. Be sure to conduct front-end evaluations early in the planning stages so that relevant information can be incorporated along the way.

Formative evaluation. Formative evaluation is also called prototyping, making mock-ups, or user testing. It is done with exhibit components before design decisions have been finalized. During exhibit development and draft label writing, prototyping can help fine-tune label texts by making sure directions, information, and vocabulary levels are expressed appropriately for the visitors that will be reading them. Data from prototyping does not tell curators what the content should be, nor does it tell designers what the exhibit should look like. Instead, it helps the team direct the content and the design so that the exhibit communicates more effectively.

Summative evaluation. Evaluation after the exhibition opens gives researchers the opportunity to test hypotheses about visitor use and impacts as well as make comparisons of exhibition success. Summative evaluations review visitor experiences in the context of the whole exhibition, providing an overall look at how well the exhibition achieved its goals, and detailing specific areas that need work. In addition, if done with systematic, universally valid tools, collaborative studies can offer opportunities to share data among institutions.

Remedial evaluation. Once a new exhibition is open to the public, remedial evaluation can reveal areas that need further refinements that could not have been anticipated earlier. Remediation can also be done of older exhibitions scheduled for renovations, existing galleries with collections that do not have any interpretive labels, or labels that need to be updated to reflect current information or standards of inclusivity.

In Praise of Small Sample Sizes

Often museum practitioners who have not done much evaluation ask, "How many people do you need to have in your sample?" They are probably thinking of the types of marketing studies that require thousands or at least hundreds of samples. The answer depends in part on what you are trying to find out (what your question is), how varied visitors' answers are, and how you plan to use the information or data.

Most front-end and formative evaluations can be informed by small sample sizes. For example, consider the question "Do visitors understand the term '*baroque*,' and can we use it in our labels without defining it?" This could be answered by testing a large sample (n = 200) to enable you to make a generalization about the museum's audience; that is, what percentage of the people understand the word. If that percentage is large enough, you might go ahead and use the term, making your decision based on numerical, or quantitative, data. On the other hand, a small sample (n = 20) could be interviewed to get qualitative data about what words visitors associate with "*baroque*." Developers can then use that information to write sensitively, weighing whether it is necessary for visitors to understand the precise definition on a case-by-case basis when the word is used. Many front-end and prototyping evaluation decisions are based on qualitative information gathered from small samples of interviews or observations.

The decisions made for one exhibit cannot usually be transferred to a new situation however, because each specific exhibit situation has its own unique set of variables. Only after doing lots of small evaluation studies and reading about studies done by others can museum practitioners build up a personal base of knowledge that allows them to make informed critical judgments about new situations. Too often, however, there is a tendency to jump to conclusions about all visitors based on one case study or even a single anecdote (n = 1). When you hear your colleagues say, "Everyone did X" or "No one did Y," be suspicious: They are probably generalizing inappropriately. Ask them, "What data was this conclusion based on?"

PROTOTYPING IN ITS VARIOUS FORMS AND FUNCTIONS

Understanding more thoroughly and specifically what visitors think, feel, and know requires some form of data gathering. Even something as simple as a label that lets visitors know they can touch an object or an iPad will require some form of testing, and it might take several versions to get to the right one. The rest of this chapter focuses on the methods and benefits of prototyping as it relates to evaluating one label, a single exhibit element, or ideas for a whole exhibition.

Testing Label Copy with Visitors

The protocol can be like this: Select a visitor and read them your recruitment statement, which should include describing what you are asking them to do, why, and how long it will take. If they agree, show them the label (hand it to them, or ask them to look at where it is posted) and ask them to read it to you (or to others in their group) out loud. If they say, "The whole thing?" consider going back to your desk and editing the label to reduce the word count before you test it again.

Testing Introductory Labels

Introductory label copy sets the stage for visitors' curiosity and expectations. The first thing to do is get the label to the point where the developers are satisfied with it. There is no point in testing something you know has problems; you'll be wasting your time and visitors' as well. You should be evaluating something you like and think is good.

Do your best to lay out the text as you'd like to see it in its final form in the gallery, down to paragraph breaks and line lengths. Now enlarge it to an approximation of the full size to be used in the exhibition. It won't be the final design, but text editing and style issues that have not been worked out in the rough drafts of the label text will become obvious when the label is made larger and placed in its context. It's amazing what you notice in the full-size mock-up that you overlooked while the label was on the computer screen.

Before asking visitors to review the label, ask yourself:

- Is the text organized in "chunks"—that is, one separate thought at a time?

- Are there natural line breaks, with one phrase or sentence per line?

- Does it look easy to read? (Big enough? Short enough?)

- Are there visuals that would help communicate the ideas?

When the label is ready to test, questions such as these can be asked of actual visitors as they react to the inexpensive mock-up:

- Do they like it?

- Do visitors still have trouble with any technical terms or words with double meanings?

- Do they think it's fun?

- Do they understand it?

- Do they find it meaningful?

■ Does their understanding coincide with (or at least not contradict) your stated communication objectives for the element?

Testing Caption Labels

When writing captions, the writer should have the real thing being captioned, or at least an image of it, in front of them as they create the draft. When testing the prototype, users should also be shown what is being captioned. Many of the questions to ask yourself before testing with visitors are the same as the ones for the introductory label, but probably a little less complicated.

Testing Labels for Interactive Exhibit Elements

The main purpose of prototyping an exhibit element is to test whether it communicates its intended message and engages visitors in positive outcomes. For interactive exhibit elements, prototyping is essential to success. You begin by cueing visitors—asking them to look at the mock-up, and use it, for as long as they want and then talk with you about it afterward. Visitors, often happy to help, are willing to ignore the crudeness of paper mock-ups and taped-together versions of an interactive. Handmade prototypes look informal, inexpensive, and easy to change. If the quality is too high, visitors might get distracted by some aspect of the design that isn't part of the issue being tested, or be less willing to give open and honest feedback because they think the prototype is already finalized and they don't want to hurt your feelings by being critical. Remember, you are testing the exhibit's ability to communicate the content, not the aesthetics of the label or device. Testing and retesting with inexpensive versions and rapid prototyping, making improvements at each iteration, is far preferable to sinking big bucks into one glitzy prototype. The main purpose of this type of prototyping is to test the ability of the exhibit element to get its point across.

Single interactive exhibit elements can be tested alone, or a group of interactive exhibits can be tested together in a dedicated space. Group testing is helpful when the elements have similar themes or design features. Some museums set aside a space or designate a room full-time for testing prototypes.

Prototyping interactives helps answer questions about mechanics, instructions, content, and visitors' intuitions. Your checklist should include the following:

■ Do label instructions start with what the visitor should do first?

■ Can visitors correctly figure out how and where to start the activity in 1.5 seconds or less?

- Is the reaction or response of the interactive intuitively clear to visitors?

- Can people follow the directions? Are the directions communicated in three or fewer steps?

- Can visitors figure out what to do without reading anything?

- If visitors act intuitively, without reading the directions, are they doing the right thing?

- Do visitors' actions reflect and/or imitate the phenomenon or concept?

- Is the reset or reaction time what it needs to be (fast enough, slow enough)?

- Do the words in the label accurately describe and/or name the structures (mechanisms) of the exhibit?

- Do the words in the label match (accurately describe and/or name) the actions and activities the visitor engages in?

- Are symbols, graphics, and/or animation needed to clarify or model the actions and structures or mechanisms?

- Does the challenge of doing the activity match most visitors' skill levels while also requiring them to "stretch" a little?

- Is visitors' attention focused, and are visitors absorbed in the experience?

- Do people feel anxious about the content or setting?

- Does it function mechanically without breaking?

- Does it function mechanically without hurting someone?

Many of the above questions should be discussed by the exhibit developers and label writers before testing begins to focus the team on the issues that formative evaluation can inform.

Mock-ups of interactive elements can reveal the need for changing the position of one object or substituting one word. A seemingly small tweak might be the difference between visitors' misunderstanding and comprehension. For example, prototyping of a bird wing exhibit revealed that visitors could make comparisons between bird feathers more easily when the examples were of wings from the same side of the bird: comparing a right wing feather from one bird with the right wing feather from another. In another case, two samples of elephant hide (one real, one fake) had to be dyed the same color so that visitors could concentrate more easily on texture and pattern, which were the relevant factors.

Visitors' reactions to mock-ups will predict, but not give complete assurance of, the exhibit's communication effectiveness in its finished iteration. The variables of context, final design, sightlines, lighting, and other factors will contribute to its success in the end. Prototyping can, however, definitely lead to a greater sense of confidence that the exhibit will work in its final installation.

Observe, Refine, Test Again, and Report the Results

When visitors don't understand a label or how to operate an interactive, some museum practitioners jump to the conclusion that either the visitors were stupid or the exhibit wasn't meant for them. But if visitors were commenting on the mount the object was sitting on instead of the object, there's something wrong with the exhibit, not the visitors. When visitors do the "wrong" thing, it's most likely because the exhibit prompts the "wrong" behavior rather than providing the conditions for the appropriate behavior.

Many ergonomic factors can only be determined by observing visitor behaviors. If visitors are using exhibits in inappropriate ways, careful observations can often reveal why, and solutions will present themselves. Often the first impulse, when users do not follow the right steps, is to add another label to explain it. It's better to try another version of the initial label, and if none achieve the desired results with visitors—i.e., more or different words are not the answer— a redesign of the interactive will be needed.

Unless there is good communication within the whole exhibit team, findings from prototyping might never be seen by the designer, especially if the exhibit is being designed by outside consultants. The ease of keeping people on track and up to date on a fast-moving design schedule is inversely proportional to the number of people involved and the distance between their desks. Sharing files online is a good idea, but it still relies on people taking the time to read them. If possible, get designers and developers out on the floor to help observe visitors and collect the data that will be used to make decisions.

Prototyping as Conceptual Development

Kathy McLean uses a newer form of prototyping to develop exhibits in which the target of the activity is the whole exhibition, not just a caption or an interactive element. For her, prototyping is not just about the object or exhibit or experience itself—it's a way of working, a philosophy and set of values, a process of inquiry. She shared her thoughts:

> As you test out your ideas and exhibit techniques with visitors, you will engage them in a conversational process that will help you make better, more informed decisions and more compelling exhibitions. It's an iterative conceptual design process. Design the mock-up, talk to visitors, redesign based on visitor input. Some elements will only need one round of testing before it is clear that visitors are engaged and understand your intentions. Other elements may need two or three or four iterations of a design before you are comfortable with the outcomes. And in the true spirit of experimentation, you will find that some ideas don't work, no matter how many times you rework them. I personally think this is the best way to develop exhibitions.

Based on their experience, the authors agree that prototyping can facilitate quick decision-making and help avoid costly mistakes, and that visitors enjoy participating in the process because they feel that their opinion is valued and can make a difference.

Other Resources

For a broader discussion of prototyping and front-end and formative evaluation and suggestions that might answer many of the questions and issues raised in this chapter, see the books *Try It! Improving Exhibits Through Formative Evaluation*; *Doing It Right: A Workbook for Improving Exhibit Labels*; *and User-Friendly: Hands-On Exhibits That Work*.

Reports on the website for Informalscience.org are good models for how to conduct a prototyping session that can be mastered by in-house staff. Outside consultants can lead training workshops and establish how-to manuals for your museum.

Institutional Objections to Prototyping

Although museum exhibit staffs systematically ramped up evaluating and prototyping of their exhibits beginning in the 1960s, some directors and museum boards have been less than sympathetic to the goals and costs (in time and money) of evaluation. They reason, "Well, you are the expert exhibit designer, why do you need visitors to tell you what to do?" Even though the prototyping process is an intuitive and logical way to experiment with creating better exhibitions, it often faces the following institutional barriers:

- First, there's the tyranny of tradition that governs the exhibition design and formalized label-writing processes. Prototyping requires an openness to discovery and the flexibility to be able to follow strange paths that might open along the way. Staff members who have spent years formalizing curatorial, design, and label-writing processes may feel that the informality of prototyping undermines their roles and the efficiency of in-place systems.

- Second, there's the specter of authority and control. It is difficult, if not impossible, to do authentic prototyping if those in charge want to limit the ideas or control the outcomes.

- Third is the fantasy of perfection. So many museum professionals believe that high production values, pristine labels, refined materials, and carefully controlled finishes are what visitors expect from museums. Most museum staff complaints about prototyping are that the process is ugly and messy and that visitors will be disappointed. And that is rarely the case. More often, visitors are so delighted to be asked their opinion of an exhibit or an idea, that the last thing on their minds is perfection.

- Perhaps the most slippery criticism is the argument that prototyping will disrupt the exhibition schedule and undermine the budget. We suggest: Plan for it. Budget for it.

Fast and Flexible

We have seen in this chapter how prototyping during the planning and design phases of creating an exhibition gives exhibit developers information while there is still flexibility in the process and time to make changes. Once the exhibition opens, there is usually little or no staff, time, or money available for remedial fixes. Unfortunately, the reverse is true of the evaluation schedule and budget, which often specifies one big final summative evaluation after the exhibition is installed and open. While evaluations done after opening may have implications for the future, they often have less practical value than front-end or formative studies conducted during development, from which recommendations can be implemented immediately. Prototyping rules!

At the Providence Children's Museum, the exhibit team went all out for prototyping as they developed new immersive installations, reporting about it in the Fall 2020 issue of *Exhibition*:

The team utilized a rigorous collaborative design process between developers and designers and with our audience. We committed to a year for the process and a $20,000 budget for this prototyping phase of work. Initially we used low-fidelity prototyping with paper and cardboard, engaging visitors and staff in quick user testing. We also designed and built a movable wall system that allowed us to configure our large public assembly space into smaller pop-up rooms for use with temporary visitor testing.

Prototyping is about making improvements. If all you want is praise, skip prototyping and do a peer review by hand-selected people who will only tell you what you want to hear: "Beautiful installation," "Stunning presentation," "Best collection west of the Mississippi." But if you want to do a better job by your visitors, and you can handle a little constructive criticism, prototyping and other forms of evaluation can lead to making a better match between what you want to achieve and what actually might happen. Learning to ask for—and listen to—criticism is a great skill to cultivate.

21

Typographic and Design Considerations

Because typography affects the legibility, readability, content, mood, and message, label writers and graphic designers must agree on how the type will look in the final production.

Museum labels are in a visual communication class by themselves. Compared with books, magazines, newspapers, and brochures, museum labels are printed in larger type sizes and are meant to be read from a distance by a standing reader. Compared to environmental graphics (e.g., building names, advertisements, directional signage, billboards), labels for outdoor museums such as living history sites, zoos, botanical gardens, and national parks use smaller type sizes, have more text, and must last longer.

Most important, a museum label's role in communication is more complex than the two-part sender-receiver model. There is a third element involved in museums: the object or phenomenon—the "stuff"—the label is about. Interpretive labels are not independent entities. The communication requirements of each label must prevail over the institutional aesthetic or personal style of the designer. This does not mean that the communication intent cannot include a personal look, voice, and point of view. But the designer must keep in mind that the label writer is enabling an experience between the visitor and the object or phenomenon, not just the visitor and the label. A label that gets remembered only for its clever style or progressive typography isn't doing its job.

WHY TYPOGRAPHY MATTERS TO LABEL WRITERS

Typography denotes the style, arrangement, and appearance of the text: the way the letters, words, and spaces are arranged to enhance how a person's eyes and brain see and comprehend the symbols. Although designers are usually the ones who make the final call about typography, most label writers find themselves confronted with typographic decisions at some point. Label writers need to understand at least the basics of typography and legibility because printed words exist as visual and verbal entities to the reader's eye and mind, and the traditions of typography are the basis for creative new ideas. With some working knowledge about typography, writers will be able to communicate their messages most effectively. All too often, the label writer's efforts—researching, writing, editing, testing, editing again, testing again, getting approvals, and delivering final copy—get torpedoed when the designer sets the text on a low-contrast background or makes the type too small.

In her book *Thinking with Type*, graphic designer Ellen Lupton describes four common "typographic diseases," some of which apply to designers of museum labels:

- **Typophilia.** An excessive attachment to and fascination with the shape of letters, often to the exclusion of other interests and object choices. Typophiliacs usually die penniless and alone.

- **Typophobia.** The irrational dislike of letterforms, often marked by a preference for icons, dingbats, and—in fatal cases—bullets and daggers. The fears of the typophobe can often be quieted (but not cured) by steady doses of Helvetica and Times Roman.

- **Typochondria.** A persistent anxiety that one has selected the wrong typeface. This condition is often paired with OKD (optical kerning disorder), the need to constantly adjust and readjust the spaces between letters.

- **Typothermia.** The promiscuous refusal to make a lifelong commitment to a single typeface—or even to five or six, as some doctors recommend. The typothermiac is constantly tempted to test drive "hot" new fonts, often without a proper license.

Although her approach is tongue in cheek, there is truth behind her humor.

DIY? Maybe Not

Computer and desktop publishing programs have put powerful and affordable tools into the hands of amateurs. These programs enable the editing and laying out of label texts on a screen. Now copy can go from the screen to final production without being arranged or designed by a person trained in typography or graphic design. According to exhibit and graphic designer

Gordon Chun, "design-made-easy" is not necessarily good design. Knowledge of basic principles of good typography is necessary to use these tools properly. Just because the computer allows stretching, compressing, slanting, and shadowing—even creating new and unfamiliar letterforms—doesn't mean you should do it.

People without knowledge of typography and design—or people born without "designer genes"—can learn about typography and how to use the computer skillfully, but not without time and effort. Even many graphic designers graduate without a good grasp of typographic design. "It's one of the hardest things to learn, and it takes a long time," says Pasadena Art Center graphic design teacher Rachael Mendez.

The Importance of Typography Cannot Be Overstated

Legibility, readability, appropriateness, design, and effectiveness of texts are all influenced by typography. The elements that make type easy to see (legible) and to read (comprehendible) have been investigated by psychologists, traffic engineers, elementary education specialists, ophthalmologists, researchers for the special needs of the visually or otherwise impaired, and graduate students. These researchers have employed a variety of methods in their investigations, including tests on the effects of distance, counts of eye movements, measures of the rate of blinking and heartbeats when people read, and studies of visual fatigue. Judging from the frequency of tiny print and long line lengths, this research—most of which results in commonsense recommendations—seems not to have widely influenced museum label practices.

We have to remember that visitors can choose to read a label or not. Ellen Lupton reminds us, "In our much-fabled era of information overload, a person can still process only one message at a time. Given the fierce competition for their attention, users have a chance to shape the information economy by choosing what to look at. Designers can help them make satisfying choices." The aesthetics of typography—from typefaces, colors, and sizes to the overall look and feel that the type gives to the design—must be balanced with the reader's need for legibility.

Design Guidelines Are Helpful

The Liberty Science Center's "Interpretive Graphic Standards" is an excellent primer on graphic design in a museum setting. Conduit is the Liberty Science Center's brand font and also serves as the default headline or title font for exhibitions that have not been assigned a special characteristic typeface.

The Getty Museum and the Exploratorium each created guides for gallery texts and graphics, in which they detail the word counts and recommended fonts for standard gallery labels. The Exploratorium advises "keep it clean and clear" and invented a unique font called "Explo" for all gallery text in its new museum. The Exploratorium isn't alone in creating its own font. The Whitney Museum of American Art commissioned Hoefler & Co. to design a unique eponymous typeface in 1996. The Smithsonian's Cooper Hewitt also created a typeface for its late-2014 reopening, recounted in the *Smithsonian* article "To Redesign a Design Museum Start with the Typeface." And the design firm Pentagram created a new font for the National Gallery of Art's rebranding in 2021.

TYPE CONSIDERATIONS FOR LABEL BODY COPY

The context in which labels will be read is an important factor to consider when making typographical decisions. Legibility and comprehensibility will be influenced by choices of typeface, type size, word spacing, letter spacing, line spacing, distance, color combinations, and lighting. The "rules" discussed below are general typographic guidelines for making interpretive labels with beautiful typography, especially for body copy. (Guidelines for titles and headlines follow those for body copy.)

Type Styles and Legible Fonts

Hundreds of typefaces offer excellent legibility for the body copy of museum labels. Styles like Times Roman, Bodoni, Caslon, Century Old Style, and Clarendon have been in use for a long time in books, newsprint, and journals and also work for museum labels. Common questions about museum text include: Should the typeface be serif or sans serif? Is bold better? Which is more legible: black on white or white on black? What size should the type be?

Typefaces: serif or sans serif?

Neither is more legible than the other in all situations. The examples in this book are from a wide variety of museums and seem to contain more sans serif type. The important thing to consider is this: Body copy type should allow the reader's eyes to glide smoothly in horizontal sweeps across the lines of type and find their way to the beginning of each new line easily. Vertical, compressed, or taller-than-wide typefaces, especially some sans serif fonts, can decrease legibility by overemphasizing verticality. Tight spacing between letters and heavy serif faces with small x-height (the distance between the base and midline of the text) can decrease legibility by making the words clump together.

Some serif faces are associated with more classical, sophisticated, or traditional looks. Sans serif faces are sometimes called "clean" or "modern." Trends or fads in typefaces, like fashions, come and go. Helvetica, a face designed in 1957 by Max Miedinger, became popular as a legible body copy style and was practically an industry and government standard for highway and airport signage. Because of its extensive use, the plea "anything but Helvetica" was the slogan in some graphic design circles by the 1970s.

Designer Gordon Chun differentiates between fonts used for exhibit texts and fonts used in print materials. He finds that type on the wall reads better when it is marginally heavier in line weight than type suited for the page. "This is particularly true for serif fonts, where I'm inclined towards traditional typefaces based on Roman serif fonts such as Garamond and Caslon," he says. "Examples of slightly heavy interpretations of these that are good for exhibits are Sabon and Athelas. For sans serif fonts, Helvetica and Univers are the well-traveled options." He adds that more recent typefaces like Avenir and Gotham also work well in exhibits.

Serif or sans serif choices have more to do with style than legibility. Some newer typefaces, such as Stone, have been designed with both serif and sans serif styles as part of the same family. Other designers have created a serif and a sans serif face to be used together, such as Gerhard Unger's Demos and Praxis.

When considering digital labels, earlier screen resolution favored sans serif over serif fonts, because sans serif fonts are simpler in design, with fewer details, and are more legible at low resolutions. The resolution of today's screens is such that either style is equally legible. The Lucida family of typefaces, designed by Charles Bigelow and Kris Holmes, was the first original typeface designed for both digital printers and screens.

Skilled designers mix serif and sans serif text with elegant effect. The design of the text panel should be considered as a whole composition with choices of fonts, colors, and proportion working together to impart the appropriate thematic message. Choose the font that works best for your subject matter. And don't be afraid to mix serifs and sans serifs when it makes sense; that is, when it serves and advances the meaning of the content.

Boldface or regular?

It is not an "or" question, really, because both have appropriate applications. Bold is often used for titles and display type, but it is not often recommended for body copy. For better legibility, consider making body copy bigger rather than bolder.

Typeface choices for label text that only allow for bold styles should be avoided. They will not give you the necessary flexibility for creating contrast between titles and body copy, or between text and credit lines. Also, boldface type takes up more space than regular.

Resist the urge to mix boldface and regular type in the same paragraph, as some people do to highlight certain words or phrases for emphasis. When bold and regular type appear together in the same paragraph, the reader's eyes get hijacked by the boldface words, and they skip over other words and lines of text. The flow of reading is interrupted, and the reader must then backtrack to fill in the skipped words. This slows reading speed and increases reading effort.

On the other hand, there's a style called "bionic reading," wherein typographic designer Renato Casutt suggests making the first letter of most words bold. Casutt reasons that because our brains read more quickly than our eyes, highlighting the initial letters lets the brain complete the word. Developed and trademarked as bionic reading typography, his idea has been around since 2009, but it has not caught on widely at the time of this publishing.

Black on white or white on black? Contrast counts!

Most people prefer to read dark type against a light background. The Americans with Disabilities Act of 1990 (ADA) recommends using as much contrast as possible, which is best achieved with black type against a white background. Reading white or colored type on black backgrounds is more tiring to the eye than the opposite.

If reverse type (light type against a dark background) is necessary for design or aesthetic reasons, a sans serif font may be a better choice. Dark backgrounds can diminish serifs by absorbing them. Making sure body copy is not too dense in the paragraphs will also help with legibility.

Regardless of the choice or combination of colors, the most important thing is contrast. Many museums make the mistake, for aesthetic reasons, of having soft-looking labels, such as white type on a gray background or brown type on tan. This renders the labels less legible than they should be for all readers.

With backlit type (clear letters in black film, lighted from behind), sans serif fonts are preferred. When serif fonts are backlit, the light can obscure or "smear" the serifs. Backlit labels can be very tiring to read because of glare. To reduce eyestrain, put sheets or strips of colored gels (gray, blue, or combinations) behind the type to diffuse the light.

What size type?

This question must be answered in the context of how the type will be used—its purpose, position, color, and lighting. Is it for a title, a caption, or donor information? How far will the reader be from the label? Is it backlit? Almost all book, magazine, and newsprint texts are smaller than 10 points. People reading on personal digital devices can, of course, expand type to comfortable sizes. Not so with printed museum wall texts.

The following are general type size guidelines for caption or group label body copy. Keep in mind that for people with less than excellent vision, these specs are minimums.

Most captions should be printed in 20- to 24-point type unless visitors are likely to be very close to the label. For most people, 18 point is the *minimum* size of body copy type for caption labels that is *comfortably* legible at twenty inches away from a standing position, with good lighting, using dark type on a well-contrasted light background.

For introductory copy, group labels, or texts that will normally be read at a distance of greater than twenty inches, the type size should be 28 to 48 point, depending on lighting, space, color, typeface, and weight. Beyond 36-point type, however, you must consider the physical setting of the label. Bigger is not always better, because large type doesn't "fit" comfortably onto a person's retina at the back of their eyeball. When you are close to large type on the wall, only a few letters fit on your retina and your reading speed is greatly slowed down. These facts are especially relevant to art museums' use of large vinyl letters mounted on walls as introductory information. If the space is not large, visitors will be forced to stand too close to the label, making reading difficult.

The best way to know for sure is by testing actual-size labels in the context in which they will be read (formative evaluation and prototyping). This will resolve many size issues.

Alignment

Ellen Lupton has the following advice about text alignment:

Flush left/ragged right: The left edge is hard, and the right edge is soft.
When it is good: Flush-left text respects the organic flow of language and avoids
the uneven spacing that plagues justified type.
When it is evil: When the editor leaves in excessive hyphenation.

Flush right/ragged left: The right edge is hard, and the left edge is soft.
When it is good: Flush-right text can be a welcome departure from the familiar.
It makes effective sidebars and marginal notes, suggesting affinities
among elements on the page.
When it is evil: Flush-right text can be an unwelcome departure from the familiar,
annoying cautious readers. Punctuation at the ends of lines can weaken
the hard right edge.

Centered: Uneven lines are centered between the left and right edges.
When it is good: Centered text is formal and classical, bearing rich associations
with history and tradition. It invites the designer to break a text for sense and
create an organic shape in response to the flow of content.
When it is evil: Centered text is static and conventional. Used without care,
it looks stodgy, static, and mournful, like a tombstone.

Justified: Left and right edges are both even. When it is good: Justified text makes
a clean shape on the page. When it is evil: Ugly gaps can occur when text is forced
into lines of even measure.

When making choices about alignment for introductory labels or captions,
careful designers will weigh the pros and cons, then create and try out full-size
alternatives before settling on one.

Line Length and Layout: How Many Characters?

Line length (the number of characters per line) and the overall layout of the
body copy will affect legibility. In running text, the reader's eyes must be able to
find their way from the end of one line back to the beginning of the next line.
When a line contains more than sixty characters, it is difficult for readers to
find the continuation of the sentence on the next line. They get lost or confused
(e.g., get started at the wrong line), and their minds will wander. The size,
weight, typeface, space between lines (leading), and number of lines can help
or hinder this movement. Fifty to sixty characters (including spaces) per line is
a reasonable maximum. It's also important to have enough words per line—at
least five is best. Two- to four-word lines of text can look very choppy.

A rule for two columns of type

To reduce the overall line length in a horizontal layout, texts sometimes need to be broken into multiple columns of type. But designers should avoid making a common mistake that can discourage reading: Don't break sentences between two columns of text. Columns that begin in the middle of a sentence interrupt reading. In books or magazines this is not a problem because readers of this kind of text are more "dedicated." Readers in museum exhibitions, however, are scanning rapidly, and many things can distract their attention. It's better to break columns after the end of a sentence. This is especially important for large introductory labels. Writers and designers need to work together to make the text fit and make it easy for readers to see the starting points or jump from one text block to the next. The label writer can edit and rewrite to make unbroken columns. The designer can let the column lengths vary to fit better.

Mixing typefaces and type design

From the time typefaces were invented, typographers have experimented with combining them, making and breaking various rules. Since digital computer type was invented, typographers and graphic designers have gone wild with the possibilities. Being radical, crude, unintelligible, angry, and anything-but-traditional is *de rigueur* for those who push the possibilities of type design. Few rules are sacred, and some designers flout the traditional rules of legibility by intertwining, overlapping, stacking, and distorting type as they explore new aesthetics of tech-expressionistic text. These techniques, easily achieved in a digital medium, create new possibilities for words on the wall. But most of this typographic experimentation is taking place among artists and advertisers, not museum graphic designers. Museum label texts, especially body copy, are not the place to be too avant-garde. Go ahead and play with wild titles and illustrations, but don't mess with the body copy.

TITLES AND HEADLINES HAVE FEWER "RULES"

Guidelines for typefaces in titles and headlines—called display type—are much more relaxed than for body copy. The acceptable variations are greater because headlines contain fewer words (e.g., one to six words, not in a full sentence). Attracting attention is the goal.

For titles and headlines, graphic designers have lots of display typefaces to choose from, or they can make one up. Questions to consider include:

- Does the typeface create the mood or symbolize the meaning of the exhibition in an attention-grabbing header?

- Will it be legible while still looking interesting and intriguing?

- Is consistency necessary for all aspects of the graphic look, including the promotional marketing materials?

Some museums restrict the choice to one typeface and use it for everything. This decision can be unifying in some cases, but very restricting in others. Ask yourself these questions on a case-by-case basis to decide which is best.

Putting It All Together

The more labels in an exhibition, the more concern there should be toward sticking to legibility guidelines and taking a conservative approach. Make labels easy to read. Visitors should not have to work to read the type.

The considerations, guidelines, and tips in this chapter will help an inexperienced writer get started using type creatively and effectively. But they are no substitute for experience or for working with skilled graphic designers.

GRAPHIC DESIGN

Between writing the right words and getting the label fabricated and installed, there is a big step called design. Graphic design does not have its own chapter here because color, layout, sizing, form, balance, and other aesthetic design principles are beyond the scope of this book.

Writers are doing a better job of being more visitor-friendly and writing shorter and more active labels. But the typical errors that result from poor graphic design choices are still too prevalent, such as reflections, shadows, too-small type, type colors with not enough contrast with the background, lack of paragraphs, unintelligible icons, and undecodeable color coding.

Museum exhibit designers and writers have the same goals—good communication—but each brings different sensibilities to bear on finding the best solutions to the problems. Working together will produce the best results. If the text is handed over to a designer and that person makes choices that detract from the meaning or message of the text, well, that's not good design.

According to museum graphics designer Gordon Chun, the best way to confirm that your graphic design is working is to produce life-size physical mock-ups. Viewing type design on the screen or on small-scale printouts from an office printer will not tell you whether the text will be legible in its final installation. Making full-size print mock-ups on paper is essential and easily done. Large-format printers are fairly affordable for institutions, and many retail copy shops have large-format capability at reasonable prices. If possible, try to replicate the conditions of the final installation, including viewing distance, lighting, and color.

Following the suggestions about typography in this chapter and those offered in earlier about label systems, chunking text, using bullets, integrating illustrations, and evaluating, testing, and evaluating again will improve label design. But they do not tell a label writer how to be a graphic designer. For that, hire a good graphic designer.

22

Production Materials and Issues

Low-technology labels can be made cheaply in-house, but the materials, methods, and prices of many other production processes are changing constantly. Environmental impacts must be considered as well.

Methods of making labels are changing quickly. Equipment names and brands come and go; new materials and software programs are being developed as you read this. *Exhibition*, the journal for the National Association for Museum Exhibition (NAME), is a good source for keeping up with changes in fabrication resources for museums. Several online Listservs enable people to ask questions and discuss the latest and best resources, including Museum Marketplace, Conservation DistList, the NAME Listserv, Museum Junction Open Forum Digest and Feedback Fridays from the American Alliance of Museums (AAM), and MuseumTrade.org. Some of these have archived questions, discussions, and threads. Other in-print resources, such as from the Society of Environmental Graphic Designers, the trade magazine *Exhibit Builder*, and the book *Signs, Trails, and Wayside Exhibits* (for materials and methods especially suited to out-of-doors), are useful but may contain out-of-date information.

Most institutions rely on their in-house or contracted designers and fabricators to stay up to date with processes. Exhibit trade shows, like the one at AAM's annual meeting, are a good source of information on the latest production materials.

No matter what label-making process you ultimately choose, the first things to think about and decide on are what size they need to be, what materials will be used, will they need to be laminated, how will they be mounted, how will they be cleaned, what's their expected life span, and will there be a budget to replace or refresh them when necessary. Don't forget environmental considerations within and beyond the museum, including protection for all from health hazards associated with the production of some exhibit materials, especially plastics.

The following are references for sustainable exhibit practices: Greenexhibits.org; Karl Abeyasekera and Geoff Matthews, *Sustainable Exhibit Design: Guidelines for Designers of Small Scale Interactive and Traveling Exhibits*; Jonathan Jager, "Environmental Correctness (EC) for Designers."

KEEP IT SIMPLE AND DIY

For many purposes, simple paper labels will suffice. Mock-ups, temporary exhibits, low-traffic areas, or low budgets can get by with practical paper products. Smaller museums often use local outside graphic fabricators for banners, vinyl title signage, and large text panels. Then they design and produce smaller labels in-house—using the same font and color palette the contracted designer used for the signage—printing them on paper and mounting them on mat board. Paper weight heavier than bond (e.g., forty-pound) works best, but the printer needs to be able to accept it. Various adhesive mounting products—spray-on glue, double-sided tape of different thicknesses—have their advantages, disadvantages, and consequences for removal. Test, experiment, and make choices based on each situation.

Desktop publishing software, or even simple word processing programs, gives label writers the opportunity and the tools to play the role of designer and fabricator as well. Some people may welcome this opportunity and, if they have the talent for it, can find good examples to follow in the sources mentioned above. If you feel confused, unprepared, and overwhelmed by the myriad choices and possibilities, stick to some of the basic typographic guidelines in this book, and seek help from local sign shops or printers.

The *Conservatory Cookbook,* created by the Huntington's Conservatory for Botanical Science, contains advice and directions for making a variety of exhibit labels in-house that, with the right equipment, can survive in high levels of humidity, light, heat, and visitor traffic. Although much of the information is related to plant exhibits, the methods, materials, and exhibit philosophies are widely shareable. A free PDF is available.

A sustainable exhibit design tool kit is available from AAM that can help us do a better job of thinking through the whole life cycle of our exhibits and materials.

Cambridge 7, in partnership with AAM, put out this resource in 2022. They encourage museums to "talk to your vendors and let them know you want more sustainable products up front. They do cost more, but as we (consumers) ask for and buy more, the technology will improve."

Simple Printing and Lamination

The simplest label production method is word-processed text laser- or inkjet-printed on paper and glued to a heavier piece of paper to prevent the label from curling. Bright white, thirty- to forty-pound coated cover stock, letter cover-weight paper, or photo paper all work well. Plain unprotected paper is a good temporary solution. Hang paper labels with one strip of adhesive at the top of the page (not four corners, not all the way around four sides) so that the paper doesn't buckle. It might even last more than a year if mounted in a low-traffic area, but sooner or later unprotected paper will be damaged by dirt and humidity.

Inexpensive adhesive application machines, such as those manufactured by Xyron, allow institutions to easily adhere paper to a firm backing to create a finished label that can be mounted on the wall. Manipulating rolls of clear adhesive requires practice to get the hang of it.

A cover of clear rigid plastic over the face of a paper label gives temporary protection from fingerprints and weathering. Be aware, however, that outdoor signs with simple plastic covers can become dripping displays of condensation or thriving colonies of algae. Furthermore, without lamination, the space between layers collects dirt and provides a hiding place for spiders and cockroaches.

Laminating graphics is more than making a paper-and-plastic sandwich. It involves actual adhesive bonding between surfaces. All types of lamination need to be done with equipment that can make the bonds clean, clear, and strong, without wrinkles or air bubbles. Eight- to ten-millimeter-thick clear laminate with a one-eighth-inch sealed border makes a reasonably durable, inexpensive solution that will even work outdoors for a while. Professional equipment is often the best choice over hand-rubbed laminations.

Information that might be picked up and read by visitors in an exhibition—such as facsimile receipts or menus in a historical museum—can be printed on waterproof and rip-proof paper such as TerraSlate. The hand feel of this product is closer to what it's meant to represent, as opposed to a stiff laminated reproduction.

SOLUTIONS THAT REQUIRE MORE OUT-OF-HOUSE HELP

For longer-lasting labels, permanent installations, and outdoor conditions, most institutions will benefit from establishing a relationship with local fabricators and reputable franchisers or dealers. Staples or AlphaGraphics can combine their skills with your needs at a reasonable price. Call other museums that have similar budgets and compare notes on who and what to use. Ask for and check the references of companies you are not familiar with. The lowest bidder is not automatically the best choice. More than one museum has had a fabricator go out of business in the middle of a project.

Computer graphics software allows the user to compose text and images on the screen with programs such as the Adobe Creative Suite. These can be printed in-house on an inkjet printer or by professional production services with larger, more expensive high-resolution equipment. Before installation, these can be laminated front and back for support and protection. Brilliant colors shown on the computer screen may not be the same as what you will get from the inkjet printer unless the monitor is calibrated to match, and lamination can further cause colors to change. Keeping designs simple (e.g., using three to five colors instead of ten) can help eliminate some problems. To avoid unpleasant surprises, request hard-copy color proof samples of the set of labels and graphics to review and approve before the printer makes the full print run. The samples will show the color and image quality of the printing machines. Keep in mind that these samples will usually incur an additional cost, so budget for it or clarify to the printer that you want hard-copy proofs, not just PDF proofs. Running hard-copy proofs takes additional time, so build that into your production schedule.

Keep the samples from each printer as references. Experimentation, practice, or buying in-house equipment can lead to better predictability for true colors. Also, when producing a set of labels for one exhibition, do all of them in one batch for consistency.

Care should be taken to work within standard size guidelines. Designers should be aware of the factory-determined sizes of paper, plexiglass, plywood, and frames so that they do not design custom graphics that are hard to fit, waste materials and money, or require oversized mounting options. The same four- by eight-foot sheet of material can yield four instead of two pieces, depending on a dimension change of only a few inches. Designers and production crews will get along better when both are willing to consider each other's needs and make compromises for the sake of economics and speed.

Flatbed or Direct Printing

Flatbed printing is an extremely versatile printing process. High-resolution digital images are printed directly onto a wide variety of surfaces, including plastic, paperboard, plywood, film, cloth, canvas, plastic, metal, wallpaper, and even carpet and glass. The only requirement is that the surface be flat. The typical in-house printer size is twenty-four inches wide, which is large enough for many label sizes. For larger jobs, go to a large-format graphics company.

Many designers like to direct print onto the versatile brand of PVC called Sintra because it's lightweight, has a low-gloss surface, is easy to cut in straight or curved lines, and comes in many colors. The strong off-gas odor of older Sintra is not present in the most recent Sintra products. Photographs reproduce well when printed on Sintra, although they have a more vivid look when printed on photo paper.

Direct printing on clear plexiglass is common and simple, but can be problematic:

- If text is screened on the face of the plastic, the letters will cast shadows on the wall behind them.

- When type is screened on the reverse surface of clear plexiglass to protect the letters, you may still get annoying shadows and decreased legibility if the labels are not mounted absolutely flush with the wall surface.

- When text printed on clear plexiglass labels is placed in cases or on top of graphics, whatever is visible behind them can and will cause distraction and decrease legibility.

- "Floating" text by printing directly onto the transparent surface of an exhibit case can be attractive, but only when the background color in or beyond the case contrasts sufficiently with the color of the type.

- Plexiglass labels, front- or reverse-screened, have highly reflective surfaces. Glare decreases legibility and is annoying and tiring.

- Nonglare plexiglass for second-surface mounting of labels offers a level of protection in situations where the labels are part of touchable areas or a hands-on activity, usually on reading rail surfaces.

Shadows behind letters are one of the most common offenses in exhibit design, committed by even by the most experienced and expensive design services. Beware! Only when type is screened on the reverse and then back-painted—usually to match the color of the wall—is clear plexiglass recommended as a substrate.

Mounting

Using cleats on the back of medium-size and large panels has three advantages: It makes the panel stand out from the wall attractively, there is no visible hardware, and the panel is easy to take off or relocate. You have many choices for visible fasteners, but the drawback is that, well, they are visible. Double-sided tape can work for smaller-size labels, but with larger signs or strong tape, when it's time to remove the label, the adhesive tears up the wall. VHB tape is more expensive, but it can be removed without damaging the wall surface.

When considering mounting heights for audiences with children, hang art and mount labels at forty-eight inches on center instead of the typical sixty inches. This provides better visual access for older children and people under five feet tall. This is also a more comfortable viewing height for people in wheelchairs.

Duratrans and Backlit Film

Labels made of color or black-and-white film mounted inside dimensional frames with internal lighting are good choices when front lighting is not appropriate. Aquariums have used backlit labels with photos and texts extensively in galleries where the fish habitats are brightly lighted and the surrounding areas are dark. Backlit film needs to be used with a diffuser or the light will "burn" in one spot instead of being evenly distributed across the sign. LED tubes give a more even light. Commercial light boxes can be purchased with their own internal lights.

More modern production for backlit signs involves a single sheet of translucent material with graphics printed directly on it and lighted with LEDs. The renovated labels for the dioramas in the dark halls of the American Museum of Natural History have individual rheostat controls so the brightness of each sign can be adjusted to its own situation.

Digital Screens

By 2015, small and large digital screens were making their way into museum galleries, and digital labels are used exclusively in some exhibitions. Their high initial cost can be offset by the ease of making changes to label text and layout, but there needs to be vigilant staff support for making edits and updates a reality.

Small interactive digital screens, such as iPads, allow visitors to touch, swipe, and scroll content for deeper exploration, for playing exhibition- or collection-related games, and even for contributing visitor-generated content.

Locking the screens to one particular use or getting an iPad to ignore alert messages such as updates can pose issues. Other considerations include securing devices to avoid theft or tampering, providing a reliable power source, cleaning the screens, and, in some cases, depending on the use, accessing a dependable Wi-Fi connection.

Formative evaluation and prototyping are key in designing apps that visitors will find attractive and easy to use and that will provide meaningful experiences beyond the novelty of a screen to play with. The evolution of the successful use of iPads and other digital interactives happens when museums share their lessons learned. Some people have found that tablets by manufacturers other than Apple have software that programmers can work with more easily than that on iPads. The annual MuseWeb (formerly Museums and the Web) conferences offer a trove of information through past talks and articles posted online.

Cut Vinyl

Computerized vinyl-cutting machines are popular for making durable indoor or outdoor signs. Vinyl comes in a wide array of colors, has a strong adhesive bond, and can be put onto a variety of smooth surfaces. Cut vinyl comes as pre-spaced letters, words, and sentences. Choose typefaces that do not have fine serifs so that the job of peeling letters off the carrier sheet will be easier. Usually, the letters are already on a transfer sheet, ready to be applied.

Simple graphics, such as silhouettes, geometric shapes, or a collage effect, can also be made in digitally cut vinyl. Skillfully combined text and illustrations can make colorful, relatively inexpensive, and attractive labels for museums. In an art exhibition, quotations made with vinyl labels in larger letters applied directly on the wall above the paintings make the text easy to read for visitors standing back from the pictures.

On the other hand, the use of vinyl letters can pose several problems involving size, location, and time:

- *Too small.* The machines can cut letters in sizes down to about one-quarter inch tall, but body copy at that size does not look good in boldface. Running text in small sizes is also very difficult to lift off the carrier sheets. Some sign makers have devised ingenious ways of "weeding" (removing the tiny insides of letters like "*e*" or "*a*"), but for the inexperienced person it can be a messy, tedious headache.

- ***Too touchable.*** Avoid applying vinyl letters on surfaces where visitors can reach them easily. As soon as one little corner of the vinyl gets lifted away, people are invariably attracted, almost unconsciously, to peel them away more. Missing letters not only make reading difficult but also make the exhibition—and, by extension, the museum—look badly maintained.

- ***Too many words.*** Art museums are especially enamored of using vinyl letters for large, long introductory labels containing hundreds of words and multiple paragraphs. It can take the designer too many hours to prep the wall and burnish all those words, and it can take visitors too many minutes to read them.

Make sure to let the vinyl type vendor know the type of wall(s) and the paint finish the vinyl labels will be applied to (matte, flat, eggshell, etc.) so they know what type of vinyl material and adhesive to use. And keep in mind that even if the vinyl letters are not tampered with, peeling may still occur because of humidity and insufficient adhesive.

The *Exhibition* journal has a good article about using vinyl type, "A Beginner's Guide to Vinyl Lettering Systems." You can pick up other production tips there and at NAME's occasional regional workshops. There's a nice instructive YouTube video of designer Matt Isble taking a day to complete a large introductory label for *The Edge of Elegance* at the Crocker Art Museum. The perennial advice is to use cut vinyl for what it does best: making headlines in large type with few words and on surfaces far from people's hands.

LABELS THAT WILL LAST OUTDOORS

Outdoor products have three desirable characteristics: They can be colorful, durable, and inexpensive. Pick any two. Because of their one-of-a-kind, text-heavy, small-typography requirements, the production of outdoor interpretive labels poses exceptional challenges compared to that of directional signs, logos, or name-only ID placards.

It is important to match the type of process to the life expectancy of the label. If the label is going to be up for a long time, it may be worth investing in something durable. This also has implications for sustainable design. Sometimes the "greener" choice is not as durable, but the less-green choice ends up being better for the environment because it won't need to be replaced.

Colorful, durable signs that are fiberglass embedded or made of porcelain enamel are not cheap. Durable, less expensive, photographically processed metal products, typically used for botanical garden plant name labels, lack color choices. Colorful, inexpensive paper products (such as color photocopying) will not last long outside, although colored pencil resists UV fading remarkably. Even when laminated, they will need to be replaced often due to fading or humidity. But frequent replacement might not be objectionable, especially if updating information is necessary or desirable.

Fiberglass Embedment

Embedding digitally printed labels in clear fiberglass makes a very durable, lightweight, and colorful outdoor sign. Fiberglass embedding was supposed to be the real deal, but it did not live up to the promises made by manufacturers—it degraded, fractured, and faded much faster than expected. The National Park Service used this technique extensively before 2000, but they favor other materials these days. See the NPS website for extensive information and recommendations for its interpretive wayside design and production.

High-Pressure Laminate (HPL) Panels

To create these panels, digitally printed paper is impregnated with a thin layer of resin and attached to a resin-impregnated substrate through intense pressure and heat. The process fuses the layers into a very durable panel. HPL panels allow bright, vibrant graphics and excellent UV protection. They are graffiti and scratch resistant, and do not rust. HPL products have warranties for ten years at Fossil Industries and twenty years at iZone Imaging.

Porcelain Enamel

Advances in enameling techniques provide excellent quality and durability for text and four-color-process photographs, but initial costs may be very high, depending on the manufacturer and number of signs produced at one time. Porcelain enamel is weather and UV resistant, but, because it is a form of glass, it can be shattered by intentional or accidental impact. Also, porcelain enamel signs are heavy and require a separate substrate to mount them.

Polyvinyl Chloride (PVC)—No More?

An exhibits fabrication company in the Chicago area, Proto Productions, has been producing graphics for indoor and outdoor installations for decades. It has tried a variety of materials and found advantages and disadvantages to them all. One favorite was the clean-looking, almost bulletproof PVC (polyvinyl chloride) panel with colorful, fade-resistant acrylic polyurethane paints and silkscreen inks that form chemically bonded adhesions. Clear finishes protected the face from graffiti, the panels did not require special framing or covers, and they could be fabricated in any shape. Unfortunately, silk-screening and PVC have proved toxic under some manufacturing processes and applications. Today, Ken Hopkins, president of Proto Productions, has switched to direct or flatbed digital printing almost entirely. Keeping up with the technology, he says, is a daily practice.

Etched Metal and Engraved Plastic

Photosensitive metal plates are commonly used by botanical gardens for small labels to identify plant species. Larger plates can be used for interpretive labels that last well out-of-doors and are relatively inexpensive to produce. Most common are black with silver or gold letters. They last a long time, even in harsh environments. Newer production methods use lasers and can produce labels with more colors.

Engraved plastic labels are also common in botanical gardens, and they have the same advantages and disadvantages as photo metal. They are relatively inexpensive and durable, but they come in limited colors and have limited capacity to show illustrations.

Direct digital printing will probably, if it has not already, become an economical and more versatile alternative to both methods.

Cast Metal

Heavy, long-lasting historical markers and donor plaques are often made of cast metal, probably because this material conveys a permanent, historically significant solemnity. Sparse graphic options and limited choices for typefaces and type sizes, plus high cost, make cast metal less suitable for an exhibition consisting of many different interpretive signs. Theft might be another problem with bronze and aluminum, which are valuable when melted and reused.

MAINTENANCE AND UPDATING

Plan for upkeep and corresponding budgets when choosing materials for indoor and outdoor labels for any "permanent" exhibition. The life span of a set of labels should be estimated at the outset and budgeted for so that in five or ten years, the need for new or replacement labels will not be a surprise.

Touchable and Replaceable?

When labels are on reading rails outside cases, visitors can interact with them more directly by running their hands along text as they read or pointing and touching parts of a label as they call a friend over to see what they have read. Rubbed-off letters indicate that visitors have been using them. Why not replace them with materials that can withstand and invite their use?

Labels on accessible reading rails outside of cases, vitrines, or dioramas have an added benefit of letting exhibit teams test them as mock-ups before final installation. Labels out of reach inside cases prevent this flexibility.

No Such Thing as Vandal-Proof

Nothing has been invented yet that is vandal-proof, but some materials are more resistant to intentional damage than others. Polycarbonate covers over signs may keep vandals from marring the original surface, but scratched or graffiti-covered covers look bad too.

Sustainable Exhibit Materials

Sustainable, or "green," design is commonly defined as something that meets the needs of the present without compromising the ability of future generations to meet their needs. The basic principles include minimizing resource consumption and reducing pollution. This is a constantly shifting arena, and new products, procedures, and philosophies are emerging at a rapid pace.

There are many ways to incorporate a sustainable approach to label design. You can start small, using paints that are less toxic and products that are recycled and can be recycled. Companies that manufacture paints, plastics, and adhesives—under the watch of the Environmental Protection Agency (EPA) and the Occupational Safety and Health Agency (OSHA)—are continually striving to produce safe, economical, long-lasting materials.

DON'T FORGET TO PROTOTYPE

After production, fabrication, and installation, it is time to step back and evaluate. Too often, time and money have already been used up, and the exhibition team has collapsed from exhaustion. The last thing they want to know is that something is not right. A better approach is to do plenty of cheap full-size paper mock-ups of the labels you plan to contract out for expensive production before the design phase is finished. Think of prototyping as one more good opportunity to improve the exhibition's communication ability—and then bask in the praise of satisfied visitors and admiring peers.

23

Evaluation After Opening

Summative evaluation of exhibitions tells you what worked as expected; what unexpected but appropriate outcomes are occurring; what did not work; and (maybe) what to do about it.

No matter how hard you try or how experienced you are, or how much prototyping you did of individual exhibit elements, you won't know how the whole exhibition will look, feel, and work until you have it up and running. It will not take a professional evaluator to tell you what the exhibition's major strengths and weakness are, because many of them will be obvious. But finding out the degree to which an exhibition is accomplishing its objectives in an overall context will require some form of systematic analysis.

Summative evaluation of an exhibition can take many forms, including in-person exit interviews, questionnaires, unobtrusive tracking and timing of visitors' behavior in the exhibition, before-and-after discussions with users, and follow-up phone interviews with visitors to see what they recall. Data is collected and analyzed quantitatively and qualitatively, depending on the nature of the data and the type of report produced. Sample sizes of the number of visitors questioned, surveyed, or observed usually run between n = 50–100 to give a high rate of confidence in the findings. These are larger than front-end or formative studies but smaller than that of market research (n = 1000s).

Effective Labels Are Key to Effective Exhibitions

Summative evaluation of labels does not have a special strategy separate from summative evaluation in general. But keep in mind that interpretive labels contribute greatly to the overall impact and effectiveness of exhibitions. It can be argued that many of the problems revealed in evaluation findings are grounded in, relate to, are caused by, and contain missed opportunities for visitors to apprehend exhibit labels in the designed environment. That is, the words are there—on labels for wayfinding, introductions, titles, interpretation, captions, and instructions—but too often visitors can't, don't, or won't see them or didn't understand them. This is because the labels were inconveniently placed, too small, poorly written, not well lighted, or not attractively designed. All of these variables are under the control of exhibit makers. Many of the biggest challenges for exhibitions—orientation, boundaries, utilization, communication—are intricately and inextricably linked to the apprehendability of texts.

SUMMATIVE EVALUATION FOR REMEDIATION PURPOSES

After an exhibition has opened, a careful walk-through review by exhibit team staff, stakeholders, and/or peers can reveal weaknesses or omissions that can often be fixed with relative ease. This is called *remedial evaluation*. Minor changes in label copy can sometimes make a dramatic difference, and it's easy to do if the labels are produced in a modular or correctable format (e.g., computer-printed, laminated, or dry-mounted paper labels). Labels printed directly on the walls or inside cases are more difficult to fix. Consider making and installing labels in easily replaceable formats, at least for an opening phase of the exhibition.

Leaving money in the budget to evaluate and fix what needs fixing after an exhibition opens carries the iterative process of exhibit development to its logical and complete conclusion. Although you can never fix everything that needs fixing, whatever you can make better will benefit everyone. Fixable things should be fixed sooner, not later, because with every day that passes, more visitors are confused or disappointed, and exhibits are ignored that could otherwise be successful. Even fixes that look temporary are better than none, because they say to visitors, "We care about making this work better for you."

Some but not many museums allocate 10 to 15 percent of the exhibition's budget for remedial evaluation. Setting money aside at the beginning of the process acknowledges that the exhibit planners expect to discover important information about the design and presentation of the exhibition after it all comes together. Some of the best solutions to exhibit problems will not be apparent until after opening. Therefore, remediation is money and effort well spent.

Problems with orientation, wayfinding, and traffic flow or circulation can be rectified by the addition of banners, introductory labels, arrows, maps and floor plans, baffles, lighting, or directional signage. New illustrations or photographs can be added to supplement texts, and labels can be repositioned to strengthen conceptual relationships.

When practiced repeatedly over the years by the same institution, remedial evaluation can lead to a shared knowledge of ways to improve many aspects of exhibit design in-house. For example, as exhibit developers at the Field Museum responded to the results of summative evaluations of their phased diorama hall projects, the clarity of later-phase floor plans and interactive instruction labels improved. But if evaluation results, findings, reports, and lessons learned are not shared, the benefits can be lost.

MULTIPLE-METHOD APPROACHES TO SUMMATIVE EVALUATION

Summative studies provide a good opportunity to use more than one technique to find out how well the exhibition is working. Using several strategies—like the ones that follow—to look at the same exhibition will give stakeholders (exhibit developers, funders, administrators) a more thorough perspective about how the exhibit is being used and what visitors are taking away with them.

The informal nature of museum learning calls for measures that challenge evaluators and educators to define learning broadly and to ask visitors holistic, contextual, and open-ended questions.

Find Out What Visitors Do *and* Say, Not Just What They Say

Many evaluators use exit surveys or interviews to learn what visitors found memorable, enjoyable, and meaningful. In addition, unobtrusive observations of visitors as they use exhibitions can answer questions that won't be self-reported as fully or accurately. For example, few visitors would be able to recall the names of all the exhibit elements they stopped at in an exhibition or which labels they read, but they may be taking away some tacit knowledge, even based on a brief exposure. By observing the number of visitors who stop at each exhibit element and engage in certain learning-related behaviors (reading labels, talking, pointing), practitioners can get information critical for constructing a picture of total exhibit use by visitors.

The tried-and-true methods of tracking and timing and exit interviews or questionnaires are the most basic and useful tools for gathering data on visitors' responses to an exhibition. At the minimum, they should be used for all summative evaluations to assess the degree to which the exhibition has achieved its objectives of attracting and holding visitors' attention and to determine how visitors have been impacted in positive, negative, and unexpected ways. This requires that exhibit developers articulate these objectives during the planning stage. Or at least articulate their objectives at the end for the purposes of evaluation. Better late than not at all.

Data from exit questionnaires or interviews about what visitors think sometimes reveal discrepancies with observational data about what visitors did. Over the years of watching and listening to visitors, evaluators realize that when visitors self-report upon leaving an exhibition that they read "most of the labels," they are probably saying that they read as many as they wanted to. For this reason, questions about how visitors used exhibit labels should be answered by watching them, not just asking them.

In a thorough study of the traveling exhibition *Darkened Waters: Profile of an Oil Spill*, a combination of data was gathered from visitor comment cards, unobtrusive tracking and timing, structured exit interviews, open-ended interviews at specific exhibit elements, and questionnaires filled out by cued visitors, who were asked to look at the exhibit and answer questions afterward. In addition, peer review and critical appraisals were conducted at the exhibit's original venue, the Pratt Museum, in Homer, Alaska, and at subsequent venues as it traveled.

The data from these multi-method evaluations showed that people responded to *Darkened Waters* positively and appropriately:

- Visitors moved through the exhibit slowly and thoroughly.

- They read many of the labels, and they used several of the interactive devices repeatedly.

- On exiting the exhibition, visitors remembered general ideas (the main communication goals) from the exhibition, and they reported learning specific new concepts, making new connections, and finding personally relevant meanings in specific elements of the exhibit.

The benefit of doing multi-method summative studies is learning about the successes as well as the missed opportunities of the exhibition's endeavor.

The open-ended cued questionnaire

During the evaluation of *Darkened Waters*, a new type of cued exit questionnaire was developed that captured rich verbal indicators of meaning-making with three open-ended prompts: What do you think is the purpose of this exhibition?

What is something you didn't know or never realized before seeing this exhibit? What did this exhibition remind you of?

Visitors were recruited to participate on their way into the exhibition and were interviewed on their way out. This "cueing" most likely motivates visitors to pay more attention while in the exhibition. The cued method intentionally creates a best-case scenario for the data gathered and shifts the emphasis to the ability of the exhibits to attract and engage rather than assess the outcomes of un-cued visitors, whose normal tendency is to casually browse. Put another way, cueing visitors measures the degree to which the exhibits communicate with a sample of motivated visitors.

This type of written feedback can be analyzed qualitatively or in quantitative, goal-referenced ways. By tallying the percentage of the comments that are specifically related to the communication objectives of the big idea and by assigning a rank (high, medium, low) to each person's sheet overall, the degree to which visitors "got" the communication objectives can be assessed. And if the cued visitors didn't get it, then it's a safe bet that a higher proportion of un-cued visitors didn't either.

This open-ended questionnaire also captures memorable "exhibit echoes"— instances in which visitors remember what they read, did, found out, or saw and then report it so clearly that you can tell where in the exhibit they probably had the encounter.

Unobtrusively observing visitors

Tracking and timing provides numerical data. Time (in seconds or minutes) is a well-understood measure. Counting the number of stops made by visitors at exhibit elements is easy when a "stop" is defined: five seconds, both feet planted on the floor, visitors' eyes looking at the element. This type of data is comparable across different types of museums and exhibitions and reveals the notion of "thorough use" to answer two quantitative questions: To what degree did visitors pay attention to the exhibition? What is the evidence for how much of the exhibition they explored and how much time they spent overall? In addition to time and stops, data collectors can record observed behaviors that indicate engagement, such as reading labels, talking with another person at an exhibit, or pointing to something in an exhibit.

To date, only a few museums have ventured to make these comparisons on a systematic, ongoing basis as part of an in-house exhibit evaluation program.

Why? Many museums are reluctant to set quantifiable goals for their exhibitions other than ticket sales, and they don't want to budget for summative evaluations that might reveal any negative findings. Many museums are content to spend money marketing outputs rather than measuring impacts.

In addition to the qualitative value of numerical data gained through tracking and timing, the careful watching of visitors gives you a much better perspective on several qualitative findings: how hard visitors try, what problems they encounter, and solid clues about how we can make improvements that will benefit their experiences.

Multisite audience comparisons

In a rare multisite summative evaluation of the American Museum of Natural History's traveling exhibition *Global Warming*, the same measurement techniques were used in six different locations. The study looked at the impact of variations in how the exhibition was installed (e.g., different layout of elements), the type of museum (e.g., natural history, science center), and the visitor demographics of the different cities (e.g., average education level). *Global Warming* interview data indicated that visitors from all venues responded rather consistently. Tracking data showed that the same exhibit elements were most popular over all the different sites.

Comparing the timing data among types of museums, however, showed an interesting trend. Visits to the same traveling exhibition were considerably shorter when the venue was a science center compared to natural history museums, as Randi Korn noted in her *Curator* article. And when the Science Museum of Minnesota staff compared their visitors' use of the exhibition *Water* to how the visitors at the American Museum of Natural History used it, they also observed that science museum visitors spent less time. Knowing more about how exhibits are used by visitors in different situations can help us develop better traveling exhibitions.

RECOGNITION FOR EXHIBIT EXCELLENCE: DISCUSSION VERSUS DATA?

Besides widely used summative evaluation methods that involve data gathering, analysis, and report writing to answer questions about how well exhibits work, there are other ways to make judgments about exhibitions. Many museum practitioners resist the suggestion that there should be standards or "best practices" because they think this will encourage sameness and stifle creativity. But without some form of guidelines, characteristics, or even a basic understanding of what is normative, we are adrift with little means of measuring our progress or direction. Fortunately, there are several resources that inform exhibit developers and museum professionals in general, including awards and books. The museum-related publishing business has expanded greatly, so only a few especially relevant sources will be covered below.

Awards for Excellence in Exhibitions

The American Alliance of Museums (AAM) hosts a competition for excellence in exhibitions each year, and the criteria are published online and include references to museum labels. These criteria were developed collaboratively by the AAM committees for curators, educators, and designers, and they have been updated several times. Judges are selected to represent various aspects of exhibition development and are rotated annually. Winners are posted in AAM's bimonthly magazine and in the journal published by the National Association for Museum Exhibition (NAME). One of the main drawbacks to these awards is that judging is based only on written and photographic presentations, as it is logistically prohibitive to require the judges to visit all the exhibitions in person.

AAM's Excellence in Exhibition Label Writing

Separately, AAM's annual Excellence in Exhibition Label Writing Competition brings together writers, editors, and enthusiasts to consider what makes a great exhibit label. The goal of the competition is "to start conversations about the process, purpose, and improvement of the primary tool we use to communicate with visitors."

While the label-writing competition has no published criteria, the writers' intentions and the judges' opinions of the winning labels are shared by NAME on the AAM's website. The free digital archive of past winners is a great resource for examples, inspirations, and grist for informal critique sessions beyond the competition.

As of 2023 the exhibition and label competition guidelines were being reconsidered because AAM disbanded the Professional Networks, including NAME. Stay tuned to the future of these two popular and useful award activities.

Are We There Yet?

The book *Are We There Yet*, subtitled *Conversations about Best Practices in Science Exhibition Development* and edited by Kathleen McLean and Catherine

McEver, is filled with discussions and opinions from many of the silverbacks of the museum field. Don't let the "science" part scare away history or art museum practitioners, because this volume contains helpful ways to think broadly about realistic impacts and expectations for all practitioners. The editors forewarn, "You will not be able to find anywhere in these pages the 'right' way to develop a science exhibition," but the contributors provide lessons learned, raise questions, dispel myths, challenge the notion of "best practices," argue about terminology, and present creative, innovative, and scholarly thinking about exhibitions. Published in 2004, the content is still extremely relevant and deals with perennial issues.

People, Places, and Pursuits

Learning Science in Informal Environments: People, Places and Pursuits is another useful book, developed by the Committee on Learning Science in Informal Environments. The "Science Learning in Designed Settings" chapter doesn't address labels specifically, but the writers do lay out the environmental and learner considerations for successful projects. The information resonates strongly with the term *"intentional design"*—referring to spaces that are designed to immerse, direct, or focus a learner's attention; give cues or prompts for engagement; and are conceived and assessed with a conceptual plan. Despite the title, this book has broad application across different types of museums.

Also of interest is the report edited by Alan Friedman, *Framework for Evaluating Impacts of Informal Science Education Projects*, especially chapter 5, "Evaluating Exhibitions" by Sue Allen.

"The Excellent Judges"

The book *Judging Exhibitions: A Framework for Assessing Excellence* resulted from a collaboration of in-house and consulting exhibit developers in Chicago who worked together for five years to develop the criteria for excellent exhibitions from a visitor-centered perspective. They visited local exhibitions, tried out different criteria and assessment formats, and evolved a final version of an interactive tool that can be used to judge exhibitions. Criteria include accessibility, orientation, transparency, ergonomics, affordances for fun, emotional and social interactions, and meaningfulness—all of which relate directly or indirectly to interpretation.

Originally the group set out to revise the AAM's Excellence in Exhibitions Award process to include having judges visit nominated exhibitions. Ultimately they steered away from AAM's award function and turned instead to a strictly professional-development domain. The main reason for the shift was that, while the members of the group (who affectionately called each other "excellent judges") were able to get solid agreement on what the criteria for excellent exhibitions should be, they could not always agree on the degree to which the criteria were met in an exhibition. The point, they decided, was not to reach consensus or call for a single democratic vote or give an award. The point was to hear other people's opinions and value thoughts that were unlike their own. The end product was not an award; rather, the outcome was the shared experience of listening to the discussion for the benefit of the people who took part in the judging and evaluating process. Probably the biggest unique outcome for users of the Judging Exhibitions Framework is hearing and valuing the opinions of people who they don't necessarily agree with.

More Resources

The Visitor Studies Association, informalscience.org postings of summative evaluations of exhibitions, the American Evaluation Association, Association for Art Museum Interpretation, and the National Association for Interpreters all have resources to share. The *Practical Evaluation Guide* (2016, third edition) is written for museums that want to learn to do it themselves. But we recommend hiring an exhibit evaluation consultant who can lead you through a few workshop training sessions and help set up in-house evaluation strategies structured to meet your needs. This could be done remotely—after an initial meeting—and over time to establish an ongoing relationship, which would be better than a single, one-off study.

Conclusions

All types of museum practitioners can personally benefit from summative evaluation, along with prototyping, remedial evaluation, judging exercises, awards, and competitions. These activities give practitioners a better understanding of the process of developing exhibit interpretive messages and ways for judging the degree to which their goals and intentions were met or even exceeded.

Photo Figures for Part V

CMOS aka *Chicago Manual of Style*

The *Chicago Manual of Style* is an editor's bible during the final stages of label writing. Writers should start with *Exhibit Labels* and other style guides available online.

Prototyping workshop

Exhibit developer Kathy McLean leads a workshop with museum staff and visitors to try out new content and designs.

Updating old labels in an existing exhibition can address issues such as colonialism and inequality in the interpretation.

before

Frogs use their vision to hunt. They have a hard time seeing things that don't move, but are good at seeing fluttering butterflies, crawling spiders, and other moving prey.

We feed our frogs both worms and venison. The frogs see the moving worms , but they can't find the venison until we wiggle it. Stand still and the frog won't see you! If you wiggle, you may become his lunch.

after

Frogs use their vision to hunt, but they have a hard time seeing things that aren't moving.

We feed our frogs both worms and meat. The frogs see the moving worms, but they don't see the meat until we wiggle it.

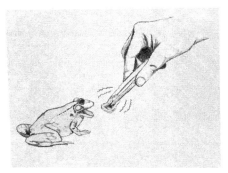

Feeding a frog

How to feed a frog

After an early draft of this label was tested with visitors, several changes were made:

- The first paragraph was shortened.

- "Venison" was changed to "meat."

- The frog photo was replaced with drawing of the action described in the text.

The final draft was shorter, easier to read, more to the point, and a lot more fun.

Scrub the deck

A label commands, "Get on your knees and scrub!" While they are scrubbing, visitors can look up and read a quote from a fictitious nineteenth-century sailor about this miserable task.

Exhibits in *All Hands on Deck* had extensive prototyping and experimentation, resulting in compelling interactives for all ages, including teenagers!

Life-sized nature

JOHN JAMES AUDUBON (1785–1851)
The Birds of America: From Original Drawings

London, 1827–38

Audubon sought to portray birds as they appeared in nature, showing them in their habitat and drawing them from life as well as from posed specimens. To do so, he needed an enormous page: small birds were often shown in flocks, yet large birds, to fit on the page, were illustrated with folded necks or frontally, rather than from the side.

Life-sized nature

The variety of typefaces and sizes in this label clearly separate the different parts: Title; author's name; name of the book and printing date; and a very legible sixty-one-word caption.

The last sentence leads your eyes back to the large Audubon drawings on display to see what the birds' necks look like.

Bridges

DREAMING BIG, BUILDING BIG

Setting out to improve on nature, people constructed massive new bridges across the water. Bridges forever changed how we live on and move around the Bay. We even see the Bay differently—zooming high above the water, we gaze at the distant waves.

Bridges

The readability of this label is due in part to the use of three versions of the same white serif font—bold, all caps, and regular text—against a black background. A compact forty-three words also helps.

THE MASH HOUSE

The malted barley is ground into a coarse powder or 'grist'. This is then mingled with heated spring water to form a thin porridge or 'mash' in which the starch completes its conversion into sugar. The resulting sugary gruel is known as the 'worts' – in a word, worthy of fermentation!

Mash house

At a whisky distillery, the steps of fermentation are elegantly interpreted with classic typography.

Fifty words set with excellent spacing and line lengths enhance the label's readability. Specimens of the products add a nice touch.

EAST OF MT. SHASTA

LARGE EYES HELP PRONGHORN LOOK OUT FOR DANGER

Millions of **pronghorn antelope** once roamed through much of California. Today, only small herds remain. Some of these live in in the brushy grasslands east of Mt. Shasta, where they browse on **sagebrush** and **antelope bitterbrush**.

Adapted to life in open spaces, pronghorn can outrun their predators, sprinting faster than 55 mph. But when they're grazing, they stay alert, pausing often to watch for danger.

Large-eyed pronghorn

This diorama label uses bold words to call out the names of the animals and plants in the scene, thereby serving two functions: identification and interpretation.

Tylosaurus proriger and Plesiosauria indet.
Lived 85–81 million years ago
Niobrara Formation, Logan Co., Kansas

REAL | CAST

Plesiosaur bones found
in mosasaur stomach

In the mosasaur
(above ↑)

In the case
(right →)

Bones found in
plesiosaur stomach

Cretaceous

THREE ANIMALS, TWO MEALS, ONE FOSSIL

This rare fossil preserves **stomach contents** that show one part of a Cretaceous marine food web. The large bones of a plesiosaur (a marine reptile) to your right were **found inside the ribcage** of the *Tylosaurus* in front of you. They have tooth damage and pitting made by *Tylosaurus*'s stomach acids. The **smaller bones come from a third species**—probably the plesiosaur's last meal.

The mosasaur *Tylosaurus* chases a group
of ammonites in Late Cretaceous Kansas.

One fossil

Bold words don't always contribute to quick and easy comprehension of the label's purpose or meaning. After the catchy title here, confusion reigns.

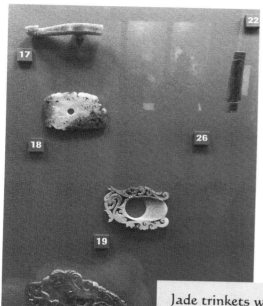

Jade trinkets were only for the rich and powerful

To the elite of the new empire, wearing and using jade in daily life were unmistakable signs of status. Different colors of jade indicated a person's rank; white jade was reserved for the emperor.

These flat, elaborate jades with center holes are pendants, made to be strung with beads and hung from the waist, neck, or shoulders. The dragon-head shape of the green belt hook was popular in the Han period and for centuries afterwards.

17 Belt hook
Han period, 206 B.C.–A.D. 220
1926.1669.183181

18 Pendant
Han period, 206 B.C.–A.D. 220
1910.1114.116553

19 Pendant
Han period, 206 B.C.–A.D. 220
1926.1669.183048

20 Pendant
Han period, 206 B.C.–A.D. 220
1910.1114.116555

Jade trinkets

When objects are placed far from the labels that identify them, legible numbers make the connection easier. But it's always more work for visitors when the words are not next to the objects.

Bending with bifocals

Labels placed too low with type too small puts a strain
on people's eyes and backs. This one should at least
be mounted at an angle to bring the label closer to the
reader, like the ones in the background.

Panel with cleats

Large panels mounted with cleats are easy to hang,
and no hardware is visible from the front.

Bedrock

Removal might be the best option when a label has
deteriorated to this extent.

The life span of a label, especially when placed
outdoors, should be calculated in the planning process,
along with replacement schedules and budgets.

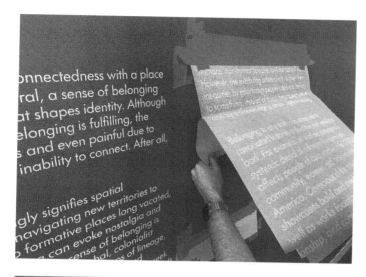

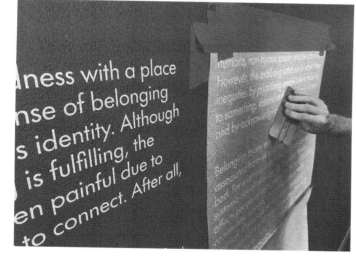

Putting up vinyl letters

The task of installing vinyl lettering involves positioning, peeling off the backing, rubbing down the letters, then peeling off the facing.

For a 350-word introductory label, this task is time consuming, difficult, and tedious. If writers had to do it, would they write less?

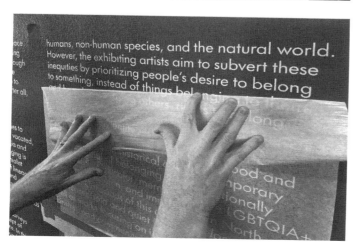

Vinyl letters rubbed off

If vinyl letters are within hands' reach, beware.

Data collector

A data collector watches visitors as they spend time looking at and reacting to the exhibits (or not).

The data will reveal the exhibits' abilities to attract and hold visitors' attention and whether visitors are reading, pointing at, and talking about the labels.

This is an actual nestling albatross that was found dead at the breeding grounds on Midway Island. An autopsy showed it to have plastics that may have contributed to its early death.

Dead albatross

Visitors reacted to this dead albatross with shock and sympathy, as well as curiosity about the impact of plastic on the ocean environment. Visitors saw what happened to the bird, and the label concisely reinforced it.

Exhibit labels competition

Winners of the 2019 Excellence in Label Writing competition were posted at the annual meeting of the American Alliance of Museums. The 2020 pandemic interrupted this tradition.

An online archive of past winning labels is available, including photos and the judges' opinions. It's a great resource for inspiring ideas about content and design as well as the helpful exercise of critiquing exhibit labels.

PART VI

Voices from the Field

Voices from the Field

This book came together thanks to many contributions from practitioners in the museum field, who gave us their time, answered our questions, showed us around their exhibitions, and much more. We have included some of their personal reflections here. For context, the authors are identified with the institutions where they worked at the time they submitted their writing to us.

Their stories are organized into the following thematic categories:

USING THE BIG IDEA
ROBIN GROESBECK, Refining Our Process

REDUCING HARM
RACHEL NICHOLSON and ARIANA CHAIVARANON, Examining Labels
LIZ GARDNER, Interpreting with Care

CHANGING VIEWPOINTS
MARIANNA PEGNO, Multivocal Labels
KRISSY O'CONNOR, Valuing all Perspectives
JESSICA BRAINARD, Confronting Colonialism

TRANSLATION
MEREDITH WHITFIELD, Authentic Voices
IVAN GUZMAN, Dynamic Bilingualism
KATHERINE BAUMANN, Enhancing Understanding

PROTOTYPING
MARC LEVITT, Questioning Paradigms
BETSY LORING, Tweaking for Engagement
AMELIA WIGGINS, Incorporating Community Voices
DEBORAH PERRY, Listening Closely
GORDON CHUN, Mock it Up

CAPTURING EMPATHY
TORI LEE, A Personal Connection
LEE DAVIDSON and LETICIA PEREZ CASTELLANOS, Evoking Other Voices

USING THE BIG IDEA

Refining Our Process

ROBIN GROESBECK, Director, Exhibitions & Interpretation,
Crystal Bridges Museum of American Art, Bentonville, Arkansas

The Big Idea has become fundamental to exhibition development at Crystal Bridges. In my previous experience, using a Big Idea sharpened our focus. But at times we ended up with compound sentences in the quest to be comprehensive. Not everyone was convinced about the power of concision!

As we began planning an exhibition about craft we decided to try a new two-step approach. Prior to the first meeting, we shared information about the exhibition content and asked colleagues to read the Big Idea chapter in *Exhibit Labels* and bring three suggestions for the subject and consequences of the Big Idea.

At the meeting, the project curator, Jen Padgett, gave a thirty-minute overview of key ideas, themes, and works of art. Most people hadn't come with specific words in mind, but the discussion was nonetheless lively.

This powerful process helped us move from:

> "Reassessing the value and excellence of traditional craft art forms opens up American Art to a broadened field of artists, voices, and histories previously hidden from view in the fine art context."

To the more pointed:

> "By highlighting craft, we expand the story of American art to include a more diverse range of artists."

The Big Idea functioned beautifully to guide decision-making. If an interpretive element didn't deepen understanding of craft as a more inclusive medium, it was eventually set aside.

The response from guests was clear: The labels were rated favorably by visitors, who reported that they learned about the diversity of artists making craft objects while in the exhibition. ■

REDUCING HARM

Examining Labels

RACHEL NICHOLSON, Director, Interpretation, Evaluation & Visitor Research, and ARIANA CHAIVARANON, Interpretive Planner, the Nelson-Atkins Museum of Art, Kansas City, Missouri

In the summer of 2020, a renewed call for racial equity in museums prompted the Interpretation team at the Nelson-Atkins Museum of Art to examine our exhibit labels through the lens of reducing harm to people who have been historically underserved by our museum. We collaborated across the museum to build a collective understanding of harm and imagine new ways of inclusive and equitable storytelling.

Harm reduction posits that, given a set of circumstances, we move forward in a way that does the least harm. In museums, harm reduction requires us to acknowledge that our institutions and collections were built in exclusionary and often colonial contexts, and then make choices that don't reproduce these legacies. Our buildings are filled with cues—the language we use, the stories we tell or don't tell—that are affirming, neutral, or negative and that affect peoples' feelings of belonging. The language in museum labels has the power to exclude, dehumanize, and uphold a system of power. Rather than simply including more voices or telling new stories, harm reduction requires us to challenge and dismantle existing narratives.

We collaborated across museum departments to define what we mean by harm, identify labels to replace, and imagine new solutions. Slow and frustrating at times, this commitment to collaboration was central to our success. It allowed us to create new principles and values that now guide all our label writing.

People ask us, "When will this work be done?" It's never done. The work we do today will quickly feel outdated because we aim for progress through constant learning and experimentation. To anyone seeking to start a large-scale label audit: Just start, listen, and let each conversation build upon the last. You will stumble and take steps back, but the conversations generated across the institution will ripple far beyond labels toward making museums more life-affirming spaces for all visitors. ■

Interpreting with Care

LIZ GARDNER, Director of Interpretation, Isabella Stewart Gardner Museum, Boston, Massachusetts

How do we interpret historic artworks with care for contemporary viewers? This was the question that our team grappled with while developing the exhibition *Titian: Women, Myth, and Power* at the Isabella Stewart Gardner Museum (ISGM). While reuniting Titian's Renaissance masterpieces was a cause for celebration, their mythological subject matter was troubling, depicting implied or impending sexual violence. Reconsidering these artworks required acknowledging the prevalence of sexual assault in our own society and the lived experiences of visitors who have survived it.

Recognizing that we were not experts in this matter, we reached out to educators at the Boston Area Rape Crisis Center (BARCC), who facilitated discussions with staff about sexual violence and suggested techniques to support survivors in our galleries. With their guidance, we created a content note: "*Titian: Women, Myth, and Power* explores themes of sexual assault and violence." We placed this language at the entrance of the exhibition and at the beginning of the online gallery guide. Staff also read it aloud before public programs and tours.

Though the words were simple, they were also powerful, enabling viewers to make an informed decision about whether they felt comfortable interacting with the exhibition. The content note was not a judgment or a warning, and while it was designed for survivors, it was also helpful for caregivers and educators.

Our work with BARCC taught us that content notes are a small gesture with a large impact, signaling to our visitors that they are welcomed here. It also asked us to think beyond the exhibition to our permanent collection galleries: What would a trauma-informed approach to the entire museum look like? With the content note as an interpretive tool, we will continue to work toward an answer. ■

Multivocal Labels

MARIANNA PEGNO, PhD, Director of Engagement and Inclusion, Tucson Museum of Art and Historic Block, Tucson, Arizona

In our attempt to be more relevant to our audiences at the Tucson Museum of Art, we are embracing a multivocal approach to exhibition development and interpretation, incorporating varying perspectives and expertise from voices in your community. Community-written labels can help create a place for active conversation and dialogue, where multiple voices share knowledge and partake in meaning making.

Since 2013 our exhibition labels have featured community expertise, offering multiple new perspectives about artworks on view. Label content and tone vary by author—some are critical investigations and direct responses to the object; some hypothesize stories within or beyond the frame; others make new connections to content, ideas, and experiences. Through this ongoing effort we have successfully built sustaining and authentic relationships with our audiences while becoming a more relevant institution that reflects our local communities.

When considering the use of community voices, I ask if they align with our museum's equity-based approach to exhibition development, engagement, and learning. Will inserting community voices into our exhibition make the museum more holistically inclusive?

I employ some basic rules of thumb when engaging in this process:

- Be considerate of time and expertise—avoid transactional experiences.

- Ask: How can this experience be mutually beneficial?

- Always offer options for potential authors to pick from; I don't assume I know what artwork the author will find interesting.

- Open-ended prompts or questions can inspire, while overly restrictive directions can mute expertise from voices beyond the museum.

- Always display community-authored labels *alongside* other descriptive texts and within the standard approach to exhibition-based interpretation, as separate treatment of these texts could inadvertently signal a hierarchy of knowledge.

This interpretative strategy is but *one* way to expand the museum's perspective and should be part of a larger initiative of building a more equitable institution. ∎

Valuing All Perspectives

KRISSY O'CONNOR, Culture and Heritage Practitioner, Aotearoa New Zealand

My question for consideration: When creating an exhibition in response to a culturally significant political commemoration, is it possible for the exhibition process and exhibition itself to avoid being politically and racially charged?

In 2019 I was contracted by the New Zealand Maritime Museum Hui Te Ananui A Tangaroa to deliver an exhibition in response to Tuia Encounters 250.

Tuia Encounters 250 was a commemoration marking 250 years since the first onshore encounters in Aotearoa New Zealand, between Māori (indigenous New Zealanders) and Europeans (specifically the crew of the HMS *Endeavour*) in 1769. *Tuia 250* endeavored to celebrate Aotearoa's Pacific voyaging heritage and spark honest conversations about the past, present, and the navigation our shared future.

The Maritime Museum commissioned seven artworks for their *Tuia 250* exhibition from artists who submitted proposals.

Writing the labels for the artworks and artifacts in the exhibition was a tense experience and has left me wondering how I valued or devalued personal oral histories in the process. In some cases, I'm proud of the discussions had and the way the artists' voices came through. In other cases, I question whether I deferred too heavily to published and accepted versions of history rather than allowing artists to completely own their family, community, and cultural history.

I also wrestled with the artists' and museum's views on managing Māori language text within English-language labels. The artists argued that cultural integrity was at stake if the Māori language didn't stand alone within the English text. The museum felt that in-text translations of Māori were paramount for visitor comprehension. While each label was presented fully in both languages, the inclusion of some Māori words within the English version was appropriate. I decided to position the Māori text without translations within the English text and included a glossary below. ∎

Confronting Colonialism

JESSICA BRAINARD, Exhibit Planner, Writer, and Evaluator,
St. Michaels, Maryland

At this time of reckoning with the legacy of slavery and colonization, we museum professionals are facing tough questions: What does it mean to decolonize a museum? How can we be more transparent about provenance? How can exhibitions confront difficult histories and "write back" against colonial narratives?

In the reinstallation of its Africa Galleries, the Penn Museum faced these questions head-on. The renovated galleries aim to recontextualize the African collections and trace their journey from their makers to the museum. As the introduction states:

> These galleries contain objects from the African continent. As with most Western museums, the foundational objects of this collection were created in or taken out of Africa during periods of enslavement and colonialism.

Working for RK&A, I conducted a summative evaluation of the Africa Galleries in the fall of 2021. Analyzing the qualitative data, I was struck by interviewees' often unprompted references to the interpretive text, using terms such as "readable," "transparent," and "thoughtfully written" to describe the exhibit labels. The gallery introductions elicited several candid comments about the problematic provenance and repatriation of museum collections, including "Maybe it's time to give the stuff back." Interviewees also cited labels associated with specific artifacts as particularly thought-provoking, including an object ID for a pair of shackles:

> Iron shackles reveal violent histories. Collected in the 1930s, these shackles were created to confine a human being.

Concise and compelling, this label drove home the object's intent and implications. As one interview commented, "It's powerful in what it says—and what it doesn't say."

Transforming the colonial paradigm in which many ethnographic museums were built is no easy task. Transparency is the first step. And, as findings from this study remind us, words matter. We can begin the difficult work of decolonization one exhibit label at a time. ■

Authentic Voices

MEREDITH WHITFIELD, Exhibition Content Developer, the Field Museum, Chicago, Illinois

Apsáalooke Women and Warriors was an exhibition at the Field Museum that interspersed cultural items with work by Apsáalooke contemporary artists. It was curated by Nina Sanders (Apsáalooke), Alaka Wali, and Meranda Roberts (Northern Paiute/Xicana). I led exhibition development with Monisa Ahmed's invaluable assistance.

Plans came together to explore the Apsáalooke emergence story, their formative physical and spiritual journey to their homeland, and what it means to live as an Apsáalooke person—highlighting the values of bravery and success. For our first draft of labels, Monisa and I interviewed Nina about these themes and the items planned for display and interpreted her knowledge using third-person "museum voice."

The labels were horrible. Flat, stilted, strange.

What were we going to do?

We recalled Crow Fair, the annual Apsáalooke cultural celebration—camping with Nina's friends and family; learning how their stories, values, and traditions are vital elements of everyday life, not curiosities to be encountered with distance. Visitors needed that understanding, emotion, and connection. The exhibition had no life without an Apsáalooke voice. We set to work revising: Nina expressed the connection among items and themes in a continuous first-person narrative, which Monisa and I carefully parceled into labels. This was tricky business: striking a balance between clarity and preserving our speaker's voice, ensuring labels were readable and connected to the items they interpreted, but still had the right emotional weight. We went back and forth, taking almost twice as long as we'd budgeted for. But in the end, the labels found the spark they had been missing.

With hindsight, this first-person approach seems obvious. Authoritative institutional voice on the lived experience of individuals or groups is one way colonialist white supremacy shows up in museums—it distances; it others. Attributed first-person voice is one step toward challenging that. ■

Dynamic Bilingualism

IVAN GUZMAN, Teens Program Coordinator, Chicago History Museum, Chicago, Illinois

Coming from an immigrant family, I was never able to experience a museum visit with my parents during my childhood. Most museums did not have any Spanish text in their exhibits, so it would have been difficult for my parents to understand what they were looking at. Furthermore, as a young, bilingual student, translating museum labels in real time wasn't something that was easy. So seeing a multilingual family interact with bilingual labels that I had created for the Packingtown Museum in Chicago, caused a sense of joy that was indescribable. Bilingual labels enabled this family to have a dynamic museum experience. The mother began by reading aloud the Spanish label to a young, elementary-aged child, who was listening intently about the slaughtering process in the Chicago Union Stock Yard. Once the mother finished, a teenager then read the English label aloud to the young child, who continued to listen intently and review the images of this process. The young child proceeded to ask both the mother and sibling questions, in both English and Spanish, receiving responses in both. The family continued on through the exhibit and the child was able to comfortably ask either their mother or sibling questions, depending on what language they could more adequately compose their question in. I am fairly confident that this child could tell you in great detail what the process of slaughtering a hog was in the packinghouses of Chicago's meat district because of this dynamic, bilingual experience. ■

TRANSLATION

Enhancing Understanding

KATHERINE BAUMANN, Production Director, Multilingual Connections, Chicago, Illinois

I work for Multilingual Connections, a translation company. The majority of our museum work is English into Spanish, followed by Chinese and Haitian Creole. Exhibits present many translation challenges, including multiple expressions for the same English word, space limitations, and gendered language.

Sometimes, what is most important is having a visual reference. For an exhibit on fire safety with an interactive component called the "firepit" where visitors "play with fire," our translators needed a full visual mock-up of what this firepit would be. This allowed them to understand what "playing with fire" meant in the context: combining combustible ingredients on an interactive screen and seeing the resulting mock "fire" in a physical firepit. The word "fire" can have many translations in Spanish: *incendio, fuego, fogata*, and more, and we needed visuals to know which translation was appropriate in the different contexts throughout the exhibit.

Gender-inclusive language is another, more modern challenge in translation. In Spanish, for example, translating with inclusive language requires both creativity and more space. For example, we don't want to use the masculine word *científicos* for "scientists" when the goal is to remain gender neutral in translation. *Comunidad científica* ("scientific community") is one alternative, depending on context, but this is two words versus the single word "scientists" in English. Since most languages already take up 15 to 20 percent more space than English, gender-neutral language can add to design challenges.

We also review the final exhibit pre-opening after our translations are incorporated (often via compiled images or design review programs). This is important because even in projects where we had comprehensive visual reference material and ongoing communication, the reference material might lack some context, or the original content might change slightly after translation. Both scenarios could affect the accuracy of the translation, and this last in-context review can catch any remaining issues. ■

Questioning Paradigms

MARC LEVITT, Archivist, National Naval Aviation Museum,
Pensacola, Florida

We were planning an exhibit on Aerospace Medicine with people who had worked in the medical field at Naval Air Station Pensacola, the active military base where the National Naval Aviation Museum is located.

After six months we began laying out concepts based on these conversations and the main points that our collaborators wanted to explain to the visitors. They had been advocating for an exhibit about their contributions for more than a decade and had created a first draft, so we included them in an iterative design process. As we began using terms like "cognitive" and "physiology" in the big idea and sectional takeaways, we wondered if the general public was familiar with these terms. We also wanted some initial reactions to the themes of the exhibit.

So we implemented online surveys and floor interviews to address these concerns. The results were surprising and illuminating. As it turned out, most visitors were familiar with the terms "cognitive" and "physiology." However, when we asked, "What comes to mind when you hear the phrase 'Aerospace Medicine'" (the very title of our exhibit), the most common response was "Medicine in Space." Well, this was quite a shock! In the Navy, "Aerospace Medicine" refers to the testing, training, and maintenance of physical, cognitive, and physiological standards of naval aviation personnel. It also includes water survival training and mishap (accident) prevention and investigation. So the evaluation really challenged our expectations. We were able to adjust our language and concepts before investing too much effort in the writing of the interpretive text.

Further, we also discovered that visitors were most interested in mishap prevention. We had wrongly assumed that visitors would find the subject too morbid. We learned that precisely because this aspect of aviation is so hidden from public view, it piques quite a bit of curiosity. ■

PROTOTYPING

Tweaking for Engagement

BETSY LORING, Principal, ExpLoring Exhibits & Engagement, LLC, Worcester, Massachusetts

For the exhibition *City Science: The Science You Live*, our team was developing a touch-screen interactive that asked visitors to create the soundscape of their neighborhood, with the prompt "What does it sound like where you live?" Visitors were having a blast with the prototype—repeating the activity, with lots of talking and laughing. Clearly, we were seeing high engagement and positive affect. However, the typical child was filling their soundscape with dozens of ice-cream trucks and fire engines, not the sound (I hope!) of their actual neighborhood. Our main goal for the interactive was to get people thinking about sounds as data: as pieces of information about natural and built environments that can be captured and examined. Front-end evaluation had told us that urban soundscapes were a potentially rich topic—sound was one of the few areas where visitors' descriptions of our city differed widely, depending upon their zip code.

So we tested a paper "introductory screen" over the touch screen with the question "What kind of neighborhood do you live in?" and three "buttons": city, suburbs, and country. After people selected their button, we flipped up the paper to reveal the exact same soundscape prompt, "What does it sound like where you live?" With this one added screen, the engagement completely changed. The sounds visitors used were much more varied and diverse. Adults got more involved, asking children, "What else do we hear?" and "Is that near to the house or far away? Okay, so should we make that quieter?" To be clear, the introductory question screen does nothing material—it functions like a "Next" button no matter which button they touch. It does something much more powerful: It puts people into the right frame of mind, and the results are dramatic. ∎

PROTOTYPING

Incorporating Community Voices

AMELIA WIGGINS, Director of Communications and Engagement, Delaware Art Museum,
Wilmington, Delaware

In 2019, as part of a museum reinstallation, Delaware Art Museum staff radically changed our approach to label writing. Before planning content, we held a series of "community salons" with diverse community members, staff, and stakeholders. These conversations helped us learn how people perceived the galleries, the art they connected with, and what they were curious about.

Guided by the prototyping model of Kathleen McLean, we tested new narratives that incorporated what we'd heard in the salons. As a team of two curators and two educators, we handwrote text on butcher paper and taped it up for visitors to comment on with sticky notes. This method provided direct access to feedback from our visitors—who called us out when information was unclear, incorrect, discriminatory, or boring:

> *Born into slavery*, not *born a slave.*

> Why is it called *Pre*-Raphaelite?

> Why are [these paintings] so dark?

We iterated and continued testing. We loosened our tone and looked critically at word choices and the perspectives we were centering. We taped up images to provide examples. We researched and responded to visitors' questions.

When we were successful, multiple visitors engaged with the ideas shared. Sometimes, they even added to each other's notes, as in the comments responding to wall text on sexism in twentieth-century illustration:

> *#metoo back in 1909*

> *Would love to see the evolution from women as objects to women as independent story leaders.*

> *The question should be, how has art changed to reflect independent women?*

Prototyping helped us recognize what was going unsaid in our galleries. Our labels changed as a result of changes in process; writing together in front of art instead of alone at a desk, drawing on the expertise of our community, and asking visitors—not just colleagues—for feedback. ■

PROTOTYPING

Listening Closely

DEBORAH PERRY, PhD, Director, Selinda Research Associates, Chicago, Illinois

You know the exhibit. *Colored Shadows.* About mixing colored lights. Three different colored lights shining onto a tabletop. You put your hand above the table and you get beautifully colored shadows. Your hands dance. Shadows dance. Visitors love this exhibit. Museums love this exhibit. (Thank you Exploratorium!)

Doing my doctoral research, I became fascinated by this exhibit. What made it so popular? Why were visitors so drawn to it? And what were they learning from it? Anything? Initial research data revealed: not much learning.

Years previously, Judy Diamond had found that visitors learn not from an exhibit, but from the conversations they have within the context of the exhibit. So I listened. Most conversations at *Colored Shadows* tended to be about "It's beautiful!" "It's fun!" " It's magic!" Rarely anything about mixing colored lights.

My research challenge thus became: Can the exhibit and labels be modified so that visitors still experience the magic, but also have meaningful conversations about mixing colored lights?

I listened some more, this time specifically to the conversations visitors had when using the labels. Too many visitors were frustrated by what the labels were asking them to do and learn: "What colored lights?" "Am I blocking a light with my hand?" "I can't do this!"

But with lots more listening and watching and prototype testing (oh my), I, along with my colleagues, identified the bottlenecks to visitors' meaningful conversations. Final data showed the revised exhibit labels resulted in a marked increase in rich meaningful conversations and learning about mixing colored lights and, equally important, no reduction in visitor enjoyment.

Next time you write an exhibit label, think carefully about the visitor conversations you want to jump-start. Test a prototype. Listen carefully. What conversations does the label stimulate? And are these the conversations you want visitors to have? ■

PROTOTYPING

Mock It Up

GORDON CHUN, Gordon Chun Design, Berkeley, California

"Nobody's reading the exhibit text! Why is the type so small?" The director of a local historical society approached me for help a couple of weeks past their grand opening reception. They had received much negative feedback about the readability of the exhibit text. The text looked great aesthetically. The problem was that visitors simply couldn't read it. There were also issues with the content—too long, too academic, etc. But the main problem was that the font was too small, line spacing too tight, formatting too complicated.

What can be done to prevent this situation? The simple answer is: Mock it up. Make full-size prototypes of your designed exhibit text and view them in conditions similar to your gallery environment. These can be inexpensive large-format prints made at a copy service. Tack them to the wall, simulate real lighting if possible, and print in final colors if feasible. Get as close to the actual gallery conditions as you can. Then make informed decisions about the accessibility of your graphic design.

In the example cited above, prototypes were not made. The designer sent the clients proofs that were reviewed on computer screens and as small printouts made on an office printer. Everything looked just fine. But the designed text was not meant to be viewed that way. The all-important step of viewing full-size mock-ups was skipped. It was not until the finals were installed that problems were revealed.

Over the years, I have seen many versions of this story played out. Often, the reason is that curators and graphic designers for exhibit projects ignore, or are unaccustomed to, the unique conditions of exhibition text: words read by people standing in low light, with various visual and environmental distractions. Exhibition text should be prototyped at full size, evaluated for its accessibility in a gallery setting, and produced accordingly. ■

A Personal Connection

TORI LEE, Exhibitions Developer, the Field Museum, Chicago, Illinois

A Natural Talent: The Taxidermy of Carl Cotton started with a photo. *Is that a Black man?* My colleague Reda Brooks and I squinted at a man perched in front of a diorama.

As I watched a video of Cotton carefully crafting individual lily pads, I knew this could become a powerful exhibition for Black History Month, one that demonstrated how African Americans had contributed to the Field Museum as taxidermists. As scientists. As exhibit makers. Like my coworkers and like myself.

Carl W. Cotton (1918–1971) was a taxidermist, artist, and exhibition preparator who worked at the Field from 1947 until his death in 1971. He was the first, likely the only, Black taxidermist employed by the museum.

Traditionally, exhibits emerge within a tight hierarchy of knowledge. Scientists and scholars provide content, informed by decades of research. But . . . there wasn't a Carl Cotton expert here. So we dug: Through archives and census records and obituaries. Through deep collection shelves. On social media, we found family members and friends with recollections and questions of their own.

With each discovery, the process grew more personal, more emotional. The labels followed suit. Chicago legend Timuel Black, oral historian and civil rights leader, swept us away with vivid recollections of growing up with Cotton on Chicago's South Side. A day with the Cotton family was filled with good food and great stories. Our archivist found three inquiry letters from Cotton to the Field Museum. I teared up at his tenacity.

The final exhibit felt like a quilt—each bit from a different conversation, a different source—a labor of love stitched together by a community that'd grown organically. Writing the labels, I sketched a portrait of the humble, passionate man I'd learned so much about—imbuing them with the same fondness I'd heard whenever people spoke of Carl. ■

Evoking Other Voices

LEE DAVIDSON, Associate Professor of Museum and Heritage Studies, Victoria University of Wellington, Wellington, New Zealand

LETICIA PÉREZ CASTELLANOS, Professor of Museology, National School of Conservation, Restoration and Museology, Mexico City, Mexico

De la Milpa a la Mesa was co-created by a Mexican–New Zealand team to enhance New Zealanders' appreciation of Mexico, beyond the clichés and stereotypes. In this vibrant, interactive space, visitors met farmers, scientists, vendors, home cooks, and acclaimed chefs from across México and heard about the challenges they face to protect their way of life.

Each exhibition theme represented stories of actual people so visitors could empathize and feel a common humanity with "real" Mexicans. We asked each Mexican what they would like to tell New Zealanders, then wrote one-hundred-word labels to accompany a photo and a short quote.

Our first attempts felt dry and impersonal. We had failed to capture people's voices and their warmth. We discussed, then had another go—forgoing some "facts" for the more evocative language of the people themselves. We also increased the length of the labels to 170 words. Everyone was happier.

Labels were drafted by a New Zealander then checked by a Mexican team member and rewritten until we all agreed. This was laborious and sometimes stressful, but it was crucial to ensure an intercultural outcome. Those in New Zealand felt the huge responsibility of representing the story and voice of the "other" authentically, and in a way that would engage local audiences and help them find points of commonality. Those in Mexico tried to maintain the meaning, tone, and spirit of the speakers. Translations were a big challenge. Sometimes a label went back and forth many times.

In the end, visitors found the labels engaging and informative, and rated them as the "most enjoyable" activity in the exhibition. As one visitor said: "Reading the personal stories made me feel closer to the real people." Our advice: Write labels that allow people to tell their own stories and create emotional connection—it's much more important that explaining all the "facts." ■

PART VII

Conclusions

24

What Research Tells Us about Visitors

Knowing what factors determine whether visitors pay attention to, engage with, and react to exhibit labels will help label writers produce texts that motivate visitors to read and are relevant to their interests and needs.

Front-end, formative, and summative evaluations, prototyping, visitor studies, and empirical evidence give us high confidence in our understanding of visitor behavior with interpretive labels in museum exhibitions.

WE KNOW THESE THINGS

The conclusions below are based on published empirical research data, unpublished evaluation studies, and the collective wisdom of label writers, designers, exhibit developers, and evaluators, who have been working to improve labels for years. There are exceptions, of course, on an individual visitor basis, but generally, the conclusions are true for many situations. So before you think, *Not in my museum*, or *Not my visitors*, consider what each would mean for your situation if they were true.

What Research Tells Us about Visitors and Labels

Paying attention is a prerequisite for engagement, and attention and engagement are necessary for learning to happen. By watching visitors as they use exhibitions, we can see the degree to which they focus on, glance at, or ignore the offered experiences.

Time spent

Visitors often spend much less time than what was imagined or hoped for by exhibit developers. These findings have consequences for how exhibits are planned and used:

1. Visitors often spend less than twenty minutes in an exhibition, regardless of the topic.

2. When visitors have good conceptual and spatial orientation in exhibitions, they are more likely to spend more time looking and reading.

3. When visitors spend more time, they tend to use more parts of the exhibition rather than spending time with one element.

4. Visitors typically stop at fewer than half the exhibit elements, especially in large exhibitions.

5. Visitors tend to use smaller exhibitions more thoroughly; they spend more time per square foot and stop at more of the elements.

6. In most cases, cued visitors spend more time than un-cued visitors.

Reading behavior

Research has shown that behavior data gathered by direct observation differs from self-reported behaviors. When asked, visitors tend to overrate engagement/paying attention, such as time spent, stops made, and labels read. This fact stresses the importance of watching what visitors do rather than only asking them what they did, especially when it comes to reading:

7. Visitors who read labels spend more time and do more things in exhibitions overall than nonreaders of any age.

8. Visitors often skip the introductory labels, except in art museums.

9. Visitors are more likely to read labels placed directly next to what the labels are about than labels keyed by a number or text or placed at a greater distance away.

10. Adults—because they are accustomed to receiving information through the written word—will work harder to understand the content of a label than children will.

11. Children will read labels if the labels provide them with easily accessible and useful information.

12. More adults will read label text to children when labels are easy to read out loud, without the need to paraphrase or translate unfamiliar vocabulary words (for themselves or their children).

13. Among adults, those who read labels and those who use interactive devices are not two separate audiences.

14. More visitors read shorter labels; fewer visitors read longer labels.

15. Visitors will read more of a label, and more thoroughly, when the text is shorter.

16. Other than caregivers reading to children, visitors do not read labels aloud to each other very often. (Why not?)

Moving through the exhibition

Data collectors who systematically watch where visitors go in exhibitions have noted several characteristics in visitor behaviors:

17. Visitors tend to not look up at labels placed higher than six or seven feet off the ground as they move through exhibitions.

18. As visitors move along the walls of an exhibit gallery, interpretive kiosks or labels in the middle of the room are often missed.

19. Visitors tend to use exhibit elements early in their visit and skip more things as they move toward the end.

20. A broad cross section of the audience is attracted to the most popular parts of an exhibition, not a special demographic subgroup, such as age, gender, or social group.

Visitors' efforts

Studies on visitors' perceived efforts to pay attention to exhibits have led to the development of a "value ratio," meaning the benefits of the effort are worth the cost of time and effort:

21. Visitors will become engaged with an exhibit when the amount of perceived effort to do so seems worth it.

22. Visitors will stop looking, reading text, or watching a video if the value of the experience is not worth the effort.

Learn from Others

Stephen Bitgood has raised many of the research questions and gathered the data that have led to many of the conclusions above. Referring to his concept of the value ratio, Bitgood says, "Studying visitors over the years has taught me, time after time, that what visitors do in museums is motivated primarily by value. Evidence for this lesson comes from several sources: (1) visitation patterns; (2) the circulation pathways visitors take as they move through museums; (3) the willingness of visitors to read (or not) interpretive text; (4) visitor reactions to interactive exhibit devices; and (5) visitor attention to the presence of videos embedded within exhibitions." Bitgood's article "Lessons Learned: The Value of the Value Ratio," featuring many bibliographic references, is available online on ResearchGate. His book *Engaging the Visitor: Designing Exhibits That Work* is also filled with actionable findings from years of research.

The Exploratorium's Department of Research and Evaluation publishes findings online from many of their excellent studies. Their reports are not guidelines per se, but they contain a wealth of information about visitor behavior, research methods, theory, and practice. Studies by Josh Gutwill and by Sue Allen are particularly helpful.

SO WHAT CAN WE DO WITH THIS RESEARCH?

Knowing these things that research tells us, exhibit developers can take important actions to increase visitors' levels of motivation to explore, engage, and enjoy exhibitions.

- If visitors tend to use exhibitions briefly and incompletely, plan exhibitions that will make sense when visitors sample less than half the exhibit elements.

- Because visitors often skip the introductory label, make these labels short and readable at a distance. Use graphics and integrate objects on the label to make them more attractive.

- Visitors need orientation. Provide orientation in several modalities and locations, including brochures, signage, floor plans, and bulleted lists of themes/sections.

- Visitors tend to use smaller exhibitions more thoroughly. Plan small exhibitions with clear big ideas.

- Visitors' attention and time spent can be increased by making exhibit elements more social, interactive, and intergenerational.

- Visitors want to feel competent, smart, and inspired. Help them think, *This exhibit was meant for me.*

IMPLICATIONS BEYOND LABELS

The scope of these recommendations takes us beyond writing interesting, short, well-crafted, visitor-comprehendible, legible labels. It makes effective communication of the whole exhibition a goal. We must pay attention to all of the following variables: (1) who the visitors are; (2) what they like; (3) what they know already; (4) what the exhibition is about; and (5) what the exhibit experiences are like (how many, what kinds). The first three are informed by audience research; the last two are the work of exhibit developers. The guidelines in chapter 1 and the essentials in chapter 25 will help show you what to do. Get busy, and have fun!

25

Essentials Takeaway

In 24 chapters we have discussed guidelines, tools, examples, and missed opportunities. Now we'd like to conclude with an answer to this question: What steps are the most fundamental for those engaged in developing interpretive museum exhibitions? There are four essentials:

HAVE A BIG IDEA

A powerful big idea will clarify and focus the nature and scope of an exhibition and provide a well-defined goal against which to rate its success. Visitors have a better experience when they know what the exhibition is about and can reflect on what it means to them.

WRITE LESS

Use fewer words. Stick to the big idea. It's a museum exhibition, not an encyclopedia or a library. It's about clarity, not simplicity. Visitors to an exhibition will appreciate the opportunity to spend more time looking and doing rather than reading. Kept it short.

PROTOTYPE

Mock it up and try it out. Prototyping during design development provides the most useful information about whether an exhibit will be understood and used correctly by visitors. Prototyping provides the best value for money and time.

DON'T FORGET ABOUT ORIENTATION

Orientation is one of the biggest challenges in exhibitions. Don't forget wayfinding aids, introductory information, and a list of all the available choices. Visitors need "you are here" clues in multiple ways to help guide their decisions and expectations.

serrell's four essentials

for interpretive exhibitions

 ## Have a Big Idea

In a single sentence:
with a subject
with an active verb and
with a so what?

 ## Write Less

It's about clarity, not simplicity:
use fewer words

 ## Prototype

Mock it up:
try it out, modify, try again

 ## Don't forget about orientation

Visitors need clues:
where it is
who it's for
what it's about

From *Exhibit Labels: An Interpretive Approach*, third edition, 2024

Acknowledgments

We give our heartfelt thanks to the people who helped make this third edition. So many things to be thankful for! They commented on the contents and graphics of the second edition and what would make it better. They contributed ideas and images, critiqued first drafts, reviewed photos and captions, submitted stories, provided quotations and examples, edited chapters, edited them again, offered revisions and additions, and Zoomed with us about issues and progress. They told us nicely when something sucked, congratulated us when they thought something was good, and suggested ways to improve it more. Special recognition goes to the efforts of our "Voices" authors and to the participants in the Feedback Friday meetings for their candid thoughts and suggestions.

We are grateful to the professors of who use *Exhibit Labels: An Interpretive Approach* in their classrooms, and who took the time to tell us what they liked and what they wanted to see in the third edition: Hope Amason, Ariana Huhn, Onnica Marquez, Ann McCleary, Therese Quinn, Elizabeth Sommer, and Jeanne Zarucchi. Thank you to our colleagues who gave us feedback about previous editions, answered our questions, and gave us new ideas to investigate and new examples to highlight in this edition: Susan Ades, Mitch Allen, Swarupa Anila, Steve Bitgood, Alex Bortolog, Kevin Boyd, Roxane Buck-Ezcurra, Eileen Campbell, John Chiodo, Carlos Diazgranados, Darcie Fohrman, Jojo Galvin, Ben Gammon, Liz Gardner, Abigail Gepner, Josh Gutwill, Christina Hellmich, Deborah Howes, Jill Kushner Bishop, Betsy Loring, Stacey Mann, Kathy McLean, Cait McQuaid, Becky Menlove, Margaret Middleton, Paul Orselli, Rhonda Pagnozzi, Lisa Suzanne Park Steskal, Deborah Perry, Molly Phipps, Jenny Sayre Ramburg, Judy Rand, Mike Rigsby, Scott Sayre, Tamara Schwartz, Susan Spero, Greg Sprick, Toni Wynn, Linda Wilson, and Loren Ybarrondo. To our colleagues who submitted writing or photos that we were unable to fit into this edition, we are so grateful for your time, insight, and efforts: Briana Cutts, Alexander Goldowsky, Linda Kellen, Nanette Kuich, Tim Lee, Héctor Valverde Martinez, Matt Kirchman, Selena Moon, Lydia Pagel, Penelope Ray, Beth Redmond-Jones, and Jason Jay Stevens. For help with editing and reviewing the manuscript, we are indebted to Ellen Bechtol, Barbara Becker, Stephanie

Downey, Karen Furnweger, Ada Mary Gugenheim, Barbara Hansen, and Nancy Levner. We are especially grateful for the sensitivity review conducted by Jackie Peterson and Sonnet Takahisa. For help with photos we appreciate Bonnie Fields, Elena Guarinello, Ron Hinton, Matt Isble, and Hannah Jennings. At the beginning and end, Kate Curto and Sam Mera-Candedo gave us the ideal forum for testing out new ideas and concepts in their virtual Feedback Fridays program. Over the course of forty months, starting in the pandemic and continuing on until the manuscript was submitted, thanks go to Jessica Sickler and Matt Sikora, who gave Beverly more than sixty Zoom cocktail hours of unsolicited alcohol-infused advice, for which she is eternally grateful. From Roman & Littlefield we thank Charles Harmon, who kept us going through the long process, and all the editors, who escorted us over the finish line. The beauty of the book's interior design, cover art, and innovative layout of the photo pages are the result of the generous and patient efforts of the talented Gordon Chun.

Photo Figure Index

PART II: OVERVIEW

Photo #	Photo Figure Names	Page #	Photo Credit
1	Plants are up to something.	44	B
2	Altered State	45	K
3	Welcome to the swamp	46	B
4	Beautiful science title	47	B
5	Shuttered context	48	B
6	Shuttered /label	48	B
7	Mirror mirror context	49	B
8	Mirror mirror label	49	B
9	Wine jug context	50	K
10	Wine jug label	50	K
11	Compassionate saint context	51	B
12	Compassionate saint label	51	B
13	Living termites context	52	B
14	Living termites label	52	B
15	Goat Mountain wayside	53	B
16	Avoiding the reptiles	54	B
17	Layered story	55	K
18	Fern Room	56	B
19	Double V	57	B
20	Silver and Gold	58	B

20 photos in Part II

Photo credits in part II:
B = Beverly Serrell, K = Katherine Whitney

PART III: AUDIENCE

Photo #	Photo Figure Names	Page #	Photo Credit
21	Douglas squirrel	120	K
22	Busted without arms context	121	K
23	Busted without arms label	121	K
24	Keep it up context	122	K
25	Keep it up label	122	K
26	Reconsidering colonialism	123	K
27	What we got from the Indians	124	B
28	"Are they real?" context	125	K
29	"Are they real?" label	125	K
30	Too many words—Geology wayside	126	B
31	Too many words—On the edge	126	B
32	Indians everywhere	127	*32
33	Kehinde Wiley context	128	B
34	Kehinde Wiley labels	128	B
35	Flip label question	129	B
36	Unicorn	130	B
37	Please don't—OK to touch?	131	B
38	OK to touch—OK to touch?	131	K

18 photos in Part III

Photo credits in part III:

B = Beverly Serrell, K = Katherine Whitney
*32, Courtesy of the Smithsonian's National Museum of the American Indian

PART IV: ENHANCING

Photo #	Photo Figure Names	Page #	Photo Credit
39	Rocks talk context	196	K
40	Rocks talk label	196	K
41	Plant petting zoo	197	B
42	Reading rail videos	198	B
43	White school—Black school	199	*43
44	Olives	200	K
45	Butterfly connection context	201	B
46	Butterfly connection close-up	201	B
47	Sticky notes	202	K
48	"Will it burn?" context	203	B
49	"Will it burn?" label	203	B
50	Galileo handset	204	B
51	Ball launcher	205	K
52	QR code iPhone	206	B
53	Iguano context	207	B
54	Iguano label	207	B
55	Welcome to evolving planet	208	B
56	Vikings entrance?	209	B
57	Arrow	210	B

19 photos in Part IV

Photo credits in part IV:
B = Beverly Serrell, K = Katherine Whitney
*43, Courtesy of Darcie Fohrman

PART V: TASKS

Photo #	Photo Figure Names	Page #	Photo Credit
58	CMOS	272	B
59	Prototyping workshop	273	*59
60	Frogs before	274	B
61	Frogs after	274	B
62	Scrub the deck context	275	K
63	Scrub the deck label	275	K
64	Life-size nature	276	*64
65	Bridges	277	B
66	Mash House	278	B
67	Large-eyed pronghorn	279	B
68	One fossil	280	K
69	Jade trinkets context	281	B
70	Jade trinkets label	281	B
71	Bending with bifocals	282	*71
72	Panel with cleats	283	B
73	Bedrock	284	B
74	Putting up vinyl lettering 1x	285	*74
75	Putting up vinyl lettering 2x	285	*75
76	Putting up vinyl lettering 3x	285	*76
77	Vinyl letter problem	286	B
78	Data collector	287	B
79	Dead albatross context	288	B
80	Dead albatross label	288	*80
81	AAM panel display	289	B

24 photos in part V

Photo credits in part V:

B = Beverly Serrell, K = Katherine Whitney

*64, Courtesy of Gordon Chun

*71, Courtesy of Ronald M. Hinton

*74, 75, 76, Courtesy of Matt Isble, MuseumTrade.org

*80, Courtesy of Gordon Chun

60 layouts total

81 photos total

Bibliography

The most commonly referenced resource for this book is the journal of the National Association for Museum Exhibition, *Exhibition* (known as *Exhibitionist* until 2016), which is filled with exhibition theory and practice for museum professionals. It is a beautifully designed, well-written compendium of really important and useful information. Find it; use it; share it.

Abeyasekera, Karl, and Geoff Matthews. *Sustainable Exhibit Design: Guidelines for Designers of Small Scale Interactive and Traveling Exhibits.* Lincoln, UK: University of Lincoln, 2006.

Adair, Bill, Benjamin Fileme, and Laura Koloshi. *Letting Go? Sharing Historical Authority in a User-Generated World.* Philadelphia: Pew Center for the Arts & Heritage, 2011.

Allen & Associates. *Secrets of Circles Summative Evaluation Report.* Report prepared for the Children's Discovery Museum of San Jose, October 2007.

Allen, Sue. *Finding Significance.* San Francisco, CA: Exploratorium, 2004.

———. "Looking for Learning in Visitor Talk: A Methodological Exploration." *Exploratorium*, 2002. https://www.exploratorium.edu/sites/default/files/pdfs/lookingforlearning.pdf.

———. "Designs for learning: Studying science museum exhibits that do more than entertain." *Science Education*, vol. 88, no. S1 Supplement: "In Principle, In Practice: Perspectives on a Decade of Museum Learning Research (1994–2004)," July 2004: S17–S33.

Allen, Sue, and Joshua P. Gutwill. "Designing with Multiple Interactives: Five Common Pitfalls." *Curator: The Museum Journal* 47, no. 2, 2004: 199–212.

Alonso, Helene, and Jeff Hayward. "Creating Apps for In-Gallery Interpretation." *Exhibitionist* 32, no. 2, Fall 2013.

Alt, M. B., and K. M. Shaw. "Characteristics of Ideal Museum Exhibits." *British Journal of Psychology* 75, 1984.

Baer, Kim, and Karen Wise. "The Role of Information Design in Sparking Visitor Interest, Engagement, and Investigation." *Exhibitionist* 33, no. 1, Spring 2014.

Batty, Jane, et al. "Object-Focused Text at the British Museum." *Exhibition*, vol. 36, no. 1, Spring 2016.

Bell, Philip, et al., eds. *Learning Science in Informal Environments: People, Places and Pursuits*. Washington, DC: National Academies Press, 2009.

Bigelow, Charles. Interview by Yue Wang, *TUGboat*, 34, no. 2, 2013.

BISE—Building Informal Science Education, Visitor Studies Association's Archives. "Research Synthesis, A Review of Recommendations in Exhibition Summative Evaluation Reports, Serrell, 2013."

Bitgood, Stephen. *Attention and Value: Keys to Understanding Museum Visitors*. Walnut Creek, CA: Left Coast Press, 2013.

———. *Effects of Label Characteristics on Visitor Behavior*. Technical Report No. 86–55. Jacksonville, AL: Jacksonville State University, Psychology Institute, 1986.

———. *Engaging the Visitor: Designing Exhibitions that Work*. Cambridge, MA: MuseumsEtc., 2014.

———, ed. "Special Issue: Exhibit Labeling." *Visitor Behavior* 4, no. 3, 1989.

———, ed. "Special Issue: Orientation and Circulation." *Visitor Behavior* 1, no. 4, January 1987.

Blackmon, Carolyn P., et al. *Open Conversations: Strategies for Professional Development in Museums*. Chicago: Field Museum of Natural History, 1988.

Boisvert, Dorothy L., and Brenda J. Slex. "The Relationship between Exhibit Characteristics and Learning-Associated Behaviors in a Science Museum Discovery Space." *Science Education* 79, no. 5, 1995.

Borun, Minda, and Katherine A. Adams. "From Hands On to Minds On: Labeling Interactive Exhibits." *Visitor Studies: Theory, Research, and Practice*, vol. 4. Arlene Benefield, Stephen Bitgood, and Harris Shettel, eds. Jacksonville, AL: Center for Social Design, 1992, 115–20.

Borun, Minda, Margaret Chambers, and Ann Cleghorn. "Families Are Learning in Science Museums." *Curator: The Museum Journal* 39, no. 2, June 1996: 123–38.

Bowyer, Emily, et al. "Making Virtual Space." *Exhibition* 20, no. 2, Fall 2021.

Brennan, Thomas J. "Elements of Social Group Behavior in a Natural Setting." Master's thesis, Texas A&M University, 1977.

Chambers, Marlene. "After Legibility, What?" *Curator: The Museum Journal* 36, no. 3, 1993.

———. "Beyond 'Aha!': Motivating Museum Visitors." *What Research Says About Learning Science in Museums*. Washington, DC: Association of Science-Technology Centers, 1990.

———. "Is Anyone Out There? Audience and Communication." *Museum News*, June 1984.

Champ, Claire. "Best Practices in Bilingual Exhibition Text: Lessons from a Bilingual Museum." *Exhibition* 36, no. 1, Spring 2016.

Coles, Stephen. "Kindle Paperwhite." *Fonts in Use*, September 7, 2012. http://fontsinuse.com/uses/2079/kindle-paperwhite.

Crane, Valerie, et al. *Informal Science Learning: What the Research Says about Television, Science, Museums, and Community-based Projects*. Dedham, MA: Research Communications Ltd., 1994.

Cron, Lisa. *Wired for Story: The Writer's Guide to Using Brain Science to Hook Readers from the Very First Sentence*. Berkeley, CA: Ten Speed Press, 2012.

Davidson, Betty, Candace Lee Heald, and George E. Hein. "Increased Exhibit Accessibility Through Multisensory Interaction." *Curator: The Museum Journal* 34, no. 4, 1991: 273–90. https://doi.org/10.1111/j.2151-6952.1991.tb01473.x.

Decolonize This Place. https://decolonizethisplace.org.

Detroit Institute of Arts. "2013 Summative Evaluation Tracking and Timing Report, Parts 1–7." Unpublished report. Detroit Institute of Arts, 2013.

———. "Phase 2 Summative Evaluation of DIA Interpretive Strategies." Unpublished report. Detroit Institute of Arts, 2012.

———. "Visitor Experience Checklist Report." Unpublished report. Detroit Institute of Arts, 2013.

Deuel, Jon, and Jessica Brainard. "Animal Attraction Summative Evaluation." Unpublished report. California Academy of Sciences, 2012. https://www.informalscience.org/search?keywords=Brainard.

Diamond, Judy. "The Behavior of Family Groups in Science Museums." *Curator: The Museum Journal* 29, no. 2, 1986.

Diamond, Judy, Michael Horn, and David H. Uttal. *Practical Evaluation Guide: Tools for Museums and Other Informal Educational Settings (American Association for State and Local History)*, 3rd ed. Lanham, MD: Rowman & Littlefield, 2016.

Doering, Zahava D., ed. "Special Issue: Focus on the Detroit Institute of Arts." *Curator: The Museum Journal* 52, no. 1, January 2009.

Faherty, Anna. "What Makes a Great Museum Label." *Museum Next*, February 1, 2022. https://www.museumnext.com/article/what-makes-a-great-museum-label/.

Falk, John. *Identity and the Museum Visitor Experience*. Walnut Creek, CA: Left Coast Press, 2009.

Falk, John H., and Lynn D. Dierking. *The Museum Experience*. Washington, DC: Whalesback Books, 1992.

Falk, John H., Lynn D. Dierking, and Susan Foutz. *In Principle, In Practice: Museums as Learning Institutions*. UK: AltaMira Press, 2007.

Felix, Dia, and Erin Fleming. "Real Talk: The Power (and Limits) of Audio Storytelling in Museums." *Journal of Museum Education* 48:1, 21–28, 2023. DOI: 10.1080/10598650.2022.2150365.

Friedman Alan J., et al. "Framework for Evaluation Impacts of Informal Science Education Projects." Report from a National Science Foundation Workshop, February 2008.

Fu, Alice, et al. "Room for Rigor: Designs and Methods in Informal Science Education Evaluation." *Visitor Studies*, vol. 19, no. 1, 2016.

Gardner, Howard. *Frames of Mind: The Theory of Multiple Intelligences*. New York: Basic Books, 2011.

———. "Multiple Intelligences: The First Thirty Years." Howard Gardener, 2011. http://howardgardner01.files.wordpress.com/2012/06/intro-frames-of-mind_30-years.pdf. Accessed March 7, 2014.

Getty Center for Education in the Arts and J. Paul Getty Museum. *Insights: Museums, Visitors, Attitudes, Expectations: A Focus Group Experiment*. Malibu, CA: J. Paul Getty Trust and Getty Center for Education in the Arts, 1991.

Giusti, Ellen. "Call of the Wild: Are Visitors Listening?: A multi-site evaluation of *Global Warming: Understanding the Forecast*." Paper presented at the annual meetings for the Visitor Studies Association and American Association of Museums, 1997.

Gregg, Gail. "Your Labels Make Me Feel Stupid." *Art News*, Summer 2010.

Gutwill, Joshua P. "Labels for open-ended exhibits: Using questions and suggestions to motivate physical activity." *Visitor Studies Today* 9, no. 1, 2006: 1–9a.

———. "Providing Explanations to Visitors Affects Inquiry Behavior: A Study of the Downhill Race Exhibit." Unpublished report. Exploratorium, June 2002. https://www.exploratorium.edu/sites/default/files/pdfs/downhill-race-2.pdf.

Ham, Sam H. *Interpretation: Making a Difference on Purpose*. Golden, CO: Fulcrum Publishing, 2013.

Harris, Neil. "Exhibiting Controversy." *Museum News* 74, no. 5, September/October, 1995.

Henry, Barbara, and Kathleen McLean, eds. *How Visitors Changed Our Museum.* Oakland, CA: Oakland Museum of California, 2010.

Hood, Marilyn. "Staying Away: Why People Choose Not to Visit Museums." *Museum News*, April 1983, 50–57.

Humphrey, Thomas. *Fostering Active Prolonged Engagement.* San Francisco, CA: Exploratorium, 2005.

Jabr, Ferris. "The Reading Brain in the Digital Age: The Science of Paper versus Screens." *Scientific American*, April 11, 2013. http://www.scientificamerican.com/article/reading-paper-screens/.

Jager, Jonathan. "Environmental Correctness (EC) for Designers." *Exhibitionist* 14, no. 2, Fall 1995.

Jennings, Gretchen. "Psychology: Understanding Ourselves, Understanding Each Other." *Are We There Yet? Conversations about Best Practices in Science Exhibition Development.* Kathleen McLean and Catherine McEver, eds. San Francisco, CA: Exploratorium, 2004, 55–59.

Jennings, Gretchen, ed. "Intentionally Designed Spaces." *Exhibitionist* 33, no. 1, Spring 2014.

———, ed. "New Media: Transforming Museums, Exhibitions and Visitors" *Exhibitionist* 32, no. 2, Fall 2013.

Johnson, L., et al. *The 2010 Horizon Report: Museum Edition.* Austin, TX: The New Media Consortium, 2010.

J. Paul Getty Museum. *Complete Guide to Adult Audience Interpretive Materials: Gallery Texts and Graphics.* Los Angeles: J. Paul Getty Trust, 2011.

Kanics, Ingrid M., and Kris Nesbitt. "Using the Goals of Universal Design to Improve Exhibitions for Kids." *Exhibition* 41, no. 1, Spring 2022.

Kapitan, Alex. "Language Is Power: Choosing Inclusive Language in Arts and Culture Institutions." PowerPoint presentation for Cultural Connections, April 28, 2022.

Kelly, E., and Leyman Pino A. "Beyond Translation, Toward Better Bilingual Exhibitions." *Exhibition* 36, no. 1, Spring 2016.

Kennedy, Jeff. *User-Friendly: Hands-On Exhibits That Work.* Washington, DC: Association of Science-Technology Centers, 1990.

Kinsley, Rose, Margaret Middleton, and Porchia Moore, "(Re) Frame: The Case for New Language in the 21st-Century Museum." *Exhibition* 36, no. 1, Spring 2016.

Korn, Randi. "An Analysis of Differences between Visitors at Natural History Museums and Science Centers." *Curator: The Museum Journal* 38, no. 3, 1995: 150–60.

Kroeger, Otto. "Exhibiting Our Differences." *Exhibitionist* 14, no. 1, Spring 1995.

Krueger, Richard A. *Focus Groups: A Practical Guide for Applied Research.* Newbury Park, CA: SAGE Publications, 1988.

Lee, Shimrit, Bhakti Shringapure (ed.). *Decolonize Museums (Decolonize That!).* New York: OR Books, 2022.

Leyman Pino, Amparo, Beth Redmond-Jones, and Vicki Wawerchak. "Blended Language Programming." *Informal Learning Review,* no. 159, November/December 2019.

Lonetree, Amy. *Decolonizing Museums: Representing Native American in National and Tribal Museums.* Chapel Hill, NC: The University of North Carolina Press, 2015.

Loomis, Ross. "Small-sample Techniques in Project Evaluations." *The Denver Art Museum Interpretive Project* by Melora McDermott-Lewis. Denver, CO: Denver Art Museum, 1990, 129–32.

Lupton, Ellen. *Thinking with Type: A Critical Guide for Designers, Writers, Editors & Students.* New York: Princeton Architectural Press, 2004, 74, 95.

Lupton, Ellen, et. al. *Extra Bold: a feminist inclusive anti-racist nonbinary field guide for graphic designers.* New York: Princeton Architectural Press, 2021.

Mackinney, Lisa Hubbell. "What Visitors Want to Know: The Use of Front-end and Formative Evaluation in Determining Label Content in an Art Museum." Master's thesis. John F. Kennedy University, 1993.

Mann, Stacey. "Crying at the Museum." *Exhibition Journal* 36, no. 1, Spring 2017.

Marino, Margie. "Prehistoric Journey Summative Evaluation Report." Unpublished report. Denver Museum of Natural History, December 1996.

Mastro, Ed. "A Beginner's Guide to Vinyl Lettering Systems." *Exhibitionist* 14, no. 1, Spring 1995: 48–51.

McCarthy, Bernice. *The 4MAT System: Teaching to Learning Styles with Right/Left Mode Techniques.* Barrington, IL.: EXCEL. Inc., 1987.

McDermott-Lewis, Melora. *The Denver Art Museum Interpretive Project.* Denver, CO: Denver Art Museum, Winter 1990.

McDonald, S. "Accessing Audiences: Visiting visitor books." *Museum and Society* 3:3, 2005, 125.

McLean, Kathleen. "Four Questions to Keep in Mind." *Human Computer Interaction in Informal Science Education Conference,* 6. Jim Spadaccini and Kathleen McLean, eds., 2013. http://openexhibits.org/hci-ise/.

————. *Planning for People in Museum Exhibitions.* Washington, DC: American Association of Science-Technology Centers, 1993.

————. "Learning to be Nimble." *Exhibitionist*, Spring 2015: 8–13.

————. "Examining Process in Museum Exhibitions: A Case for Experimentation and Prototyping." *The Future of Museum and Gallery Design.* Suzanne Macleod et al., eds. New York, NY: Routledge, 2018.

McLean, Kathleen, and Catherine McEver, eds. *Are We There Yet? Conversations about Best Practices in Science Exhibition Development.* Walnut Creek, CA: Left Coast Press, 2004.

McLean, Kathleen, and Wendy Pollock, eds. *Visitor Voices in Museum Exhibitions.* Washington, DC: Association for Science-Technology Centers, 2007.

McManus, Paulette. "It's the Company You Keep . . . The Social Determination of Learning-Related Behavior in a Science Museum." *International Journal of Museum Management and Curatorship* 6, 1987: 263–70.

————. "Watch Your Language! People Do Read Labels." *What Research Says About Learning Science in Museums.* Washington, DC: Association of Science-Technology Centers, 1990.

Meijer, Renate, and Minnie Scott. "Tools to Understand: An Evaluation of the Interpretation Material used in Tate Modern's *Rothko* Exhibition." *Tate Papers* 11, 2009.

Miles, Roger S. "Lessons in 'Human Biology': Testing a Theory of Exhibition Design." *The International Journal of Museum Management and Curatorship* 5, 1986.

————. "Museums and Public Culture: A Context for Communicating Science." *Science Learning in the Informal Setting.* Chicago: Chicago Academy of Sciences, 1987.

Multilingual Connections. "The Nuance of Gender in Translation." *Multilingual Connections*, June 1, 2022. https://multilingualconnections.com/blog/gender-inclusion-in-translation/.

National Research Council. *Learning Science in Informal Environments.* Committee on Learning Science in Informal Environments. Philip Bell et al., eds. Washington, DC: The National Academies Press, 2009.

Neumann, Ann. "Interpretive Graphic Standards." Unpublished document. Liberty Science Center, 2005.

Neurwith, Jessica, and Hillel O'Leary. "What You Bring With You, and What You Take Away: Strategies for Supporting Creativity and Making Meaning in Immersive Exhibitions." *Exhibition* 41, no. 2, Fall 2022.

Orselli, Paul. "Many Ways to Say Thanks." *ExhibiTricks: A Museum/Exhibit/Design Blog,* March 7, 2013.

Packer, J. "The Visitor Motivation Scale: An Instrument for Measuring the Relative Importance of Reasons for Visiting Educational Leisure Sites and Activities." Paper presented at the annual meeting of the Visitor Studies Association, Grand Rapids, MI, July 27, 2006.

Parker, Melanie, Allison Crites, and Amelia Wiggins, "Towards Shared Authority: Community-Authored Labels Expand Expertise, Spark Relevance, and Build Relationship," *Exhibition* 41, no. 2, Fall 2022, 62.

Pekarik, Andrew J., et al. "IPOP: A Theory of Experience Preference." *Curator: The Museum Journal* 57, no. 1, 2014: 5–27.

Penney, David. "Reinventing the Detroit Institute of Arts: The Reinstallation Project 2002–2007." *Curator: The Museum Journal* 52, no. 1, January 2009: 44.

Perkins, D. N. "What Constructivism Demands of the Learner." *Educational Technology* 31, no. 9, 1991.

Perry, Deborah. *What Makes Learning Fun? Principles for the Design of Intrinsically Motivating Museum Exhibits.* Plymouth, UK: AltaMira Press, 2012.

Plaza, Carlos. "In Other Words: Developing Bilingual Exhibitions." *Association of Science-Technology Centers Dimensions,* July/August 2009. http://www.astc.org /blog/2009/07/30/in-other-words-developing-bilingual-exhibitions. Accessed December 20, 2013.

Postman, Neil. *The End of Education: Redefining the Value of School.* New York: Alfred A. Knopf, Borzoi Books, 1995.

Preston, Jennifer. "So Many Stories to Tell For Met's Digital Chief." *New York Times,* October 27, 2013.

Punt, Barbara. *Doing It Right: A Workbook for Improving Exhibit Labels.* Brooklyn, NY: The Brooklyn Children's Museum, 1989.

Rabb, George B. "The Unicorn Experiment." *Curator: The Museum Journal* 12, no. 4, 1969.

Rand, Judy. "Finding Your Voice." Presentation at the American Alliance of Museums Annual Meeting, New Orleans, LA, 2004.

———. "Fish Stories that Hook Readers." Technical Report No. 90-30. Jacksonville, AL: Center for Social Design, 1985.

———. "The 227-Mile Museum or A Visitor's Bill of Rights." *Curator: The Museum Journal* 44, no. 1, 2001: 7–14.

———. "Write and Design with the Family in Mind." *Connecting Kids to History with Museum Exhibitions*. D. Lynn McRainey and John Russick, eds. Walnut Creek, CA: Left Coast Press, 2010, 257–84.

Randi Korn & Associates, Inc. "Summative Evaluation: *Race Are We So Different?*" Unpublished report. Randi Korn & Associates, Inc., November 2007.

Raphling, Britt, and Beverly Serrell. "Capturing Affective Learning." *Current Trends in Audience Research and Evaluation*, vol. 7. AAM Committee on Audience Research and Evaluation, 1993.

Ravelli, Louise J. *Museum Texts: Communication Frameworks*. London and New York: Routledge, 2006.

Reitstatter, L., K. Galter, and F. Bakondi. "Looking to Read: How Visitors Use Exhibit Labels in the Art Museum." *Visitor Studies*, vol. 25, no. 2, 2022.

Roberts, Lisa C. *From Knowledge to Narrative: Educators and the Changing Museum*. Washington, DC: Smithsonian Museum, 1997.

Rorimer, Anne. "Michael Asher and James Coleman at Artists Space." *Michael Asher / James Coleman, June 2–July 2, 1988*. New York: Artists Space, 1988.

Rounds, Jay. "The Curiosity-Driven Museum Visitor." *Curator: The Museum Journal* 47, no. 4, 2004: 389–412.

Rudzinski, Mark, and Linda Wilson. "Segmentation Studies and Their Application." Workshop, Visitor Studies Conference, Albuquerque, NM, August 2004.

Schloder, John E., Marjorie Williams, and C. Griffith Mann. *The Visitor's Voice: Visitor Studies in the Renaissance–Baroque Galleries of The Cleveland Museum of Art 1990–1993*. Cleveland, OH: The Cleveland Museum of Art, 1993.

Science Museum of Minnesota. "Water: Comparative Timing and Tracking Report." Unpublished study. Science Museum of Minnesota, June 2009.

Screven, C. G., ed. *Visitor Studies Bibliography and Abstracts*, 3rd ed. Shorewood, WI: Exhibit Communications, Research, Inc., 1993.

Serrell & Associates. "Cornell Lab of Ornithology: Summative Evaluation of the Interpretive Elements in the Visitor Center." Unpublished report for the Cornell Lab of Ornithology. Serrell & Associates, 2006.

———. "From Stuffed Birds on Sticks to Vivid Feathers, Gleaming Talons and Sparkling Beaks: A Summative Evaluation of the Bird Halls at Field Museum of Natural History." Unpublished report. Serrell & Associates, November 1992.

———. "Gallery of California Natural Sciences, Oakland Museum of California Summative Evaluations." Unpublished report. Serrell & Associates, August 2014.

———. "Profile of an Exhibit: Evaluation Report." Unpublished report. Serrell & Associates, 1992.

———. "The Dena'ina Way of Living, Summative Evaluation." Unpublished report. The Anchorage Museum, Serrell & Associates, 2014.

Serrell, Beverly. "Are they Watching: Visitors and Exhibition Videos." *Curator: The Museum Journal* 45, no. 1, January 2002: 50–64.

———. "Building Informal Science Education (BISE) Research Synthesis, A Review of Recommendations in Exhibition Summative Evaluation Reports." *Visitor Studies Association—BISE*, October 12, 2013. https://visitorstudies.org/resources/archive?high light=WyJiaXNlIiwiYmlzZSSdzIl0=.

———. *Judging Exhibitions: A Framework for Assessing Excellence.* Walnut Creek, CA: Left Coast Press, 2006.

———. *Paying Attention: Visitors and Museum Exhibitions.* Washington, DC: American Association of Museums Press, 1998.

———. "Paying More Attention to Paying Attention." *Informal Science: Learning Sciences*, March 15, 2010. http://www.informalscience.org/perspectives/blog/paying -more-attention-to-paying-attention.

———. "Something Smells." *Exhibitionist* 23, no. 1, Spring 2004: 14–15.

———. "The 51% Solution Research Project: A Meta-Analysis of Visitor Time/Use in Museum Exhibitions." *Visitor Behavior* 10, no. 3, Fall 1995.

———. "The Question of Visitor Styles." Paper presented at the annual meeting of the Visitor Studies Association, 1994. Available from serrell&associates website.

———. "Using Behavior to Define the Effectiveness of Exhibitions." *Museum Visitor Studies in the 90s.* S. Bicknell and G. Farmelo, eds. London: Science Museum, 1993, 140–45.

———. *The Big Idea* eBook. 2020. Online and Free to you at serrellassociates.com.

———. "The Aggregation of Tracking-and-Timing Visitor-Use Data of Museum Exhibitions for Benchmarks of 'Thorough Use,'" *Visitor Studies*, vol. 23, no. 1, 2020.

Serrell, Beverly, and Hannah Jennings. "We Are Here: Three Years of Wayfinding Studies at Brookfield Zoo." Proceedings of the American Association of Zoological Parks and Aquariums. Oglebay Park, WV, 1985.

Serrell, Beverly, Matt Sikora, and Marianna Adams. "What Do Visitors Mean by 'Meaning'?" *Exhibitionist* 32, no. 1, 2013: 8–15.

Shellman, Cecile. *Effective Diversity, Equity, Accessibility, Inclusion and Anti-Racism Practices for Museums: From the Inside Out.* Roman & Littlefield/American Alliance of Museums, 2022.

Shettel, Harris. "Exhibits: Art Form or Educational Medium?" *Museum News* 52, no. 1, 1973: 32–41.

———. *An Evaluation of Visitor Response to "Man in His Environment."* Report no. AIR-43200-7/76-FR. Washington, DC: American Institutes of Research, 1976.

Silverman, Lois H. "Of Us and Other 'Things': The Content and Functions of Talk by Adult Visitor Pairs in an Art and History Museum." PhD dissertation. University of Pennsylvania, 1990.

Silverman, Lois H. "Visitor Meaning-Making in Museums for a New Age." *Curator: The Museum Journal* 38, no. 3, 1995.

Silvers, Dana Mitroff, et al. "From Post-its to Processes: Using Prototypes to Find Solutions." *Museums and the Web 2014.* N. Proctor and R. Cherry, eds. Silver Spring, MD: Museums and the Web, 2014. Accessed June 19, 2014.

Simon, Nina. "Design for Participation." *Exhibitionist* 28, no. 2, Fall 2009: 12–17.

———. *The Participatory Museum.* Santa Cruz: Museum 2.0, 2010. http://www.participatorymuseum.org.

Spero, Susan, guest ed. "Museum Educators and Technology: Expanding our Reach and Practice." *Journal of Museum Education* 36, no. 3, Fall 2011.

Spock, Daniel. "What the Heck Is Experience Design?: Theoretical Underpinnings." Donna Braden, Ellen Rosenthal, and Daniel Spock, eds. *Exhibitionist* 24, no. 2, Fall 2005: 14–16.

Stamp, Jimmy. "To Redesign a Design Museum Start with the Typeface." *Smithsonian Magazine*, August 14, 2014. http://www.smithsonianmag.com/arts-culture/redesign-design-museum-start-typeface-180952040/?no-ist.

Taylor, Samuel, ed. *Try It! Improving Exhibits through Formative Evaluation.* Washington, DC: Association of Science-Technology Centers, 1991.

Tilden, Freeman. *Interpreting Our Heritage*, 3d ed. Chapel Hill, NC: University of North Carolina Press, 1977.

Trapp, Suzanne, Michael Gross, and Ron Zimmerman. *Signs, Trails, and Wayside Exhibits: Connecting People and Places.* Interpreter's Handbook Series, no. 4, Stevens Point, WI: University of Wisconsin-Stevens Point Foundation Press, 2006.

Trench, Lucy. "Gallery Text at the V&A: A Ten Point Guide." *Victoria & Albert Museum.* https://collectionstrust.org.uk/resource/gallery-text-at-the-va-a-ten-point-guide/.

Veverka, John. *Interpretive Master Planning*. Cambridge, MA: MuseumsEtc, 2011.

Wallace, Mike. "The Battle of the Enola Gay." *Museum News* 74, no. 4, July/August 1995.

Wells, Marcella, Barbara H. Butler, and Judith Koke. *Interpretive Planning for Museums: Integrating Visitor Perspectives in Decision Making*. Walnut Creek, CA: Left Coast Press, 2013.

Werner-Avidon, Maia. MWA Insights. "Giants of Land and Sea Summative Evaluation Report." San Francisco, CA: 2019.

Whitehead, Alfred North. *The Rhythm of Education*. University of California Libraries. Digitized 2007.

Williams, Joseph M. *Style: Ten Lessons in Clarity and Grace*, 3d ed. New York: Harper Collins Publishers, 1989.

Winter, Marcus. "Visitor perspectives on commenting in museums." *Museum Management and Curatorship* 33, no. 5, September 2018, 484–505.

Wolf, Lisa F., and Jeffrey K. Smith. "What Makes Museum Labels Legible?" *Curator: The Museum Journal* 36, no. 2, June 1993.

Wolf, Maryanne, and Catherine J. Stoodley. *Proust and the Squid: The Story of Science and the Reading Brain*. New York: Harper Collins, 2007.

Yalowitz, Steven, and Ava Ferguson. "Sharks Myth and Mystery Summative Evaluation." Monterey, CA: Monterey Bay Aquarium, 2006. http://informalscience.org/images/evaluation/report_227.pdf.

Yalowitz, Steven, et al. Bilingual Exhibits Research "Initiative: Institutional and Intergenerational Experiences with Multilingual Exhibitions." Report NSF DRL #1265662, September 2013. https://www.informalscience.org/sites/default/files/2013-10-01_BERI_Research_report_Final_Sep_2013.pdf.

Zapf, Hermann. "Future Tendencies in Type Design: The Scientific Approach to Letterforms." *Visible Language* 19, no. 1, Winter 1985.

Index

About the Authors

Since 1979, **Beverly Serrell** has been an exhibit and evaluation consultant with art, history, natural history, and science museums, as well as zoos and aquariums. She was previously head of a museum education department for eight years and worked as a high school science teacher and a research lab technician. Serrell holds an MA in Science, teaching in informal settings, and a BS in Biology. In 1995 she was a guest scholar at the J. Paul Getty Museum and has received two National Science Foundation grants to conduct research on visitor behavior in museum exhibitions. She has been a frequent museum visitor all her life.

Katherine Whitney is a museum consultant specializing in exhibit development and label writing. Her work has taken her into art, science, history and children's museums, as well as zoos and aquariums. She is particularly interested in how families engage with museums and has written about her own family's experiences. Whitney has an MA in Museum Studies and a BA in Art History. She is co-editor and a contributor to the nonfiction anthology *My Shadow is My Skin: Voices from the Iranian Diaspora* (University of Texas Press, 2020). In 2014 she collaborated with Beverly Serrell to produce the second edition of *Exhibit Labels: An Interpretive Approach*.